HEALTH AND MEDICINE IN
EARLY MEDIEVAL SOUTHERN ITALY

THE
MEDIEVAL MEDITERRANEAN

PEOPLES, ECONOMIES AND CULTURES, 400-1453

EDITORS

Michael Whitby (Warwick)
Paul Magdalino, Hugh Kennedy (St. Andrews)
David Abulafia (Cambridge)
Benjamin Arbel (Tel Aviv)
Mark Meyerson (Notre Dame)

VOLUME 11

HEALTH AND MEDICINE IN
EARLY MEDIEVAL SOUTHERN ITALY

BY

PATRICIA SKINNER

BRILL
LEIDEN · NEW YORK · KÖLN
1997

The paper in this book meets the guidelines for permanence and durability of the Committee on Production Guidelines for Book Longevity of the Council on Library Resources.

Library of Congress Cataloging-in-Publication Data

Skinner, Patricia, 1965–
  Health and medicine in early medieval southern Italy / by Patricia Skinner.
      p.   cm. — (Medieval Mediterranean, ISSN 0928-5520 ; v. 11)
    Includes bibliographical references and index.
    ISBN 9004103945 (cloth : alk. paper)
    1. Medicine, Medieval—Italy, Southern—History. 2. Diseases--Italy, Southern—History. I. Title. II. Series.
    [DNLM: 1. History of Medicine, Medieval—Italy. 2. Social Conditions—history—Italy. 3. Attitude to Health. WZ 70 GI8 S62h 1996]
    R518.S55   1996
    610'.9457'09021—dc21
    DNLM/DLC
    for Library of Congress   96–45334
                                                                                                                         CIP

Die Deutsche Bibliothek – CIP-Einheitsaufnahme

Skinner, Patricia:
Health and medicine in early medieval Southern Italy / by Patricia Skinner. – Leiden ; New York ; Köln : Brill, 1996
  (The medieval Mediterranean ; Vol. 11)
    ISBN 90-04-10394-5
    NE: GT

ISSN   0928-5520
ISBN   90 04 10394 5

PRINTED IN THE NETHERLANDS

CONTENTS

PREFACE

As always with any major undertaking, there are friends and colleagues to thank. The research work for the project was generously supported by a Wellcome Trust Research Fellowship in the History of Medicine, held at the Wellcome Institute in London, where Vivian Nutton offered encouragement and valued criticism. I also benefited from the financial support of the British Academy in the course of my preliminary investigations.

I am not an archaeologist, and Gill Clark patiently guided me to possible sources of information. I hope that my efforts meet with her approval; any errors remain firmly my own. Drafts of individual chapters were read by Chris Wickham and Monica Green, and I am grateful for their insights. The idea for the study developed from a paper given at Birmingham University's postgraduate medieval seminar, and subsequent chapters were read at the Early Medieval History seminar at the Institute of Historical Research in London; the Accordia Research Seminar at the Institute of Archaeology; the History of Science and Medicine seminar at the Wellcome Institute; and at the second International Medieval Congress at Leeds. I received many fruitful lines of enquiry to follow up at all four meetings and extend warm thanks to all concerned. That the project has finally appeared in print is due wholly to the initial encouragement of David Abulafia and to the efforts of Julian Deahl and the staff at Brill.

Michael Brooks and Irene Skinner have frequently helped me in my pursuit of the sick of medieval southern Italy, offering assistance and acute suggestions as the manuscript took shape: they remain my most valued critics.

LIST OF TABLES

ABBREVIATIONS
(see Bibliography for full publication details)

Alexiad	Anna Comnena, *Alexiad*
AESC	*Annales, Economies, Sociétés, Civilisations*
Apulia	F. Caraballese, *L'Apulia ed il suo Comune*
ASCL	*Archivio Storico per la Calabria e la Lucania*
ASPN	*Archivio Storico per le Province Napoletane*
BAR	*British Archaeological Report*
BHM	*Bulletin of the History of Medicine*
Caiazzo	*Pergamene dell'Archivio Vescovile di Caiazzo*
Carbone	G. Robinson, "The history and cartulary of the Greek monastery of S. Elias and S. Anastasius of Carbone"
CDA	*Codice Diplomatico Amalfitano*
CDB	*Codice Diplomatico Barese*
CDC	*Codex Diplomaticus Cajetanus*
CodCav	*Codex Diplomaticus Cavensis*
CP	*[Il] Codice Perris*
ChronSal	*Chronicon Salernitanum*
Cusa	*[I] Diplomi Greci ed Arabi di Sicilia*, ed. S. Cusa
DCDN	*Diplomata et Chartae Ducum Neapolis* in *Monumenta ad Neapolitani Ducatus Pertinentia*, IIii.
Donato	V. de Donato, "Aggiunte al *Codice Diplomatico Barese*".
Donnoso	*S. Nicolas de Donnoso*, ed. A. Guillou
Ducs	*Recueil des Actes des Ducs Normandes d'Italie*
Garufi	*[I] Documenti Inediti dell'Epoca Normanna in Sicilia*, ed. C. A. Garufi
Magistrale	F. Magistrale, "Aggiunte al *Codice Diplomatico Barese*".
Mileto	L.-R. Ménager, "L'abbaye bénédictine de la Trinité de Mileto".
Morea	*Il Chartularium del Monastero di S. Benedetto in Conversano*, ed. D. Morea
Nardò	*[Le] Pergamene della Curia e del Capitolo di Nardò*
NSK	*Die Urkunden der normannisch-sizilienischen Könige*
Oppido	*[La] Theotokos de Hagia-Agathe (Oppido)*, ed. A. Guillou
PAVAR	*[Le] Pergamene degli Archivi Vescovili di Amalfi e Ravello*
PBSR	*Papers of the British School at Rome*
PC	*Le Pergamene di Conversano*, ed. G. Coniglio
QFIAB	*Quellen und Forschungen aus italienischen Archiven und Bibliotheken*
RN	*Regesta Neapolitana*
RNAM	*Regii Neapolitani Archivii Monumenta*
SG	*Pergamene del Monastero Benedettino di S. Giorgio*
SGA	*[Le] Pergamene del Monastero di S. Gregorio Armeno di Napoli*
SLS	*Regesto di S. Leonardo di Siponto*, ed. F. Camobreco
SMML	*[Les] Actes Latins de S. Maria di Messina*, ed. L.-R. Ménager
Trani	*[Le] Carte che si conservano nello Archivio del Capitolo metropolitano della Città di Trani*
Théristes	*S. Jean-Théristes (1054-1264)*, ed. A. Guillou
Tremiti	*Codice Diplomatico del Monastero Benedettino di S. Maria di Tremiti (1005-1237)*, ed. A. Petrucci
Trinchera	F. Trinchera, *Syllabus Graecarum Membranarum*
Troia	*Les chartes de Troia*, ed. J.- M. Martin
Venosa	Briscese, "Le pergamene della cattedrale di Venosa"

INTRODUCTION

Good health is an essential prerequisite to most human activity. If an individual suffers illness, it impairs his or her ability to work effectively, or to participate in leisure pursuits. In short, ill-health sets an individual apart from normal personal and communal activities. In the middle ages, this inability to function could have extremely serious consequences. Being too ill to work could bring rapid destitution; non-participation in community events might engender suspicion and fear. In the early middle ages, public activity defined an individual's place in his or her community. Illness could, therefore, be devastating to an individual's social position, particularly if it manifested itself in physical deformities or was recognised as infectious.

Yet it is in fact very rare to find meaningful references in certain types of medieval written evidence to the health problems experienced by the medieval population. Most charters concentrated on the transfer of wealth, and most chroniclers, if they mentioned the sick at all, usually represented them in the context of charitable works. The most frequent references occur in hagiographical texts, but these have all sorts of associated problems for the historian due to their generic structure and often formulaic descriptions and incidents. Can we trust the often graphic descriptions of suffering in this type of evidence, or are they so derivative as to have little value? This study attempts to answer such questions and to understand the day-to-day health problems of the rich and poor as presented by a variety of texts.

Specifically, the study will attempt to link the rich documentary references to poverty and sickness in southern Italy in the period between the ninth and twelfth centuries to Italian chronicle evidence of famine and disease, hagiographical texts and the relatively sparse archaeological and epigraphic remains. I hope that this will shed some light on people's experience of, and reactions to, ill-health in their community. I shall also investigate possible causes of ill-health and the measures available to alleviate it. The study also seeks to explore the attitudes of society to those who were ill, and the fears and collective mentality surrounding sickness. Were the sick viewed negatively? Are the assumptions that little effective medical care was available, and that the aetiology of a given illness was poorly understood, correct? The differing interpretations placed on sickness in different societies will also be addressed from southern Italian examples.

The study will also investigate whether social class played any part in an individual's susceptibility to disease or the care that he or she could call upon. If the sick are elusive in our documents, then the poor sick are even more so. Nevertheless, it is likely that a reciprocal relationship existed between poverty and ill-health, each, in many cases, leading to the other. Marc Bloch quotes the French scholar Simiand to illustrate this relationship: 'For a doctor, the cause of an epidemic would be the multiplication of a microbe and its conditions the dirt and ill health occasioned by poverty; for the sociologist and philanthropist, poverty would be the cause, and the biological factors, the condition.'[1] With sufficient evidence, we may be able to test these relationships in the southern Italian context.

At the outset it is necessary to decide what is meant by 'poverty'. Hunger in a household might be caused by the sickness, or more often death, of a functioning member, but might not, for example, be linked directly to poverty.[2] Similarly, natural disaster could threaten people's livelihoods.[3] Many of the people featured in this study may not have been poor, but they were needy as a result of such circumstances, and this had the effect of reducing them to a similar set of actions.[4]

Medieval charters might at first seem unpromising as sources of evidence for ill-health. They are, first and foremost, records of individuals' transactions in land—by sale, lease, exchange or dispute or wills. But the survival of the latter allows us to glimpse the circumstances in which such documents were drawn up, and a careful combing of the charters, numbering some two to three thousand for the period, may also reveal instances of poverty. For example, movement to more fertile areas, land clearance, alternative foods, the exchange of service or property for food and the recording of loans, gifts or charity might all have been responses to hardship of some kind.[5]

---

[1] M. Bloch, *The Historian's Craft*, trans. P. Putnam, with preface by P. Burke (Manchester, 1992), pp.159-60.

[2] *Hunger in History*, ed. L. Newman et al. (Oxford, 1990), p.18.

[3] E.g. in Salerno in 1009, the tenants of a piece of land came to request a reduction in the rent in kind paid to their landlord, Amorus the priest, after the land they leased had been flooded: *CodCav*, IV, doc. 621.

[4] Even the language used is emotive: when a mother and son asked permission from the local judge to sell off land in Salerno in 1017, the document records that the child's request was made 'in order to avoid starvation': *CodCav*, IV, doc. 698. This phrasing derived from Lombard law, which forbade the sale of a child's land for any reason but impending starvation. On this, see P. Skinner, 'Gender and poverty in the medieval community', in *Medieval Women in their Communities*, ed. D. Watt (forthcoming).

[5] *Hunger in History*, pp.20-21 elaborates these responses.

These actions may be recorded in the medieval documentation with or without their direct cause, be it poverty, illness or neediness. However, we must be wary of assigning all such actions to hardship and poverty: many southern Italians were active entrepreneurs, and the clearing of new land or movement might be signs of economic prosperity rather than hardship.

The period under examination is relatively under-represented in studies in the history of disease and medicine. This is partly, I suspect, because the latter discipline seeks signs of intellectual activity, such as the transmission of medical texts. The 'dark ages' in western Europe rarely provide evidence of such activity, and so therefore have formed a lacuna between the classical era and that of the twelfth-century 'Renaissance'.[6] But southern Italy was exceptional, as we shall see. Intellectual activity is documented here, albeit sparsely, from at least the seventh century. The area has already attracted attention from historians whose main interest is in the medical texts emanating from the area, the development of the so-called 'school of Salerno', and the transmission of ancient sources.[7]

However, the copying and production of medical texts, and the precocious professionalisation of medicine in this region is only part of the story. A strict definition of medical history might be the study of the transmission of theoretical and practical medical skills through research into such medical texts and tools. Indeed, the introduction to a recent collection of essays on the subject has stressed that, since medicine was shaped by Judaism, Christianity and Islam and that all three religions had respect for the written word, then medical writings must be studied to reveal how these communities' minds worked in the face of disease.[8]

I shall make references to such learned medicine in the main text but, as Nancy Siraisi points out, 'medical texts are essentially prescriptive ... unreliable and inadequate sources of information about

---

[6] Nowhere is this more apparent than in the medieval contribution to a recent volume on *Medicine in Society*, ed. A. Wear (Cambridge, 1992), pp.59-90, which was able to condense 1000 years into just one chapter: K. Park, "Medicine and society in medieval Europe, 500-1500".

[7] An introductory, and useful, overview is provided by S. Vryonis, *The Medical Unity of the Mediterranean World in Antiquity and the Middle Ages* (Crete, 1991). See also G. Cavallo, "I libri di medicina: gli usi di un sapere", in *Maladie et Société à Byzance*, ed. E. Patlagean (Spoleto, 1993), pp.43-56, for the subsequent use and transmission of one late antique text. For a rapid general overview of the major developments in intellectual, medical activity in southern Italy prior to 1200, see N. Siraisi, *Medieval and Early Renaissance Medicine: an Introduction to Knowledge and Practice*, (London, 1990), p.58.

[8] F. M. Getz, "Introduction", in *Health, Disease and Healing in Medieval Culture*, ed. S. Campbell, B. Hall and D. Klausner (London, 1992), p.xiv.

actual medical activity and its social context.'[9] She calls for more localised studies to fill out that background. My previous research in southern Italy lead me to believe that it could provide such a detailed study and produce a complementary picture of those in southern Italy whose lives were never touched by such intellectual activity. They may not all have been peasants, 'the neglected ninety-plus per cent of the population',[10] but then, since medical care came at a price, neither were they wealthy enough in most cases to afford it.

The present study therefore broadens the definition of medical history to include the environment in which the southern Italian population lived, their diet, the relationship between sick people and their community, the availability and use of medical doctors, and alternative sources of care and cure.

A major issue to address is whether those medical practitioners who are documented represent the level of care available. Much literature about medieval medicine as a whole has tended to divide practitioners and their charges on the basis of sex. Traditionally, male doctors were trained and regulated, literate and demanded high fees; women, on the other hand, practised remedies from folk knowledge, rarely recorded their activities in writing and, if they charged at all, were cheaper and more accessible. Thus the evidence that we have for medical practitioners, almost all male, may not be truly representative of the pattern of healthcare. This may be particularly true of southern Italy, which had at least one literate, female medical practitioner in Trota of Salerno.[11] Taken together with evidence of high levels of lay literacy in this area, it might be suggested that the division outlined above may oversimplify the picture.[12] We cannot reconstruct a network of informal healthcare delivered by men and women in their communities without evidence of their activities, but we must remain alive to the possibility that they existed, and that the picture

---

[9] Siraisi, *Medieval and Early Renaissance Medicine*, p.xi.

[10] Chris Wickham, *Land and Power: Studies in Italian and European Social History* (London, 1994), p.1.

[11] See below, chapter 5.

[12] Apart from one "Virdimura of Catania, Jewess and wife of one Doctor Pasquale, who was licensed in 1276 to practise on paupers 'who cannot afford the immense fees of medics and physicians'", Monica Green has found little direct evidence of the type of wage differential mentioned: M. Green, "Recent work on women's medicine in medieval Europe", *Society for Ancient Medicine Review*, XXI (1993), quoting from F. Pierro, "Nuovi contributi alla conoscenza delle medichesse nel regno di Napoli negli ultimi tre secoli del medioevo", *Archivio Storico Pugliese* XVII (1964); see also M. Green, "Documenting medieval women's medical practice", in *Practical Medicine from Salerno to the Black Death*, ed. L. Garcia-Ballester et al. (Cambridge, 1994), p.334.

we build up from the surviving sources may be only a small part of the whole.

It is also entirely possible that the types of sources available to us fail to record precisely those whom we are seeking, the poor and the sick, simply because it was these sections of the community who were least likely to need records of property or to attract the attention of chroniclers. It is here that alternative sources, such as hagiography and archaeology, can be of such immense value. Hagiography is all too often dismissed as too stereotypical and full of *topoi* or set themes to illuminate medieval lives with any great reliability. However, if read closely, saints' lives are in fact much more diverse in content than might be expected, and can be tremendously valuable. Archaeological work can also bring us closer to the poor and sick, but as yet there is relatively little southern Italian material to work on.

The history of medicine and health are still in their infancy in Italy.[13] Only in the areas of text transmission and the rise of the Salerno medical school has any significant work been done.[14] The social history of medicine has remained largely neglected, and so many of the parallels I shall be using are from other, better-studied parts of Europe. Byzantium, in particular, furnishes considerable comparative evidence and has attracted much interest from scholars.[15] Its hegemony over parts of southern Italy in this period and continuing cultural and economic links, however, do not necessarily imply that the patterns here were the same.

This brings me to a brief historical introduction, setting the political frame within which the developments I shall be describing took place. Between the ninth and twelfth centuries, southern Italy was a political patchwork. The expansion of the Lombards southwards in the eighth century had created the vast duchy of Benevento, pushing the Byzantines, heirs of the Roman empire, down into the southern

---

[13] See, for example, the discussion by Luigi Faccini, "Storia sociale e storia della medicina", *Studi Storici* XVII (1976), pp.257-64. Although focusing on more modern history, it highlights the tendency of any work in this field in Italy to be by foreign scholars.

[14] On the texts: A. Beccaria, *I Codici di Medicina del Periodo Presalernitano (Secoli IX, X, e XI)* (Rome, 1956); on the school: P. O. Kristeller, "The school of Salerno: its development and its contribution to the history of learning", *BHM*, XVII (1945).

[15] On Byzantium, recent work includes: *Maladie et Société à Byzance*; the *Symposium on Byzantine Medicine*, ed. J. Scarborough (= *Dumbarton Oaks Papers*, 38, 1984); and numerous articles by Peregrine Horden: "Saints and doctors in the early Byzantine empire: the case of Theodore of Sykeon", *Studies in Church History*, XIX (1982), pp.1-13; "The Byzantine welfare state: image and reality", *Society for the Social History of Medicine Bulletin*, XXXVII (1985), pp.7-10; "Responses to possession and insanity in the earlier Byzantine world", *Social History of Medicine*, VI (1993), pp.177-94.

tips of Apulia and Calabria, isolated outposts on the Tyrrhenian coast around Naples, and the island of Sicily. In the ninth century Sicily was lost to the Arabs, and would remain under Moslem control until the middle of the eleventh century. On the mainland, an Arab emirate was briefly created in and around Bari; Amalfi and Gaeta broke away from Neapolitan suzereignty to become independent polities; and Salerno and Benevento split into separate Lombard states after a bitter civil war. Byzantium, however, went on the offensive under Basil I, and reconquered not only Bari but also large parts of Calabria and Apulia as well, and administrative *themes* of Longobardia and Calabria were created. Whilst the far South was being reconquered, further fission occurred in the Lombard states, with the creation of a separate polity centred on Capua. This pattern would endure until the eleventh century.

During our period, therefore, the peninsula was home to Latin- and Greek-speaking Christians, Sicily to Moslems and a few Greeks. In addition, there was a vibrant, although patchily-recorded, Jewish community in most urban centres of the South. In the eleventh century another group emerged: through the efforts of their energetic leader Robert Guiscard, the mainland gradually fell to the Normans. Theirs was not the first attempt to unify the area politically, but it was arguably the most effective, and would have repercussions on the social and cultural life of its inhabitants. The creation of the Norman kingdom in 1130 marks the end point of our detailed investigations.

The study is arranged in three parts. The first examines diet and environment, the two bases of good health and the areas in which social differentiation might be most visible. It includes a chapter on reproduction, with its implications for the health of both mother and child.

Part II moves away from environmental and biological factors to present the evidence from written sources for the impact of disease on the individual and his or her family. It will go on to examine the distribution of documented medical practitioners and places of healthcare in the South in this period, and assess whether these were the sole sources of care. The evidence for supernatural cures will also be discussed, and a chapter will investigate the impact of death on the community. Although archaeological investigations are still in their infancy in this area, some comments can be made about the types of disease visible on skeletal remains and the ways in which death was recorded.

Part III then attempts to briefly re-examine the types of medical text emanating from southern Italy in this period and to investigate the rise of the Salernitan medical school. It will set both of these

developments into the wider context of what we know about the
distribution of medical practice in the region. Some tentative conclusions will then be drawn as to why this area produced texts of such
quality and how they link into the activities of the medical school.
The conclusion will attempt to draw these threads together, to show
that what appears to be a disparate collection of fragmented evidence
may in fact have been different aspects of a strong medical tradition
in the South.

Very little of the material I shall be using for this study is new or
unmined. The charters under examination will be familiar to scholars
of this area: many have been accessible in published form for over a
century. Saints' lives from the South have frequently been examined
to augment the often sparse documentary record. Medical historians,
too, will recognise the texts that are referred to. The key lies in com-
bining sources of information which have previously been studied in
isolation from each other. Without devaluing the need to establish the
integrity of medical texts, the historian's task must also be to examine
the underlying conditions of lifestyle and to record the evidence for
incidents of ill-health and care, if such evidence is available.[16] As we
shall see, not all ill-health is attributable to lower standards of living.
Sickness does not stop at class boundaries, as the young patricians
featured in Giovanni Boccaccio's *Decameron* found out before they fled
the ravages of the plague in Florence in the fourteenth century. But
their wealth facilitated that flight.[17] Did privileged position make a
difference to health in preceding centuries? In the following two
chapters I shall examine two major indicators of status: diet and
living conditions.

---

[16] See, on this, M. D. Grmek, "Préliminaires d'une étude historique des maladies",
Annales ESC, XXIV (1969), pp.1473-83.

[17] Giovanni Boccaccio, *The Decameron*, trans. G. H. McWilliam (London, 1972),
p.64: the seven ladies and three young men described by Boccaccio took refuge in a
rural palace, having sent on supplies ahead. Their leisurely arrangements underline
their wealth.

PART ONE

INDIVIDUAL AND ENVIRONMENT

CHAPTER ONE

FOOD AND FAMINE

What did the inhabitants of southern Italy eat, and how did their diet affect their health? This chapter attempts a systematic survey of the foods mentioned in our sources and considers their nutritional value. The documentary evidence from southern Italy provides perhaps the fullest record anywhere, with the possible exception of the Iberian peninsula, of medieval crops, food and diet of the population. The bulk of the material available is in the form of charters referring to crops grown, for most documents were concerned with the recording of land transactions. As such, it could be argued that they reflect more the pattern of production than that of consumption. I shall return to this issue later in the chapter.

How much and what types of food were needed by the medieval population is a matter of some debate. The effect of diet upon health was well-known in antiquity. Galen's *De alimentorum facultatibus* specifically dealt with the issue.[1] As far as I can tell, this text was not one of those preserved in southern Italian compendia; even if it was, it is unlikely to have reached more than a tiny handful of people in the region, or to have had much impact on those who grew the food consumed. Any lessons about the beneficial or harmful effects of certain types of food would more likely have been learnt through empirical observation. Some of this observation finds its way into the written record.

In a satirical passage, for example, Liutprand describes what might await the inmate of a Byzantine foundation, putting his words into the mouth of the deposed emperor Romanus:

> Here is boiled water for you colder than the Gothic snows: here are soft beans, greenstuff and fresh cut leeks. There are no fishmonger's delicacies to cause illness; that is rather brought about by our frequent fasts.[2]

In fact, nutritionally, the monastic diet described may have been more beneficial than harmful! There are also comments such as that of Peter of Blois who, expelled from Sicily in 1168, criticised the

---

[1] His work is mentioned as a background to T. Scully, "The *Opusculum de Saporibus* of Magninus Mediolanensis", *Medium Aevum*, LIV (1985), pp.178-207.

[2] *Antapodosis*, V, 23

Sicilian habit of eating raw celery and fennel as bad for the health. Such statements are illuminating if only for the prejudices they reveal.[3]

A still more contentious issue is whether levels of nutrition and disease were linked. In his influential essay, Massimo Livi-Bacci acutely summarises the evidence that has been marshalled in recent years on the effects of nutrition on population changes,[4] and comes to the conclusion that whilst, 'In the short term, the negative effects of poverty and famine (coinciding with epidemic outbreaks) on population are well-established... the greatest mortality crises have generally been brought about by epidemics not linked to nutritional factors.'[5]

Livi-Bacci suggests that adequate calorific intake per head in pre-industrial societies was probably around 2000 calories.[6] How this broke down nutritionally could vary. A lack of variety in the diet or of any one particular element could be very damaging to health, as Table 1 illustrates. It can be seen from the table, based on modern dietary requirements, that vegetable sources could provide many of the nutritional elements necessary for good health. The Mediterranean diet, rich in leguminous vegetables and cereals, would appear to be quite adequate in terms of proteins.[7]

This has implications for the relative health of rich and poor in medieval society, where meat was something of a luxury if not caught in the wild. Even if 'pre-industrial populations were, for the most part, consumers of cereals which, in the form of bread, loaves, buns, porridge and so forth, constituted the staple diet,'[8] they could frequently supplement this monotonous regime with fresh vegetables and fruit, more so in the Mediterranean than in other parts of Europe. Indeed, the Neapolitans were known as *mangiafolie* (leaf-eaters)

---

[3] B. Henisch, *Fast and Feast: Food in Medieval Society* (London, 1976), p.109.
[4] M. Livi-Bacci, *Population and Nutrition* (Cambridge, 1991).
[5] Livi-Bacci, *Population and Nutrition*, p.xii.
[6] Livi-Bacci, *Population and Nutrition*, p.27.
[7] Livi-Bacci, *Population and Nutrition*, p.30. He elaborates this statement later, p.91: a survey of available data on food intake in Italy between the 14th and 18th centuries shows that between 500 and 800 grams of bread was available to the individual each day, or roughly 2/3 or 3/4 of a person's average daily requirement of 2000 calories a day. "So for example, a half-kilo loaf of bread, complemented by 100 grams of black olives, 100 grams of cheese, half an onion and the odd fruit or vegetable in season would have satisfied the 'average' requirement, and has constituted the most normal diet of Mediterranean countries from the time of Homer to virtually the present day." However, M. S. Mazzi, *Salute e Società nel Medioevo*, (Firenze, 1978), p.10, disagrees with this optimistic view: she states that the availability of beans, peas and chickpeas could not compensate for the reduced use of meat in protein terms.
[8] Livi-Bacci, *Population and Nutrition*, p.48.

Table 1. Nutrients and Diseases

(after Livi-Bacci, *Population and Nutrition*, pp.28-9)

Nutrient	Food sources	Deficiency causes
proteins	meat, fish, beans (high) cereals (av.) fruit, veg (low)	wasting disease
vitamin A	meat, fish, beans, milk, leguminous veg malformed bones	vision disturbance, rickets, anaemia,
vitamin D	animal and veg fats	rickets, osteomalacia
vitamin E	vegetables	anaemia
vitamin C	fruit, greens, liver	scurvy
vitamin B6	fish, meat	depression, convulsions
folic acid	many foods	anaemia
vitamin B12	meat, eggs, milk	pernicious anaemia
calcium	milk, beans, cereals	rickets, osteoporosis
phosphorus	many foods	rickets, fragile bones
magnesium	many foods	vasodilation, arteriosclerosis
iron	meat, eggs, veg some greens	anaemia
zinc	many foods	dwarfism, retarded growth
iodine	fish, milk, greens	goitre, cretinism

up until the sixteenth century, on account of their high dietary intake of greenstuff.[9]

Thus, although the availability of different crops varied greatly depending on which part of the region one inhabited, it could be argued that southern Italian peasants and poor families were comparatively well-nourished in relation to their northern European counterparts.

Livi-Bacci points out that it is in fact difficult to demonstrate clearly a link between privileged diet and better health. But some types of disease can be shown to have a clear link with poor nutrition. They include cholera, diarrhoea, herpes, leprosy, respiratory problems, measles, intestinal parasite, whooping cough and tuberculosis.[10] Ironically, poor nutrition may have been the result rather than the cause of some infections, as the illness reduced the individual's capacity to absorb nutrients from food. Diarrhoea, in particular, is known to have this effect, and is especially dangerous for infants and children.[11]

With these thoughts in mind, it is time to examine what the inhabitants of medieval Italy grew to eat. Did the population receive an adequate diet in terms of nutrition?

Fruit and vegetables

Around Salerno, apart from the ubiquitous vine, crops included a preponderance of orchard fruits (apples, pears, plums) and nuts on the hill slopes. The latter were mostly chestnuts, which could be used for flour as well as eaten whole, and hazelnuts. Although only rarely documented,[12] almonds may also have been a popular crop. A foreshadowing of this area's conversion to intensive citrus cultivation is a tenth-century reference to the growing of lemons.[13] Figs and damsons are also recorded.[14]

---

[9] Mazzi, *Salute*, p.18. This image is borne out by the charter evidence, where the cultivation of "leaves" appears solely in Neapolitan documents: *RN*, doc. nos. 443 (1033), 493 (1063), and 533 (1084).

[10] Livi-Bacci, *Population and Nutrition*, p.38.

[11] Livi-Bacci, *Population and Nutrition*, p.35.

[12] Up to 1050, only one document, *CodCav*, IV, doc. 545 (1002) refers to their cultivation.

[13] *CodCav*, II, doc. 382 (986).

[14] Figs: *CodCav*, I, doc. 187 (955), and V, doc. 773 (1025); plums, figs and damsons: *CodCav*, V, doc. 740 (1022).

Vegetables are far less frequently documented, reflecting perhaps their cultivation for domestic consumption rather than commercial exploitation. Gardens, after all, would change hands far less frequently than fields and vineyards, and so do not show up so prominently in the documentary record. Pulses are recorded in 868 and 1014,[15] unspecified vegetables in 999,[16] and onions in 1002,[17] but these rare references are unlikely to represent the true occurrence of these crops. Olives were grown as well, and their oil used for both lighting and consumption.[18]

Cereal crops are rarely documented in the Cava archive, perhaps reflecting the limited areas in which they could be grown around Salerno. Bread is mentioned in only one document,[19] but this again reflects the nature of the evidence, which was more concerned with the raw materials grown to produce it. Grain, wheat and barley are documented in 1018, when they formed part of the rent for a mill on the river Liri.[20] Barley occurs in other documents,[21] but whether it fed humans or animals is unclear, as it is mentioned alongside acorns. The latter were a common source of food for domestic animals, especially pigs.[22]

Documents from Naples reveal a similar diversity of crops and foodstuffs. Once more, the growing of vines was common. As might be expected from an area which had more exploitable arable land, grain crops are frequently documented, mostly wheat, from the earliest charter. Apples also appear frequently.

The records pertaining to ecclesiastical estates are particularly valuable when examining foodstuffs, for they are likely to present a reliable picture of locally-available produce. For example, in 921 the convent of St Gregory Armeno at Naples was benefiting from the cultivation of barley, wheat and millet.[23] The convent's archives also reveal the growing of cucumbers,[24] perhaps reflecting the docu-

---

[15] *CodCav*, I, doc. 64; *SGA*, doc. 14

[16] *CodCav*, III, doc. 524.

[17] *CodCav*, IV, doc. 542.

[18] Refs to olives: *CodCav*, I, doc. nos 137 (919) and 194 (956), II, doc. nos 294 (976), 399 (988), and 424 (990), III, doc. 476 (995), IV, doc. 688 (1015), V, doc. 740 (1022), Refs to oil: *CodCav*, II, doc. 249 (966), IV, doc. 576 (1005).

[19] *CodCav*, II, doc. 323 (980): the proprietors of a church gave the priest the bread belonging to their foundation, suggesting communion bread.

[20] *CodCav*, V, doc. 709.

[21] *CodCav*, IV, doc. 641 (1011), V, doc. 747 (1023).

[22] Acorns: *CodCav*, IV, doc. 572 (1005), V, doc. 862 (1033).

[23] *SGA*, doc. 2.

[24] *SGA*, doc. 11 (996). *Caucumenas* also grown for SS Sergius and Bacchus as well: *RN*, doc. 314.

mented occurrence of kitchen gardens in the city. An early example of the 'leaf' cultivation which gave the Neapolitans their nickname occurs in a document of 1033. When the abbess of St Gregory Armeno leased a mill with a garden, the rent comprised half the milling profits plus greens, onions and leeks.[25] The convent may have obtained the rent from its own tenants: a lease of a suburban garden owned by the convent carried a rent of cash in instalments plus ten quarts of greens and 200 chicken eggs each year.[26] The same or a similar garden provided greens, eggs and onions in 1084.[27]

A lease of land belonging to the monastery of SS Sergius and Bacchus in 1019 also reveals rent demanded in kind, including wheat, millet, wine, apples and nuts.[28] Two years later, the monastery was receiving apples, chestnuts and acorns,[29] and red beans.[30] The convent of SS Marcellinus and Peter also took advantage of rent in kind, receiving wine, chestnuts and hazelnuts and wheat in a lease of 1022.[31] Pulses, still a staple of Mediterranean cuisine, occur frequently in the Neapolitan evidence.[32] Olive cultivation appears frequently in the earlier charters from Naples, but less so later on. Either the crop became rarer, or a change occurred in the way it was grown, with a move away from formal olive groves to perhaps the odd row of trees among other crops, or simply less groves changed hands.[33]

The habit of recording rent in kind in Neapolitan documents is extremely useful, revealing the types of crop grown and, occasionally, processed. Thus mill leases of 990 and 1016 reveal the miller paying both flour and bread.[34] This may indicate the means of production in Naples, with bread being made at the mill as well as or rather than in private or public ovens.

Around Amalfi, the predominant food crops grown appear to have been apples and chestnuts, reflecting the mountainous and wooded

---

[25] *RN*, doc. 443 (1033): the mill lay at *Fullotani* (unidentified) and perhaps was not urban.

[26] *RN*, doc. 493 (1063).

[27] *RN*, doc. 533.

[28] *RN*, doc. 379. The monastery continued to receive these crops from its tenants: *RN*, doc. 399 (1023): wine and apples.

[29] *RN*, doc. 388.

[30] *RN*, doc. 391.

[31] *RN*, doc. 396.

[32] *RN*, doc. nos 3 (915), 67 (953), 233 (982), 277 (992), 281 (993) red beans, 267 (990) 275 (992); white beans in a lease of 1022 (*RN*, doc. 395).

[33] References to olives: *RN*, doc. nos 25 (934), 96 (957), 102 (958), 121 and 125 (962), 128 (963), 155 (966), 161 (967), 165 (968), 177 and 182 (970), 209 (976), 244 and 247 (985), 273 (992), 319 (1003), 334 (1009), 358 (1016).

[34] *RN*, doc. nos 268 and 367.

terrain of the Lattari mountain spur. In addition, a significant number of documents refer to the growing of pulses. Where these are specified, beans and chickpeas appear to have been the favoured crops.[35] A few documents refer to olives or olive groves,[36] but these are all early in date (the latest being 1004), suggesting, as at Naples, that a change of cultivation may have taken place, or that olives were grown along the edges of orchards and rarely recorded, or that their cultivation was extremely rare anyway. A couple of documents mention vegetables, without specifying types.[37]

I have discussed the cultivation patterns around Gaeta in some detail elsewhere,[38] but a brief survey reveals the cultivation of vines and cereals as major crops. Other foods are rarely documented: isolated documents record pears, figs and chestnuts.[39] Although much of the grape crop must have gone to make wine, two Gaetan documents record the use of raisins.[40] A further charter records loaves, another rare example of bread being recorded rather than its raw ingredients.[41]

Further south, the peninsula becomes less hospitable to any kind of cultivation, and there is a distinct change in the types of foodstuffs grown. There is also a notable decrease in the number of documents featuring cultivated foods. Lucania and Calabria are particularly poorly-documented. Like Campania further north, these areas produced nuts,[42] and fruit growing is heavily documented around Oppido, although types are not specified. A document from Carbone, dated 1007, provides useful evidence of the range of products from a monastic estate. Cosmas, abbot of St Basil, handed over control of the monastery, its vines 'which I myself have planted', animals, a mill, corn and 300 jars of wine.[43]

---

[35] References to pulses generally: *CDA*, I, doc. nos 36 (1020), 47 (1036), 55 (1043), 61 and 62 (1051), 76 (1081), 77 (1084), 79 (1086); *PAVAR*, I, doc. 13 (1037); *CP*, doc. nos 6 (1036) and 49 (1067). References to beans and chickpeas: *CDA*, I, doc. 60 (1048); *CP*, doc. 80 (998). Both the latter documents refer also to the cultivation of *mauci*, which I have been unable to translate.

[36] *CDA*, I, doc. nos 4, 15 and 18.

[37] *CDA* II, doc. 591; *CP*, doc. 91.

[38] P. Skinner, *Family Power in Southern Italy: the Duchy of Gaeta and its Neighbours, 850-1139* (Cambridge, 1995), pp.247-59.

[39] *CDC*, I, doc. nos 28, 96 and 27 respectively.

[40] *CDC*, I, doc. nos 147 (1025) and 150 (1026).

[41] *CDC*, I, doc. 181 (1047).

[42] Walnuts: *Carbone*, doc. 6 (1056); chestnuts: *Oppido*, doc. nos 11 (1052) and 43 (undated).

[43] *Carbone* 1.

Still more detailed information comes from the unique list, compiled in the mid-eleventh century, of possessions and revenues of the archbishopric of Reggio di Calabria. Primacy is given to listing the see's plantations of mulberry bushes, presumably for the production of silk, but the remainder of the seven-metre roll reveals numerous olive-groves, fruit trees, vines (often irrigated, suggesting the inhospitable conditions here), pastures and fig trees.[44]

In Apulia, figs are frequently documented, reflecting that tree's greater resistance to the drier conditions there.[45] The ubiquitous crop here, however, was the olive, and groves are recorded in all the major document collections relating to the Apulian and Salentine peninsula. This may explain why Amalfitans came to live and own land here, since olives were, as we have seen, less common in their homeland.

This survey of vegetable and fruit growing reveals some important points. The first concerns availability. In a region like Naples and its hinterland a variety of food crops seems to have been readily available. Other regions were less fortunate. If food of any type had to be transported, its price inevitably rose. This had implications for the less well-off, who may have found even the most basic foodstuffs prohibitively expensive. Worthy of note is the likelihood that both Amalfi and Gaeta had to import a considerable amount of their grain requirements, the former in particular having no easy access to cultivable land. Tied in with the fact that milling facilities were tightly controlled in both territories, it may well be that here bread was in fact a luxury foodstuff. We may have to revise our notion that it was a freely available staple: the substitution of chestnut flour, producing an inferior quality loaf, has already been noted.

That the agricultural pace was quickening in the South during this period is suggested by numerous contracts, again particularly from Campania, to improve and bring land under cultivation. A typical example occurs at Nola in 1038, a lease by archpriest of St George in *castellum de Cicala* of land to be planted up with vines and apple trees at one-fifth of the crop as rent.[46] However, we must be cautious about interpreting such evidence as a clear indicator of population growth: such contracts may have more to do with entrepreneurial activity than increasing the food supply. Even if the latter was the aim, the

---

[44] *Le Brébion de la Métropole Byzantine de Règion (vers 1050)*, ed. A. Guillou (Vatican City, 1974).

[45] Around Bari: *CDB*, I, doc. 4 (962), IV, doc. nos 2 (962) and 16 (1025), V, doc. 21 (1095); at Corato: *CDB* IX, doc. 13 (1098); at Troia: *Troia*, doc. 21 (1088).

[46] *RN*, doc. 465.

regionalised nature of southern Italian food crops suggests that provision and distribution must have been extremely patchy.

Fish

An important supplement to the medieval diet, particularly if meat was too expensive, was fish. Many of the documents from southern Italy come from coastal cities and churches, and reveal different ways of exploiting fish stocks. As well as fishing off the coast, we have several references to distinct fisheries, all in the hands of the wealthy and powerful. For ecclesiastical institutions, fish replaced meat when the latter was forbidden, and there are numerous instances of monasteries and churches owning fisheries. The church of SS Peter and Paul in Taranto, for example, received half a fishpond by the sea in that city in 981.[47] In 986 princess Aloara of Capua offered the monastery of St Laurence there a fishery in lake Patria.[48] Fisheries were a valued part of the dukes' property in Gaeta, and fish are recorded several times.[49] Lake Patria lay on the border between Gaeta and Capua, and Gaeta's rulers had rights here too, as did the dukes of Naples. Duke Sergius of Naples gave Peter, the abbot of SS Severinus and Sossus in the city, the right to fish in the Neapolitan part of the lake in 998.[50] Other, similar donations are also recorded in other parts of southern Italy,[51] and the value of fisheries is reflected in disputes over their ownership. In 1030 the bishop of Canne near Barletta won a dispute over a stretch of river near Siponto, but the losers were permitted to keep a third of the *kyppe* (?kippers ?mackerel) they fished there.[52] And in 1063 it took the combined weight of the local bishops and a papal order to persuade a group of noblemen including the count of Loritello to restore two fisheries to the abbot of the monastery at Banzi, recorded in a document written at Venosa.[53]

In Salerno, the ownership of fisheries was again a preserve of the rich, but here tenants were allowed to hold and exploit the stocks. In 1018, for example, the sons of Disigius the count leased out their lake

---

[47] *Trinchera*, doc. 8.
[48] *RNAM*, doc. 206.
[49] *CDC* I, doc. nos 55 (957) and 135 (1019); II, doc. nos 218 (1063) and 231 (1066).
[50] *DCDN* 6.
[51] E.g. in 1082 Robert Guiscard and his wife Sikelgaita gave a fishery in Taranto to the church of St Laurence in Aversa: *Ducs* 40; and in 1092 Robert Borrell gave a church and some fishing rights to St Angelus at Mileto: *Mileto* 10.
[52] *CDB* VIII, doc. 9.
[53] *Ducs* 12.

called Paulinum to two tenants at a cash rent for one year.[54] Fish
were also included in food rents from other tenants: the priest of a
church in Naples in 1028 was obliged to give its owners a meal of
meat and fish or chicken every year.[55]

It is unclear whether the towns of southern Italy made extensive
use of moats in their defences—few survive today if they did— but
Guillerme draws attention to the northern French practice of fishing
in the town moat.[56] Certainly for the inhabitants of many southern
Italian towns the possibility existed of fishing in nearby rivers and
ditches as well. Capua, for example, lay in the bend of a river, as did
Benevento. Nonetheless, it may well be that once again the wealthy
were able to have fish far more frequently as part of their diets,
simply because they had jealously-guarded fisheries from which to
exact rentals in kind. King Roger of Sicily combined recreation with
practicality: he had pleasure gardens at Favara, where there were
well-stocked fishponds.[57]

Meat

Meat is a rather more elusive thing to find in the southern Italian
documentary record. Later material from northern Italy is more explicit about the movement and consumption of animals: 'In terms of
the medieval period in Italy, three major sources of food may be
defined: firstly food was obtained from agriculturally-orientated units,
both large and small, at indeterminate distances from the urban mar-
kets: secondly, a discrete amount of livestock kept in and around the
town itself could provide some meat and milk: thirdly, food and other
animal products were acquired through hunting and fishing.'[58] Findings from later periods also suggest that meat consumption may have
been relatively high among the Italian population, as there was plen-
tiful land for flocks and herds to graze.[59]

---

[54] *CodCav*, V, doc. 710. Earlier leases, such as that of Manso the Amalfitan, again
the son of a count, to his tenant Legori in 963, asked for a portion of the fish caught
as part of the rent: *CodCav*, II, 223. Manso's son left the fishponds to the church of St
Maximus in his will of 1012: *CodCav*, IV, doc. 646.

[55] *RN*, doc. 417.

[56] A. Guillerme, *The Age of Water: the Urban Environment in the North of France, 300-
1800* (College Station, Texas, 1988), p.98.

[57] Henisch, *Fast and Feast*, p.34.

[58] G. Clark, "Town and countryside in medieval Italy", *Anthropozoologica*, XVI
(1992), p.76.

[59] Livi-Bacci, *Population and Nutrition*, p.92. See also G. Clark, "Animals and animal
products in medieval Italy: a discussion of archaeological and historical methodol-

Terry O'Connor points out that many medieval towns contained 'substantial areas of waste ground, orchard and garden', in which small livestock might be kept. The most amenable to this spatially limited way of life were goats, pigs, fowls and geese.[60] The southern Italian evidence rarely reveals the existence of urban animal husbandry, but is concerned with property blocks. We might, then, be able to assess the likelihood of such husbandry, and the documented offerings of eggs certainly presupposes the existence of fowls.[61] Chickens appear extremely frequently in the documents, and were mostly demanded as part-payment of land rents.[62]

In the South, stock-rearing revolved around pigs and sheep or goats. Documentary references to the latter are particularly useful, as their archaeological remains are notoriously difficult to distinguish.[63] Also, in direct contrast to crops, we know more about the consumption of meat through archaeological investigation than about the methods of animal husbandry.

The hilly slopes of much of the Amalfitan peninsula were ideal grazing ground for sheep, and they are documented in this area in the eleventh century.[64] Lambs are specified in two documents,[65] suggesting a taste for their more tender meat. Ecclesiastical rents in Naples reveal other uses: as well as rents including specified numbers of sheep,[66] documents relating to the lands of SS Severinus and Sossus and SS Sergius and Bacchus include the stipulation that sheep are to be kept for lard.[67]

---

ogy", *PBSR*, LVII (1989), p.162, on the records of 14th-century pensions in Sicily. She also, p.156, draws attention to the discovery of an intensive beef-raising policy at Farfa abbey.

[60] T. O'Connor, "What shall we have for dinner? Food remains from urban sites", in *Diet and Crafts in Towns*, ed. D. Serjeantson and T. Waldron (BAR British Series 199, Oxford, 1989), pp.14, 17.

[61] Neapolitan documents again provide a rich hunting ground for eggs: *RN*, doc. nos 493 (200 were demanded as part of payment of rent to a church), 533 and 548.

[62] Salerno: *CodCav*, I, doc. 151; III, 529; IV, 540/1, 654, 680 and 701; V, 757, 762 and 812; Naples: *RN*, doc. nos 1, 8, 158, 212, 244, 314, 330, 331, 336, 370, 391, 417, 448, 465 and 493; *SGA* 2; Mileto: *Mileto*, doc. 5; Amalfi: *CDA*, II, doc. 589; I, doc. nos 41, 73, 76, 86; *CP*, doc. nos 18, 80, 35; Gaeta: *CDC*, I, doc. nos 96, 143, 181. The vast majority of these references are in lease payments to churches on major feast days, and vary from one to 26 chickens per year.

[63] P. Baker and G. Clark, "Archaeozoological evidence for medieval Italy", *Archeologia Medievale*, XX (1993), p.51.

[64] References to sheep: *CDA*, I, doc. 60; II, doc. 591; *CP*, doc. nos 45 and 35.

[65] *CDA*, I, doc. nos 36 and 55.

[66] *RN*, documents 285 (994: 50 sheep payable to SS Severinus and Sossus); 336 (1009: 20 sheep payable to SS Marcellinus and Peter); and 385 (1020: 50 sheep payable to SS Sergius and Bacchus).

[67] *RN*, documents 281 (993) and 292 (996) respectively.

Elsewhere sheep are rare, but are recorded around Carbone in Lucania,[68] and Conversano in Apulia,[69] areas of significant uplands. Sheep featured among the possessions of the church of St Menna in the territory *rusiani*, possibly Rossano, given to the monastery of the Holy Trinity, Cava, in 1086.[70] A document from Mileto does not specify whether the animals referred to as flocks are sheep or goats, but at least gives some idea of numbers.[71]

Goats are less frequently referred to: again they may have been rendered invisible by the nature of the documents, which were more interested in the land they grazed on.[72]

Although cattle are mentioned occasionally, their numbers are smaller.[73] A Gaetan document refers to a cow and calf,[74] and seems to reflect a common pattern that cattle were kept singly and were a prized asset. A document from Salerno refers to a co-owned cow and slave-girl (indicative also of the status of slaves!), and a church in the city later numbered a cow amongst its livestock.[75] Ecclesiastical institutions are also documented owning herds of cattle. The monastery of SS Sergius and Bacchus in Naples received a herd from two brothers seeking its support in 953, and the *igumenos* of St Basil left a herd to his community in 1007.[76] Finally a gift to St Nicolas in Terlizzi in 1098 included two cows and a *stracarium* (a young cow?). Oxen are often referred to,[77] and were presumably slaughtered for food and/or hides when their working lives were over.

In the twelfth century, the monastery of St Maria Latina in Messina is documented exporting cattle from Sicily to Jerusalem. In a concession made in 1168, the Norman king, William II, and his mother Margaret listed the produce that could be exported without paying tolls. The annual allowance included two hundred cattle, lambskins, ox hides and seven hundred cheeses, the last item testifying to an active and rarely-documented dairy industry on the island.[78]

---

[68] *Carbone*, doc. 1 (1007).

[69] *PC*, doc. 3 (915).

[70] *Trinchera*, doc. 49.

[71] *Mileto*, doc. 10 (1092).

[72] Salerno: *CodCav*, III, doc. 459; V, doc. 812; Gaeta: *CDC*, I, doc. 4 (831).

[73] This corresponds with the pattern found in a late medieval site further North, Tarquinia-Corneto, where pigs and sheep/goats were more common than cattle: Clark, "Town and countryside", p.77.

[74] *CDC*, I, doc. 19, the will of Docibilis I (906).

[75] *CodCav* I, doc. 108; V, doc. 812.

[76] *RN*, doc.81 and *Carbone*, doc. 1 respectively.

[77] At Salerno, *CodCav* II, doc. 324, and at Carbone, *Carbone* doc. 4.

[78] W. Holtzmann, "Papst-, Kaiser- und Normannen-urkunden aus Unteritalien I: San Filippo—S. Maria Latina in Agira", *QFIAB*, XXXV (1955), doc. 7.

References to pigs are scattered and isolated.[79] If they were, for the most part, kept in areas of woodland where they could scavenge for nuts and acorns, they may not appear as frequently as their actual numbers. Pigs are, however, the most frequently documented animal in Gaetan charters.[80] Their importance to the local diet, at least for the elite, may be indicated by the fact that both Docibilis I and Docibilis II, his grandson, had men whose task was specifically to care for their pigs.[81] Pork seems to have been a popular food here: on two occasions bishop Bernard of Gaeta leased out properties and demanded as part of the rent pork shoulders and loins.[82] The consumption of meat may have followed quite a regular pattern according to the time of year: it is interesting that among the twelve signs of the zodiac depicted in the twelfth-century mosaic in on the floor of Otranto cathedral, February is represented by a woman cooking a piglet.

Indeed, much of the evidence about animal stocks seems to be linked to payments of rental in church documents, perhaps reflecting a tendency for slaughtering to occur at religious festivals. Certainly the pattern of payments, often in instalments at Christmas and Easter with, sometimes, a further delivery of meat on a specified saint's day, tallies with the idea that meat was consumed on what were, literally, feast days. Taken together with the pattern of ownership of livestock, which favours the elite in at least one archive—that of Gaeta—we may surmise that meat was a luxury that few poorer families were able to enjoy, apart from perhaps the odd chicken, or small game caught in the wild.

Although hunting traditionally enjoys an image as the preserve of the elite in medieval society, it is highly likely that in the woods and marshes of southern Italy a diet could be relatively easily supplemented with the occasional game bird or rabbit. Around Amalfi, quails are recorded several times, suggesting that these birds, too, could be hunted or reared.[83] As with chickens, their eggs may also have been consumed. Pigeons, blackbirds and ducks are also mentioned in Neapolitan documents.[84]

---

[79] Salerno: *CodCav*, III, doc. 459; V, doc. 812; Conversano: *PC*, doc. 3 (915), and a later one from Amalfi, *CDA*, I, doc. 60 (1048); Naples: *RN*, doc. nos 244 (985), 330 (1006) and 336 (1009).

[80] *CDC*, I, doc. nos 10 (855), 19 (06), 54 (957), 56 (958), and 62 (962); II, doc. 213 (1061).

[81] *CDC*, I, doc. nos 19 (906) and 52 (954).

[82] *CDC*, I, doc. nos 96 (997) and 181 (1047).

[83] *CDA*, I, doc. nos 36 (1020) and 60 (1048); II, doc. 591 (1033); *CP*, doc. 45 (1033).

[84] Pigeons and blackbirds: *RN*, doc. 212 (977); ducks: *SGA*, doc. 8.

Other foods: salt and honey

An essential corollary to the use of meat and, to a lesser extent, fish, was the availability of salt to preserve it. There is considerable charter evidence for saltpans in southern Italy. Anna, the widow of Kataspites the priest, handed over half of her saltpans to the cathedral of Oppido in 1054.[85] The revenue-list of the archbishopric of Reggio also includes saltpans.[86] When Theodore *pettacarus* received a saltpan at S. Elia near Bari in 1061, he agreed to pay a rent of 20 barrels of salt and one *modium* of fine white salt each year.[87] It is possible that the distinction here was between preserving and table salt. A major centre of salt production appears to have been the lowlying area around Siponto. The value of its product is clearly indicated by the series of disputes over saltpans there between the bishop of Siponto and the abbot of the monastery of St Maria on the Tremiti islands off the Apulian coast.[88] The bishop of Rossano was granted the saltpans in his town by king Roger II, a gift confirmed by the empress Constance and Frederick II in 1198.[89] Salt is also documented at Oppido in 1054/6.[90] The occurrence of the placename Salini indicates that Gaeta, too, had saltpans.

Honey formed a rather more luxurious part of the diet. It is recorded in Naples in 994 and Salerno in 1029.[91] Wild honey was probably available to those who knew where to look. Beehives are recorded at Carbone in 1007,[92] reflecting perhaps one of the essentials of a well-stocked estate.

The food products documented in the southern Italian sources would seem to satisfy Livi-Bacci's list of essential nutrients, and the nature of the evidence suggests that much more food was produced that is in fact documented, both in terms of quantity and, probably, variety. However, this is only part of the equation, for we must also consider how many people actually had access to the full range of foods on offer. Can any comment be made about the levels of 'food entitle-

---

[85] *Oppido* 33.
[86] *Brébion de la Métropole Byzantine de Reggio.*
[87] *CDB*, IV, doc. 41.
[88] *Tremiti*, doc. nos 23 (1033/8), 75 and 76 (1064) and 79 (1068).
[89] W. Holtzmann, "Papst-, Kaiser- und Normannen-urkunden aus Unteritalien II: San Giovanni di Fiore, Erztbistum Rossano, Bistum Bova, Sant'Elia Carbone", *QFIAB*, XXXVI (1956), p.24.
[90] *Oppido*, doc. 33.
[91] *RN*, doc. 285; *CodCav*, V, doc. 811.
[92] *Carbone*, doc. 1.

ment'[93] in this part of medieval Europe? Was an inflated value, derived from rarity, placed on certain types of food? These questions may ultimately be unanswerable, but some account must be taken of the issue of food entitlement if we are to decide whether food, or lack of it, was responsible for differing levels of health in different social classes. The differing levels of food entitlement become apparent if we compare documents. For example, fisheries were strictly controlled by the ruling elites of different areas (even if it was, in practice, probably fairly simple to catch fish elsewhere). The record of meat frequently occurs in the context of payments by tenants to their landlords, the latter being almost entirely major ecclesiastical foundations. One wonders how many tenants actually ever ate the types of food they handed over. Chickens, in particular, were a favoured part-payment of rent. They almost came to symbolise subjection, if a document from Gaeta is anything to go by. Freed in a will, a group of slaves still had to make annual offerings of chickens to their former master's family.[94] Nevertheless, the fact that tenants often had to pay a proportion of the food they produced as rent suggests that they were able to keep and consume the remainder.

As we have seen, stark regional differences also existed in the types of foodstuffs grown. It is by no means a certainty that the diversity of foods available could be had in all regions of the South. Even if a lively internal market existed, there was no guarantee that crops would always be available, and the poor in any case would not be able to afford what was on sale. This brings us to the problem of food shortage.

Rich and poor alike suffered a drop in their food intake during times of famine, even taking into account the greater ability of the wealthy to cushion themselves against its effects. A serious famine hit the Byzantine empire in 927-8.[95] Liutprand is an eloquent witness to another which struck the Byzantine empire at the time of his visit of 968, during which in the Greek territory, 'one gold piece did not purchase two of our Pavian measures of corn.'[96] Its effects at Constantinople were such that 'three gold pieces were insufficient to pro-

---

[93] That is, the number of people who owned or had the means to purchase food or had a right to a dole of some kind: L. A. Tilly, "Food entitlement, famine and conflict", in *Hunger and History*, ed. R. I. Rotberg and T. K Rabb (Cambridge, 1983), p.136.

[94] *CDC*, I, doc. 143.

[95] Morris, "Powerful and the poor", p.8.

[96] Liutprand of Cremona, *Embassy to Constantinople*, chapter 44, in *The Works of Liutprand of Cremona*.

vide one meal for my twenty-five attendants and our four Greek guards.'[97]

This type of evidence, relating as it does to the Byzantine capital rather than the provinces, is too anecdotal to be of much value in determining what impact famine had. It is unlikely that much food was moved long distances between the heart of the empire and its provinces, so we cannot assume that the Byzantine famine had any effect in southern Italy. But Liutprand also provides detailed information about a famine in Italy which may have more relevance for the present study. The bishop of Cremona's precise account can provide a fairly accurate date for the occurrence of the famine:

> In this year, as you yourselves know well, there was a great and terrible eclipse of the sun, on the sixth day of the week at nine o'clock in the morning. On that day your king Abderahamen was overcome in battle by Radamir, the most Christian king of Galicia. Moreover in Italy for eight nights in succession a comet of wonderful size appeared, drawing after it a very long and fiery trail. This foreshadowed the famine destined soon to follow which by its severity caused lamentable havoc in Italy.[98]

The following chapter says that this occurred after king Hugh had been driven from Rome, which happened in 932.[99] The defeat of Abderahamen, mentioned in the text, can probably provide a closer date, for it may refer to the victory of king Ramiro II of Leon's victory over Abd al-Rahman III at Simancas in 939.[100]

If, then, we take the years around and after 939 as the time of famine, can this be seen reflected in the evidence of the time in the South? There may be some correlation with another narrative source, the *Chronicon Salernitanum*. This relates that during the reign of prince Gisolf I (943-78) 'a furious plague hit the principate, very many died and many houses were empty. With great insistence the citizens raised prayers to God, until the plague ended.'[101] Before the plague struck, storms and rain had dislodged part of the mountain above the city. Now famine and plague are obviously not the same thing, but one can only imagine the devastation wrought by the plague on a population only just recovering from famine conditions.

Salerno had been hit by famine before, during the Saracen siege of the city. The Salernitan chronicler tells us that the defenders were

---

[97] Liutprand of Cremona, *Embassy to Constantinople*, chapter 34.
[98] Liutprand of Cremona, *Antapodosis*, V.2, in *The Works of Liutprand of Cremona*.
[99] C. J. Wickham, *Early Medieval Italy* (London, 1981), p.178.
[100] R. Collins, *Early Medieval Spain* (London, 1983), p.241.
[101] *ChronSal*, chapter 168.

worn out with hunger to the point of eating dogs and mice.[102] The very unusual sale by one Wiletruda the widow of her *morgengab*, her portion of her husband's lands which was designed to be kept to support her, reflected the hardship in the city at this time: she cited as the reason for the sale the fact that she had no food.[103] From the evidence of the chronicle, it seems that attacks, whether by Christians or pagans, were planned to cause as much disruption to the enemy's food supply as possible. There are instances of attacks on Capua both at harvest time and the grape-picking season.[104] Similarly, the fighting season meant that double damage was caused to the Neapolitans when their city was besieged between May and July.[105]

, In times of crisis such as these, the poor were the first to suffer. Southern Italian sources reveal remarkably little concern for the needs of the poor. The key point to note when attempting to describe their lives in this period is the ambivalence with which they were viewed by contemporary authors. The poor were at the same time a burden on society and an opportunity for Christians to imitate Christ.

To be charitable was both a Christian duty and a virtue, winning praise and respect for the giver.[106] Thus the Byzantines' action of killing or imprisoning the Latin-speaking beggars who came to Liutprand of Cremona's lodgings in Constantinople merely reinforces his black picture of his hosts.[107]

Looking at tenth century evidence, Rosemary Morris identified a rather more tolerant attitude towards the needy in Byzantium, but linked it rather with the emperors' attempts to curb the power of the *dynatoi*, or powerful officials, than with genuine concern for the plight of the poor. Emperors were expected to take part in public displays of charity,[108] but their rhetoric against abuses of power served only to reinforce their authority over their mighty subjects.[109]

Apart from imperial doles, however, other institutions catered for the needs of the starving, the sick and the disabled. Several of Naples' churches functioned as *diaconiae*, that is, ecclesiastical foundations

---

[102] *ChronSal*, chapter 115.

[103] *CodCav*, I, doc. 97 (882).

[104] *ChronSal*, chapter 125: Guaiferius (861-80) besieged Capua at time of harvest; chapter 134: Athanasius of Naples attacked the city during the grape harvest.

[105] *ChronSal*, chapter 64.

[106] See for example Liutprand's praise of king Hugh of Italy: *Antapodosis*, III.19, in *The Works of Liutprand of Cremona*.

[107] Liutprand of Cremona, *Embassy to Constantinople*, chapter 46.

[108] Morris, "Powerful and the poor", p. 21.

[109] Morris, "Powerful and the poor", p.27.

which regularly gave out help to the poor, on a Byzantine or more accurately a late Roman model.

Charity towards the poor seems to have been a popular way of winning spiritual reward amongst southern Italian individuals as well. Particularly worthy of praise were the very wealthy and powerful who nevertheless remembered their less fortunate subjects. The author of the *Chronicon Salernitanum*, writing in the tenth century, contrasted those like prince Arechis II who 'tied himself to God's precepts' and distributed alms to the poor, and gave food and clothes to the crippled,[110] while others like Roffred the nobleman and prince Grimoald IV of Benevento brutally oppressed the poor.[111]

Lesser men made gifts to the poor. For example in 1188, Peter Coci, going on a pilgrimage, made his will and stipulated that 10 *tari* be paid each year to support the infirm and ill.[112]

In the Jewish community as well, care of the poor was seen as a meritorious act. Although there is very little direct evidence of the Jews' activities in southern Italy, it would not be hazardous to suppose that the tradition of baking a few extra loaves and doing charitable works, associated with the women of the community in Fustat in Egypt and recorded in the Cairo Genizah,[113] extended to other parts of the Mediterranean Jewry as well.

A final comment by Liutprand of Cremona adds an interesting twist to our picture of food intake. We often assume that the medieval population ate according to their status, and that the rich dined better than the poor. The survey of southern Italian foodstuffs and consumption patterns supports this analysis, and it is further reinforced by the ideal image of contemporary saints who eschewed most foods in favour of greenstuff and water.[114] This may well be true as far as the quality of food is concerned. However, Liutprand describes the mistresses of the miscreant pope, John XII, thus: 'some of them fine ladies who, as the poet says, are as thin as reeds by dieting,

---

[110] *ChronSal*, chapters 14 and 18.
[111] *ChronSal*, chapters 48 and 49.
[112] *Garufi*, doc. 92.
[113] S. D. Goitein, *A Mediterranean Society II: the Community*, (Berkeley, 1971), pp.105-113.
[114] See, for example, the life of St Fantinus, whose ascetic diet of crude greenstuff and water is stressed: *La Vita di San Fantino il Giovane*, ed. E. Follieri (Brussels, 1993), chapter 21; St Nilus, too, is praised for his simple diet of bread, water and sometimes cooked vegetables: *Vita di San Nilo*, ed. G. Giovanelli (Grottaferrata, 1966), chapter 3.16.

others everyday buxom wenches.'[115] This suggests that dieting for
fashion was already well-known in the medieval West.[116]

To sum up, various regions of southern Italy produced a wide
variety of foodstuffs to feed their population. There is little evidence
in the documents of the aristocratic classes that food shortage was
ever a problem, and they enjoyed a diet including a variety of meat
and fish. Although clerics are most visible demanding such foods as
rental, we must remember that they may also have catered for distinguished guests visiting their foundations.

The majority of the population, however, may have subsisted on
much simpler fare. A question mark must hang over the availability
of bread to the poor in areas where grain was scarce and/or imported, but alternatives such as chestnut flour and, perhaps, even
pulse flour may have been used. Nutritionally, if others besides the
Neapolitans were 'leaf-eaters', their total diet may have been deficient
only in certain proteins. Nevertheless, what little we have been able to
glean suggests that cultivators and tenants did not begin to approach
the sophistication of diet of their social superiors, and that this may
have had health repercussions. Was this carried through into the
environment in which rich and poor lived? The following chapter
attempts to discuss this issue.

---

[115] Liutprand of Cremona, *Chronicle of Otto's Reign*, chapter 4, in *The Works of
Liutprand of Cremona*.

[116] *Contra* Henisch, *Fast and Feast*, p.16, who argues that 'dieting for fashion had not
yet been invented.'

CHAPTER TWO

INDIVIDUAL AND ENVIRONMENT

Nutrition was one major factor in the preservation of good health. Another was the environment in which individuals found themselves. Written sources can provide some information on living conditions likely to affect health. Archaeological investigations provide even more evidence, since they pick up factors which were not thought necessary to record in the written sources. Archaeology may allow us some insight into possible class differences in living conditions, and can illuminate hidden health problems.

It is now, for example, more possible than ever to retrieve valuable information about people's lifestyles and state of health from careful investigation of skeletal remains. Burials and incomplete cremations allow the science of paleopathology to open up a window on such issues as age at death, diseases and nutritional stress, all of which leave tell-tale signs on the individual skeleton.[1]

There has, as yet, been very little work on southern Italian cemeteries in order to begin reconstructing a general picture of the population's health in the early medieval period. This is partly due to the paucity of archaeological investigation itself, which has still to produce significant samples of medieval material to analyse. Maria Ginatempo, in a recent review article, highlighted the tendency, until relatively recently, of Italian archaeology to pass over the human remains excavated, even on necropolis sites. This she attributed to a lack of interdisciplinary cooperation.[2] Even now, much Italian investigation is of prehistoric and ancient sites. Where medieval cemeteries were excavated in the eighteenth and nineteenth centuries, the human remains tended not to be kept at all, or at best the skulls were preserved.[3]

---

[1] See the very useful survey by Tony Waldron, "The effects of urbanisation on human health: the evidence from skeletal remains", in *Diet and Crafts in Towns*, pp.55-74; also, the very useful overview provided by A. Chamberlain, *Human Remains* (London, 1994).

[2] M. Ginatempo, "Corpi e uomini tra scienza e storia: studi di osteo-archeologia umana per l'Italia medievale", *Archeologia Medievale*, XV (1988), p.7.

[3] Ginatempo, "Corpi e uomini", p.18.

Nevertheless, some limited work has been done in central and southern Italy which, along with documentary and environmental investigations, can provide further information.

In a recent excavation at Otranto in Apulia, although samples of human bone were found in later strata than the Roman cemetery, they were explained in terms of disturbance of the cemetery layers, and so could date to anywhere between the first century B.C. and the fifth century A.D. It is tempting, however, to suppose that the "gracile population at Otranto", which had "females with very fine features and extremities, but coarse limbs and stocky bodies",[4] did not significantly lose those characteristics between the ancient and medieval eras. Similarly, the pathologies of these samples, which revealed extensive osteoporosis and osteoarthritis,[5] can begin to suggest the types of problems that the medieval population may have faced as well, particularly when the people represented in this bone sample seem to have died from natural causes with little outside evidence of disease. The average age of death is unfortunately not stated.[6]

It is perhaps not very useful to try to gain evidence from individual pathologies, however. Recent work in the field has stressed the need to look beyond the individual, and to try to assess instead the general health of the population—the "biocultural" approach.[7]

In Italy, the Farfa Project, an integrated study of the Farfa region using both its rich documentary sources from the eighth century onwards alongside a campaign of field survey and excavation, is currently using this more wide-ranging approach to try to illustrate the changes in settlement pattern in this region between the late Roman and medieval periods.[8] The site has so far yielded signs of early medieval occupation and a late medieval/early modern cemetery, and it is to be hoped that further investigations in this far-reaching project will furnish further information.

Another major excavation, still in progress, is that on the site of the early medieval abbey of St. Vincent on the Volturno river. Two burial sites have so far been found in this rural location, dating from

---

[4] M. Becker, "The human bones", in *Excavations at Otranto I: the Excavation*, ed. D. Michaelides and D. Wilkinson (Lecce, 1992), p.156.

[5] Becker, "Human bones", p.158.

[6] Becker, "Human bones", p.160.

[7] H. Bush and M. Zvelebil, "Pathology and health in past societies: an introduction", in *Health in Past Societies*, ed. H. Bush and M. Zvelebil (BAR Int. series 567, Oxford, 1991), p.4.

[8] See the report by J. Moreland, M. Pluciennik et al., "Excavations at Casale San Donato, Castelnuovo di Farfa (RI), Lazio, 1992", *Archeologia Medievale*, XX (1993), pp.185-228, including references to earlier interim reports.

the late Roman and early medieval periods. The sample excavated between 1980 and 1986 formed the subject of an investigation by Valerie Higgins, who sought to examine the changes in health of S. Vincenzo's late Roman and early medieval populations.[9] Unfortunately, the skeletal samples were poorly preserved, and produced few positive findings except for the fact that the stature of women seems to have increased between the two periods.[10] Nor did the recent publication of the report on the excavation of the hill-top cemetery furnish any further data.[11] Nevertheless, the San Vincenzo project offers the prospect of further investigations.

The social environment had far-reaching consequences for health, and could cause illness as much through mental stress as physical hardship.[12] However, the physical surroundings in which people found themselves were just as important.

Housing

A person's living place could have a significant effect on the health that they enjoyed. Lack of light or fresh air, overcrowding, or the early medieval tendency to share living space with livestock might all be detrimental to mental or physical well-being. An analysis of sixteenth and seventeenth century data suggests that it was the urban crowding, density and transmissibility of infection that were the primary causes of disease and death, and these overrode any benefits that a richer, more varied diet might bring.[13]

The southern Italian documents offer some information on living conditions in an urban environment but, unfortunately, little about rural settlement patterns. What sort of housing was available to the medieval inhabitants of southern Italy? We are in no position as yet to assemble an equivalent to the medieval housing typologies which have been attempted for England on the basis of archaeological data,[14] but the documentation provides some descriptive detail and a

---

[9] V. A. Higgins, *Health Patterns in Rural Agricultural Communities of the Late Roman and Early Medieval Periods, Including a Study of Two Skeletal Groups from San Vincenzo al Volturno*, 2 vols. (Sheffield, Ph.D. thesis, 1990).

[10] Higgins, *Health Patterns*, I, p.108; this in itself may be an indicator of better nutrition.

[11] C. Coutts, 'The hill-top cemetery', in *San Vincenzo al Volturno 2*, ed. R. Hodges (London, 1995), pp.98-118; a further report on the skeletal remains is, however, due to appear in the third volume of the excavation report.

[12] H. Bush, "Concepts of health and stress", in *Health in Past Societies*, p.15.

[13] Livi-Bacci, *Population and Nutrition*, p.67.

[14] J. Schofield and A. Vince, *Medieval Towns* (Leicester, 1994), pp. 63-74.

number of dimensions. The latter are rather sparsely scattered, reflecting the fact that in some places measurements were required in property transactions, whereas in others a generic description of the property was sufficient.

In Salerno dimensions do appear to have been important: the *Codex Cavensis* includes numerous transactions in specifically measured pieces of land, and this tendency extended to urban properties as well. For example, a wooden house in the city exchanged for another by two clerics in 853 measured 3 *passus* by eight, or about three metres by seven.[15] A series of land leases by the church of St Maximus in the city in the late tenth and early eleventh centuries is more informative. In 966 Peter Bisantius the cleric leased a plot of land measuring just under five metres by five for 29 years. On it, he was to build a house to share with his sons and daughter (and, crucially, he stated that he would live there).[16] Fifteen years later, Mauro the Amalfitan and Stephen son of Peter received another plot from the church to build another house, this time measured as twenty by seventeen feet.[17] Many other, similar examples survive.[18] None, however, provide much detail on the houses to be built, apart from occasionally to specify wood as the building material, and to make provision for the drainage of water through *sericidia*.[19] Two exceptions are documents of 1023 and 1026. In the first, the abbot of St Maximus renewed a lease, originally made to John the priest, for John's eponymous son. John the elder had built a one-storeyed house on the plot, measuring fifteen feet by eighteen and, with two years and four months remaining on his tenancy, had presumably died. His son, also a priest, now received a lease of twenty-two years, and was permitted to build a wooden path and to renew the old wooden

---

[15] *CodCav*, I, doc.36.

[16] *CodCav*, II, 249.

[17] *CodCav*, II, doc. 331. This appears to have been an average size, to judge by other examples. A two-storey house divided into three portions in 1028 measured 22 feet by ten: *CodCav*, V, doc. 796.

[18] E.g. *CodCav*, II, doc. nos 372 (984), 432 (990) and 452 (992); III, doc. nos 496 (996) and 508 (997); IV, doc. nos 537 (1001), 598 (1008), 604 (1008) and 705 (1018). The smallest plot leased by St Maximus measured fourteen feet by nine, and was to be held by two men: *CodCav*, V, doc. 749 (1023). The relatively late date of this document, and the fact that the men were offered the choice of building a one- or two-storeyed house, reveals how crowded the city was becoming. Apart from St Maximus, we also have a lease by one Peter the priest to his brother in 996, on much the same lines: *CodCav*, III, doc. 499.

[19] For example, the specification that Ligori, son of John the Sorrentan, was to build two drains when he constructed his house on a plot of land, measuring 23 feet by 22, leased from St Maximus in 1000: *CodCav*, III, doc. 536.

columns, apparently a portico of some sort. This house also had a drain.[20] The second document records the sale of a house by Ermesenda, widow of a cleric, and probably includes more detail because of the permanent alienation of the property. The house was two-storeyed and measured eighteen feet by eleven. By the path along one wall, there was a balcony and small wooden stair case, two feet wide and ten long, and the house also benefited from a drain-pipe.[21]

An interesting document of 991 reveals how crowded the city had already become: a plot of land measuring forty-nine feet by thirty-one contained several houses described as "Jewish".[22] However, we should not assume that the well-documented Jewish community of the city lived in poorer conditions than their Christian neighbours: in 1012 two brothers named Maio and Samuel leased a site measuring 38 feet by eighteen for just one house.[23]

Although we are reasonably well-informed about the nature of housing, including the internal arrangements of several two-storeyed structures, in medieval Naples, we are nevertheless unable to gain any accurate idea of their floor area.[24] A wooden house recorded at Gaeta in 980, on the other hand, was measured at approximately six metres by seven.[25] The limited space of some properties is quite striking: in 1031 Mila gave a house site in Caputaquis, next to the house of Peter the cleric, to a father- and son-in-law. It measured just four feet by eighteen, and they were to share the communal exit and waterpipes on the site. Given that the plot is described as a house site, we must assume that the two men were intending to build on it.[26] A house sold in Troia in 1043 was recorded as being five feet on the street frontage by eleven, and there is no indication that this tiny space was compensated by more than one storey.[27] Another property sold in the city in 1083, with a well and a ditch, measured about three metres across its street frontage, but extended some twenty metres backwards.[28] House sites sold in Lecce in the twelfth century seem to confirm this width as

---

[20] *CodCav*, V, doc. 750.

[21] *CodCav*, V, doc. 787. The price of this property was twenty *solidi*. Land and a house next to a well, sold in 1028, and totalling fifteen by 23 feet, went for fifty *solidi* two years later: *CodCav*, V, doc. 807. The wealth of house owners, it seems, was far in excess of that of their tenants.

[22] *CodCav*, II, doc. 442.

[23] *CodCav*, IV, doc. 651. The lessor was the monastery of St Maria.

[24] Skinner, 'Urban communities', discusses Neapolitan houses

[25] *CDC*, I, doc. 75.

[26] *CodCav*, V, doc. 839.

[27] *Apulia*, doc. 6.

[28] *Troia*, doc. 18: the dimensions are given as 18 by 60 feet.

an average: a site sold in 1109 measured about nine metres across, whilst another in 1130 was just three metres wide.[29] We do not know how far back these house sites may have extended from the street, of course, nor whether the houses themselves filled the entire plot. It seems likely that the living space would have been similar to that in the Gaetan case, but with an open piece of land behind. This would correspond to English examples of the same century, and might belie a certain amount of planning by the Norman rulers of both areas.

In striking contrast, we have a fairly full description of the most prestigious housing available: the ducal palace at Gaeta, built by John I and surveyed in the will of his son, Docibilis II (fl. 914-54). This stretched from the centre of the town all the way to the sea (and on present-day remains was terraced to do so), and included in its accommodation baths, other houses, separate kitchens and even aviaries.[30]

That the Gaetan palace took up so much space in the cramped Gaetan peninsula was itself a sign of high standing. The boundary clauses in documents describing most houses reveals their proximity to other, similar properties, and gives some idea of the level of urban crowding throughout the period. It emerges that, whilst Campanian towns soon saw structures of more than one storey from the tenth century onwards, including some of the smaller centres like Nocera,[31] the Pugliese centres retained single-storey housing rather longer, only beginning to build upwards in the twelfth century.[32]

But in both areas the crowding is noticeable, with repercussions for the towns' sanitation and water supply. How well did the inhabitants of southern Italy fare in these respects?

Sanitation

That hygiene and public sanitation were recognised as integral factors in the health of the population is illustrated by the measures taken in late medieval Italian cities to regulate both.[33] Were any such

---

[29] *Le Carte del monastero dei SS. Niccolò e Cataldo in Lecce*, ed. P. de Leo (Lecce, 1978), p. 143, doc. 3 (27 feet) and p. 147, doc. 5 (10 feet).

[30] *CDC*, doc. 52.

[31] A two-storeyed house is recorded here in 1033: *CodCav*, V, doc. 856.

[32] For more on this, P. Skinner, "Urban houses and households in medieval southern Italy", in *Houses and Households in Towns*, ed. R. Holt (forthcoming)

[33] Siraisi, *Medieval and Early Renaissance Medicine*, p.38, summarises the main provisions in the northern cities. See also the discussion in V. Fumagalli, *Landscapes of Fear: Perceptions of Nature and the City in the Middle Ages* (Cambridge, 1994), p.92.

measures in force in the earlier period in the South? The evidence
available to answer this question again comes entirely from an urban
perspective. Rural areas provided more space for waste disposal, and
presumably might even have used the waste as fertiliser for crops, but
in discussing the urban population we must not fall into the easy trap
of seeing the countryside as in some way more "healthy": the evidence is just not available to make such a judgement.

Standards of hygiene were perhaps more important than nutrition
when it came to health in medieval southern Italy. Paul Arthur suggests that under its independent dukes from the end of the eighth
century onwards, the level of deaths in Naples decreased as the city
prospered. His explanation for such a phenomenon is that the growth
of a more efficient system of waste disposal under the dukes.[34] It must
be said that Arthur does not provide much evidence for his statement,[35] and both Naples and the other large medieval city of the
South, Bari, provide evidence of private arrangements and occasional
disputes over the disposal of human waste.[36] But in neither case can
the solutions found be described as improvements in standards of
hygiene: agreements not to throw waste into communal alleyways
hardly equates to an effective "system" of waste disposal.

Nevertheless, Naples may, by the standards of the time, have appeared advanced in some aspects of hygiene. It is from this city that
the earliest southern Italian reference comes to lavatory facilities: a
small house used as a *monimen* in 924.[37] The next occurs in Salerno (a

---

[34] P. Arthur, "Archeologia urbana a Napoli: riflessioni sugli ultimi tre anni",
Archeologia Medievale, XIII (1986), p.521.

[35] The report of the excavation in the city centre at vico Carminiello ai Mannesi
reveals waste blocking up an entire street in the same century, and a possible wall
built to contain it or form a terrace in the same century: *Il Complesso Archeologico di
Carminiello ai Mannesi (Scavi 1983-1984)*, ed. P. Arthur (Rome/Lecce, 1994), p.74.
This might be interpreted as ducal control, and Arthur, p.433, describes the fifth-
century reuse as a dump as "?official", but I am sceptical whether it was in any way
systematic.

[36] Naples: Stephen had to agree in 1005 not to throw his refuse out of a new
window he proposed to make overlooking a communal alleyway which he shared
with at least twelve neighbours: *RN*, doc. 323; in 1032 a dispute arose over a drain
made in the first floor of a house which poured water onto a church roof next door:
RN, doc. 435; in a dispute over a common courtyard in the city in 1077, its function
as a dump for water and refuse is explicitly stated, *RN*, doc. 524, but this was not to
block the common entrance to the yard. Bari: Nicolas and Porfiro agreed in 1026 to
building work to prevent *aqua et suzzimen* falling on Nicolas' house in Bari: *CDB*, IV,
doc. 17; in 1034 Kalocuri was forced to build a drain in the same city to prevent
water falling on the houses of his two neighbours: *CDB*, IV, doc. 23.

[37] P. Arthur, *Naples in the Dark Ages* (forthcoming), ms p.57; I am grateful to Paul
Arthur for the opportunity to read his book in advance of publication.

camera necessariorum) only in the late twelfth century.[38] Later evidence suggests, however, that conditions in Naples saw little improvement through such innovations. A decree of the Angevin king Robert in 1313 suggests that Neapolitan streets, full of *sporcizie*, were as unsavoury as any other city's.[39] Some idea of the reputation of cities as unhealthy places is suggested by the fact that during the "dog days" of summer, the fierce heat in the city and hills of Rome kept Otto I from entering the city.[40]

The creation of the Norman kingdom of Sicily in 1130 seems to have brought with it a higher level of regulation in city sanitation, at least in Palermo, where the kings were based. A unique document of 1187 records how Richard *camerarius* (chamberlain) leased a piece of land near the royal palace from the archbishop to serve as a public dunghill (*pistilentia*).[41] Arthur suggests that in Naples at least human faecal remains were carefully disposed of on account of their value in the fertilisation of agricultural land.[42] There is no evidence to confirm whether the dung collected outside the palace at Palermo would serve the same purpose.

Water Supplies

The supply of fresh water was even more important than effective waste disposal for the lives of the medieval population. The benefits of running water for sanitation are not attested to in our evidence, but there are frequent references to urban water supplies.

"We must presume that many town dwellers succumbed to cholera and intestinal infections",[43] both related to the imbibing of polluted water. A recent study suggested that wealth could not reduce exposure to disease because aristocrats drank from the same rivers and streams as the rest of the population.[44] Both assumptions, of course, rest on the belief that the medieval town dweller actually drank water. In medieval Italy, wine was freely available and may

---

[38] A. R. Amarotta, *Salerno Romana e Medievale* (Salerno, 1989), p.242.

[39] Mazzi, *Salute*, p.22.

[40] Liutprand, *Chronicle of Otto's Reign*, chapter 8.

[41] *Garufi*, doc. 88.

[42] Arthur, *Naples in the Dark Ages*, p.57.

[43] *Death in Towns: Urban Responses to the Dying and the Dead, 100-1600*, ed. S. R. Bassett (Leicester, 1992), p.1.

[44] S. Cotts Watkins and E. van de Walle, "Nutrition, mortality and population size: Malthus' court of last resort", in *Hunger and History*, p.26.

have been the preferred beverage of most people. This is supported
by clear evidence that the connection between poor water and poor
health was being made in the tenth century. Liutprand of Cremona
explicitly relates the sickness that he and his companions suffered in
Constantinople to the brackish water that they were forced to drink
instead of wine.[45] This, ironically, in a city where the system of water
provision was particularly sophisticated.

Guillerme has also recently pointed out a possible connection in
France between "the authority of Jewish doctors attendant on nobles
during the tenth and eleventh centuries" and the fact that "the aris-
tocracy was not insensitive to the concern for preserving the purity of
drinking water. The Old Testament and Talmud contain numerous
precepts on the subject, and Jews drank only well water."[46] His suggestion could apply equally well to southern Italy, particularly since
Jewish physicians were active here.[47]

What sources of water supply were available? It is clear that many
towns were sited on rivers in order to benefit from both the water
available and the defensive protection that they afforded. Nowhere is
this proximity more apparent than in Benevento - a house sold here
in 845 was called "de fluvio Sapatu" and must have been extremely
close to that river.[48] Where no rivers flowed, settlements often benefited from springs and wells instead - the immediate hinterland of
Gaeta is an example of this. Further inland, the benefits of winter
snows might also come into play. It is clear, however, that where
water was not directly accessible, measures were taken to manage a
supply from a distance. This served both agricultural purposes—
channels and aqueducts appear quite frequently in this context[49]—
and supplied urban centres.

Roman Naples had certainly had aqueducts: were these still functioning? During the Gothic wars in the sixth century, the citizens of
Naples had held out until the aqueducts were cut, suggesting that at
that date there were no other supplies of water available. Later, one
aqueduct gave its name to a region outside Naples near modern
Pomigliano, but no clues survive as to whether it still functioned.[50]
Paul Arthur suggests that the wells referred to in Neapolitan docu-

---

[45] Liutprand of Cremona, *The Embassy to Constantinople*, chapter 13, in *The Embassy
to Constantinople and other Works*, trans. F. A. Wright (London, 1930).
[46] Guillerme, *Age of Water*, p.101.
[47] See below, chapter 5, for more on Jewish physicians.
[48] *CodCav*, I, doc. 26.
[49] *PC*, doc. 10 (954, Bari); *Troia*, doc. 22 (1089); *CDB*, I, doc. 36 (1096, Bari).
[50] *RN*, doc. nos 137 (964), 217 (978), and 286 (994). Later evidence would suggest
not: in 1073 the arches are described as "once an aqueduct": *RN*, doc. 517.

ments may have been relics of the Roman system of water supply to that city, drawing water from an aqueduct running to the Serino river near Avellino.[51] The availability of water in the area is illustrated by the sale of a *fundus* with oven, bath and well in 1042.[52] Within the city in the *Furcillense* district, the *Aqua Fistola* is documented as flowing down the road in 1073.[53] In a document of 1092, Ursus received an *excatorium* from the monastery of SS Sergius and Bacchus in the marshes at Tertium outside Naples. From this he was to provide water for the monastery and its land for seven years.[54] A relatively early document provides evidence that running water may have been available in private dwellings in Naples as well. In 958, the three sons of Sergius the monk swore that the water running through their *solareum* had run out into the courtyard of their neighbour, Maru, for a long time and that their father and Maru's mother had agreed this.[55] It is entirely possible that, under relatively stable ducal rule, the aqueducts were to some extent repaired and maintained.

This also seems to be the case in the survival of a medieval aqueduct at Salerno (plate 1), suggesting that the inhabitants of this city fared rather better than their contemporaries elsewhere. Their well-being is certainly supported by the sheer presence of water in charters relating to the city, and the distinction made in terms to refer to it.[56] Crucially, a ninth-century document refers to "public water",[57] indicating that the Lombard princes took measures to ensure its supply to their centre of power, at least early on. The aqueducts are referred to in several charters,[58] distinguished from the rather more common term for a channel or conduit,[59] suggesting that they were still func-

---

[51] Arthur, *Naples in the Dark Ages*, ms p.10.

[52] *RN*, doc. 474.

[53] *RN*, doc. 514; the road begins to take its name from the watercourse soon after: the *vico de Fistola* is documented in 1076, *RN*, doc. 517.

[54] *RN*, doc. 551.

[55] *SGA*, doc. 6.

[56] Apart from the specific references in following footnotes, water occurs in *CodCav*, I, doc. 63; II, doc. nos 330 and 400; III, doc. 482; IV, doc. 555 (all of these references are rural); fountains (largely in the sense of rural springs) occur in *CodCav*, I, doc. 148; II, doc. nos 286 (975: a fountain in the Plaiu district of the city) and 296; IV, doc. 577.

[57] *CodCav*, I, doc. 36 (853): the "public water" is referred to near "empty land" in new Salerno, that is, the part of the city expanding eastwards.

[58] *CodCav*, III, doc. 535 (the builder of a new house in the Plaiu district is ordered to construct a *sericidia* or water-channel); IV, doc. 608 (rural aqueduct); V, doc. 814 (an aqueduct associated with milling on the river Lirino).

[59] References to waterpipes and channels: *CodCav*, I, doc. 101 (a waterpipe bearing the evocative name *Puteo Regente*); III, doc. 469; V, doc. nos 749, 750, 787, and 807.

tioning. Water from these may well have been distributed to various parts of the city and stored in the cisterns which recur in the charter evidence; a further source of water for the Salernitans was a number of wells.[60]

The Cava archive also reveals urban water management and supply in smaller centres. In 1004 and 1021 houses in Avellino are documented with both aqueducts and gutters.[61] A two-storeyed house had a waterpipe in Nocera in 1023;[62] and in the relatively new settlement of Caputaquis, waterpipes associated with a house are documented in 1031.[63]

Elsewhere, a document of 1001 from the city of Canne, later deserted for nearby Barletta, refers to the *aquaro* at one end of a section of the city wall.[64] References to aqueducts and cisterns in Amalfitan material suggest water management in that region as well, essential in such a mountainous area.[65] There is also evidence for wells,[66] springs and cisterns.[67] Lakes may have been managed to provide drinking

---

[60] *CodCav*, II, doc. nos 372 and 438; III, doc. 488: all of these are urban wells.

[61] *CodCav*, IV, doc. nos 564 and 653.

[62] *CodCav* V, doc. 745.

[63] *CodCav* V, doc. 839.

[64] *CDB*, VIII, doc. 2.

[65] Amalfi, aqueducts: *CodCav*, IV, doc. 564 (1004); *CDA*, I, doc. 33 (1018); cisterns: *PAVAR*, II, doc. 11 (1037); *CP*, doc. 47 (1061).

[66] *Morea*, doc. 2 (889): two wells; *Trinchera*, doc. 4 (899): dispute over wells near Conversano; *RN*, doc. 6 (920): well in garden next to church of St Eufimia in Naples (the church is later documented in 985 with a pool, *RN*, doc. 245); *CDB*, IV, doc. 1 (939): well associated with two houses in Bari; *PC*, doc. nos 8 (941) and 9 (944): wells in Castellana; *RN*, doc. 74 (951): land with wells at Tertium outside Naples; *PC*, doc. 14 (960): well and pool; *CDB*, IV, framm. 3 (993): houses and well in Bari; *PC*, doc. nos 20 (969) and 31 (1009): lands and wells near Conversano; *CDB*, IV, doc. 11 (1011): well near house in Bari vicinity; *PC*, doc. 33 (1014): church and well in or near Conversano; *CDB*, VIII, doc. 5 (1018): well below Canne; *Trinchera*, doc. nos 35 (1047): well of St John near Taranto; and 39 (1052): land near the well Abbatissa given to Bartholomew of SS Apostles (?Taranto); *PC*, doc. 38 (1052): well; *Théristes*, doc. 1 (1054): wells; *Troia*, doc. 18 (1083): house with well and ditch in city of Troia; *CDB*, V, doc. nos 5 (1085), 13 (1089), 29 and 30 (1099): houses next to a wells in Bari; *PC*, doc. 46 (1085): well; *Donato*, doc. 3 (1093): well by vineyard in Pallizzo outside Bari; *PC* 56 (1095): division of well near Conversano; *Nardò*, doc. 1 (1099): church and well near Nardo. Some wells are particularly well-documented, for example that named Malo in or near Conversano, given to the abbey of St Benedict there by Domnico in 957, *PC*, doc. 11. His wife gave her portion in 960, *PC*, doc. 14, and the monastery subsequently defended it in a courtcase, *PC*, doc. 38 (1052). In 1053, however, a further *portiuncula* (tiny portion) of the well was sold to St Benedict's by Letitia: *PC*, doc. 39.

[67] *PC*, doc. 3 (915): two cisterns and houses in Conversano; *CodCav*, I, doc. 146 (927): house with cistern in *platea Furcillensis*, Naples; *RN*, doc. 17 (930): gift of cistern from which the donors had drawn water for 30 years in/near Naples; *CDC*, I, doc. 36

water too, if a reference to the "well in lake Flaburra" near Conversano is to be taken literally.[68]

Water consumption is sometimes indicated. In 1085 two brothers received a gift of land near St Benedict's in Conversano together with a well from which they were allowed to draw one *quartara* of water each day.[69] We do not know the use to which this water was to be put, however.

Baths

Cleanliness does not appear to have been a major concern of the southern Italian population. Public bath-houses, such a part of Roman life, may have fallen out of use, and references to public baths are rare. But does the assertion of G. Rosen, that "throughout large periods of human history, cleanliness has been next to godliness... and not for hygienic reasons", hold true in medieval southern Italy?

Beginning with Naples, it is worth noting that a district of the city was named *Thermense*, suggesting not just baths, but hot springs.[70] The tenth-century chronicle of the bishops of Naples records that bishop Nostrianus (*fl.* mid-fifth century) built two baths in the city, one of which "until today" was named after the bishop.[71] This suggests that at least one of the bishop's baths was still in use. It is unclear where exactly these baths lay, but a street in Naples, which retained the name *vicus Nustrianus* and lay just a few hundred metres from the *Thermense* district, is the most likely site.[72]

The link between the clergy and bathing is repeated in the life of the seventh-century bishop of Naples, Agnellus. Founder of the

---

(934): the church of St Erasmus in Formia has a pool, but this may be related to the functioning of its watermill; *RN*, doc. nos 47 (942): garden and pool in *vico Ficariola*, Naples; 55 (945): sale of garden and pool in/near Naples; 139 (964): house in *forum* of Naples with pool; 181 (970): house with pool in upper part of Naples; *CDB*, I, doc. 19 (1036): pool near garden in Bari; *PAVAR*, I, doc. 11 (1037): house with cistern near Ravello; *RN*, doc. 502 (1067): a *piscina commune* documented in Naples in the Marmorata district; *CP*, doc. 57 (1069): a house with "an old basin" near Amalfi; *CDB*, IX, doc. 7 (1074): vineyard and cistern in Casalicclo near Trani; *CDA*, II, doc. 594 (1098): two two-storey houses with water cisterns at Pogerola

[68] *PC*, doc. 12 (957).
[69] *PC*, doc. 46.
[70] *RN*, doc. 137: it lay in the city centre.
[71] *Chronicon Episcoporum S. Neapolitanae Ecclesiae*, in *Monumenta ad Neapolitani Ducatus Historiam Pertinentia*, ed. B. Capasso, I (Naples, 1881), p.171.
[72] For a plan of the city in the tenth and eleventh centuries, P. Skinner, "Urban communities in Naples, 900-1050", *Papers of the British School at Rome*, 62 (1994), p.282.

church of St Ianuarius within the walls, which would function as a *diaconia* or charitable house, Agnellus stipulated that the brothers resident there would have food and wine from the bishopric each year. In addition, *pro labandis curis bis in anno, nativitatis, et resurrectionis Domini anni*, he allowed the brothers to be given soap.[73] Here we have a clear indication that the former, pleasurable function of baths in the Roman world had given way to a more ritual (and less frequent) form of bathing. The running water in a private house mentioned earlier was specifically intended for the inhabitants to 'wash their hands and feet'.[74]

Nevertheless, even if hygiene was not the main priority of bathers in this area, good health may still have been a factor. Nearby Pozzuoli appears to have had several baths still in use at the beginning of the thirteenth century, if the evidence of Peter of Eboli's *De Balneis Puteolanis* is correct.[75] His poem is only the latest piece of evidence for the restorative qualities of bathing in the bay of Naples area. I have found no evidence in the charters of steam baths, but Michael Dols asserts that the prevalence of leprosy amongst the crusaders may have contributed to the "reintroduction of public bathing into Europe — of the Islamic type (the hot steam bath or *hammam*) rather than the Roman."[76] The steam bath is certainly represented amongst those mentioned by Peter of Eboli.

Roman and early medieval sources had already identified the benefits of the baths at Pozzuoli, and although we cannot say whether they were in continuous use throughout the early middle ages, the evidence of John the Deacon in c.920 suggests that at least some were in operation. Among the crowds flocking to the translation of St Sossus at Misenum, he says, were some who had come simply to bathe for health reasons.[77]

The charter evidence provides more information about Neapolitan baths. A record of 983 survives of the building of a bath for the

---

[73] *Chronicon Episcoporum*, p.190.

[74] *SGA*, doc. 6.

[75] E. M. O'Connor, "Peter of Eboli, *De Balneis Puteolanis*: manuscripts from the Aragonese scriptorium in Naples", *Traditio*, XLV (1989/90), pp.380-91, at p.380, points out that some of the descriptions are not authentic. This does not invalidate the evidence of the text for *some* baths in this area, however.

[76] Dols, "The leper in medieval Islamic society", *Speculum*, LVIII (1983), p.905, n.83.

[77] *Translatio Sancti Sosii Auct. Iohanne Diacono*, in *MGH SRL*, p.462: 'Affluebant enim plurimi non tantum ex adiacentibus castellis, sed etiam ex illis qui pro fovendis corporibus ad ipsas venerant thermas...'

nuns of SS Marcellinus and Peter, and the usage is more clearly visible.[78] The abbess of the convent at the time, Drosu, was clearly a shrewd businesswoman. She handed over the site for the bath to one John son of Peter the monk and his wife Anna. They were to oversee the construction of a bath and well, an *expoliatorium* and a *lenarium* (possibly a place to wash or prepare linen?) which the nuns would have exclusive use of when they visited it. If John and Anna died without heirs, the convent would inherit half of the bath and would buy the rest, thereby gaining the use of an amenity with very little investment. Paul Magdalino highlights this role of churches in the construction of new baths in Constantinople and other parts of the Byzantine empire throughout this period.[79] He argues that the clergy need not have had exclusive use of the bathing facilities, and may well have run the baths as a commercial concern for general use outside their own bathing times; he contrasts this with Bryan Ward-Perkins' suggestion that ecclesiastical baths in medieval Italy were only used by the clerics and the poor.[80] The Neapolitan example seems to support Magdalino's argument, as the nuns of SS. Marcellinus and Peter seem only to have required exclusive use of the bath for part of the time, and the builder, John, clearly retained ownership of the property. We must be careful of seeing baths in this context as representative of a desire for cleanliness, however. The grant of a flow of water through its *solareum* to wash hands and feet to the convent of St Gregory Armeno in the same city seems to owe more to Christian ritual than sanitary concerns.[81] The association of two rooms of a bath building with yet another religious foundation, the later church of St Clare, seems to confirm the importance of bathing in clerical life.

References to baths elsewhere provide a rather different picture. In a division of property at Amalfi in 1009, a bath was included in the portion with a house and oven.[82] In 1054, two houses, a fountain and a bath were sold near the same city.[83] Most baths in fact seem to have been the private preserve of the very rich. The use of a bath, of course, denoted control over a supply of water, which was almost

---

[78] *RN*, doc. 241.

[79] P. Magdalino, "Church, bath and *diakonia* in medieval Constantinople" in *Church and People in Byzantium*, ed. R. Morris (Birmingham, 1990), p.167.

[80] B. Ward-Perkins, *From Classical Antiquity to the Middle Ages: Public Building in Northern and Central Italy 300-850* (Oxford, 1984), p.140.

[81] *SGA*, doc. 6 (958).

[82] *CodCav* IV, doc. 627.

[83] *CP*, doc. 77.

always the prerogative of the wealthy and powerful in medieval southern Italy.[84]

This group may have bathed regularly, judging by the way bathing is represented in the *Chronicon Salernitanum*. There are two detailed tales relating to bathing in the early ninth century. In an episode from the time of Grimoald IV (806-17), the baths in Benevento function as a meeting place for political intrigue, and give some insight into bathing habits:

> One day Sico went to bathe and Roffred, seeing this, ordered his slaves to carry him to the bath too because, if he could not speak to him in public, at least he would be able to speak during a bath. Going in, he found Sico in the bath and positioned himself nearby. Whilst Sico was washing his body with soap, Roffred suddenly began to wash his [Sico's] shoulders. Sico wondered at this and asked: 'Who is that pouring water on my shoulders?' The other stopped washing his shoulders and poured water over his head, saying: 'Sshh, Sico. Be quiet, it's me, Roffred.' Sico, recognising his voice, was afraid and said: 'What's the meaning of you tricking me and joking like this? If anyone finds out, they'll laugh at me.' And Roffred said: 'Soon your head will be crowned, with Christ's help'....[85]

One of the key elements to note from this tale is the stress on the privacy of the baths as a place to meet, in stark contrast to Roman practice. The other is the fact that Sico's bath does not appear to have been in any way unusual: this is not the twice-a-year ritual wash that we have met in a Neapolitan, ecclesiastical context.

The second example from the *Chronicon* supports the idea that bathing was a regular habit. It was a cause for comment that the wife of Nannigone, raped by prince Sicard, refused to bathe, use perfumes, wash her face or wear clean clothes.[86] On her husband's return, she explained what had happened and asked him to cut her throat from the shame of it, but his reaction was to order her to bathe and wear bright clothing again.[87]

---

[84] The other context in which a water supply was essential, milling, shows the same high level of exclusivity: Skinner, *Family Power*, pp.72-8. An example of water control: in 1018 Sergius, duke of Amalfi, gave all the water running through the aqueduct to the church of St Peter to the abbess of St Laurence: *CDA*, I, doc. 33.

[85] *ChronSal*, chapter 48 [my translation].

[86] *ChronSal*, chapter 65.

[87] Cf. *CodCav*, I, doc. 106: a certain Adelghisa claimed in 894 that Teodelgardus had raped her. He admitted the charge and, unable to pay the fine levied, was enslaved and became the joint property of Adelghisa and the palace of Salerno. Neither chronicle and charter evidence from Salerno seems to be at all concerned with the injuries suffered by rape victims. Nannigone was unable to take action against a much more powerful man, and simply ordered his wife to put on a brave face as if nothing had happened; Adelghisa's case was simply one of monetary compensation, which ended up with her co-owning her assailant.

The evidence of baths in Salernitan charters supports the chronicle references. In 955, public baths are even mentioned in the much smaller settlement of Nocera, suggesting that Salerno's water supply system may have been actively maintained.[88] but it is hard to believe that the larger city, where the princes had their palace, was lacking in bathing facilities. The excavations of Arechis' palace in Salerno have revealed it overlaid a *frigidarium*, possibly of an earlier Roman bath complex.[89] Even if this no longer functioned, it suggests that a water supply may have been available.

As early as 906 we have evidence of bath ownership in the city of Gaeta. In his will the *hypatos*, Docibilis I, left his son John the house with a tower and bath in which John was living, and a similar bequest to his other son Leo.[90] Since most of the houses built for his other children lay near the port, it is likely that both the properties with baths were situated in this area as well. By 954 the ducal palace had been constructed, probably replacing some of the houses, and was described in the will of Docibilis II as having baths and running down to the sea.[91] Indeed, the shore area of Gaeta appears to have become the preserve of the city's elite. Another property nearby, again with a bath, was bequeathed to Docibilis' son Marinus, and Marinus' brother Gregory received a small house with a bath near the port. In 983 the then duke, John III, received a share of a bath in the *forum* of Gaeta from the bishop, Stephen.[92] It is possible that this was one of the baths referred to in the earlier document, which in the interim had fallen into the hands of the bishopric.

The control of water was, I have argued elsewhere, a central theme of the power of the Docibilan family over Gaeta and its territory.[93] In addition to their bath ownership, members controlled mills and cisterns near the city. In 980, for example, dukes Marinus and John III donated a cistern just outside the city to a church there.[94] The main problem is finding evidence of the use to which all these facilities were put. John III had agreed with bishop Stephen that the bishop and twelve clerics could use the bath in the *forum*, but we do

---

[88] *CodCav*, I, doc. 187. A note of caution should be sounded about these particular baths, however. An earlier document from Nocera refers to land *super terme*, *CodCav*, I, doc. 23, so the baths here may have owed their existence to hot springs.

[89] P. Peduto, M. Romito, M. Galante, D. Mauro and I. Pastore, "Un accesso alla storia di Salerno: stratigrafe e materiali dell'area palaziale longobarda", *Rassegna Storica Salernitana* (1988), pp. 9-62, at 12.

[90] *CDC*, I, doc. 19.

[91] *CDC*, I, doc. 52.

[92] *CDC*, I, doc. 82.

[93] Skinner, *Family Power*, p. 72ff.

[94] *CDC*, I, doc. 78.

not know how often. Otherwise, we are completely lacking in information about the use of the baths in the palace and houses near the port. Were they simply for show? Certainly the documents in which they are mentioned also stress the marble decoration on the houses and palace, and describe many of the buildings in some detail. Perhaps the ownership of baths simply topped off an already impressive complex. The family were, after all, proud of their building achievements, as still extant inscriptions in the city demonstrate.

Nevertheless, further South we find a similar pattern of ecclesiastical control but public use of bathing facilities. In the parchment roll listing the revenues, benefactors and properties of the archbishopric of Reggio di Calabria, prepared around the middle of the eleventh century, we learn that the archbishopric's hospital of St Peter had a public bath (*louetron dhimosion*) at *Mésina*. Unfortunately, the roll provides no details as to the income that this generated for the church.[95]

By the twelfth century, bathing may have become a regular part of convent life, if the 1174 confirmation of the rules of the newly-founded St Maria Latina in Palermo, including the injunction against bathing outside the convent, reflects Sicilian reality rather than archetypal documents of this kind.[96]

Some baths may not have reached great heights of sophistication in their construction, to judge by the brief description of some near Lucera. These lay next to vineyards (the subject of the document) by the river Perticata, suggesting that the baths were in or near the river itself.[97]

Only one document mentions a bath in Bari, and this again appears to be a private foundation which has fallen into public hands, as the *turmarch* of Bari grants "the house and bath of Moisi" near the city's ditch among other properties.[98]

Once again we are at the mercy of the skewed survival of evidence when it comes to discussing environmental factors in health. It seems that the two essentials of life, good housing and relatively clean water supplies, were confined to the highest elites of southern Italian urban society. It is striking to see that in the only city with sufficient evidence to draw conclusions, Salerno, the small house plots were being leased by tenants of relatively modest status: members of the clergy,

---

[95] *Brébion de la Métropole de Règion*, ed. A. Guillou (Vatican City, 1974), pp.181 (Greek text) and 51 (French translation).
[96] *Garufi*, doc. 64.
[97] *CodCav*, I, doc. 127 (911).
[98] *CDB*, V, doc. 1 (1075).

labourers like John the *portarius*,[99] outsiders from Amalfi and one free-man, Peter the Frank. Only later on would such tenants achieve sufficient wealth to begin buying these properties.[100]

Susceptibility to illness may have also depended upon whether the individual was able to buy wine to drink or had to rely on standing water. It is unclear whether drinking water actually formed a commodity for sale in the area in this period: the level of control over water supply would indicate that it was. Although urban cisterns provided an accessible supply, they also carried health hazards of their own. The occurrence of dysentery must have been a regular part of urban life. For one section of the population, such disease could be fatal: in the following chapter we shall look at the risks of infant mortality and the process of childbirth.

---

[99] *CodCav*, IV, doc. 604 (1008).
[100] E.g. in 1044, Leo the Atranian is documented as lessor of a house and land measuring sixteen feet by thirteen in Salerno: *CodCav*, VI, doc. 1033.

CHAPTER THREE

PREGNANCY AND CHILDREARING

Children occupied a primary place in the lives of medieval laypeople. The wealthy depended on the production of heirs to continue a noble or aristocratic line, to make marriage alliances and to prevent its property falling to another line of the extended clan.[1] The birth of prince Gisolf I of Salerno (943-978), for example, was hailed by the Salernitan chronicler as a blessing, since his father was already advanced in age.[2] The less wealthy relied on the production of children to maintain a workforce within the house or on their fields, always balancing this need with the peril of producing too many extra mouths to feed.

For the majority of medieval women, therefore, childbirth was an expected and repeated event in their lives. A child was an asset to the family, and despite Philippe Ariès' pessimistic view of medieval children as adults in miniature,[3] it provided more than just practical help to its parents. Sufficient authors have now demonstrated the real emotional bond that existed between parents and their children, even if such affection was displayed only infrequently.[4]

This chapter seeks to examine the evidence for the care and attitudes surrounding childbirth and infancy. It is a popular motif in medieval and modern historiography to stress the perils of pregnancy and childbirth for women's health. Demographic data, it is argued, prove that lower numbers of women must be due to the hazards of pregnancy and delivery.[5] Yet such an easy explanation for the early

---

[1] This is not to say that parents did not sometimes take steps to limit the number of children they had. Among the poor such limitation was an economic necessity: E. Patlagean, 'Sur la limitation de la fécondité dans la haute époque byzantine', *AESC* 24, (1969), 1353-69.

[2] *ChronSal*, chapter 159.

[3] P. Ariès, *Centuries of Childhood* (New York, 1972); for one, of many, refutations of Ariès' viewpoint, see S. Shahar, *Childhood in the Middle Ages* (London, 1990), pp.1-4.

[4] P. Skinner, "'The light of my eyes': medieval motherhood in the Mediterranean," *Women's History Review* (forthcoming); J. Nelson, "Parents, children and the church in the earlier middle ages", *The Church and Childhood*, ed. D. Wood (Oxford, 1994), pp.81-114, esp.81-2.

[5] Clarissa Atkinson, *The Oldest Vocation: Christian Motherhood in the Middle Ages* (Ithaca, NY, 1991), p.52, highlights the concern over the perils of childbirth in medieval texts; H. Dillard, *Daughters of the Reconquest* (Cambridge, 1984), 156, assumes that in Reconquest Spain 'the parturient death rate was high', but provides little concrete evidence; G. Minois, *History of Old Age from Antiquity to the Renaissance* (Cam-

deaths of women may not accurately reflect the experience of having children. Were women really at greater risk or is our perception of the evidence coloured by the fact that, inevitably, deaths in childbirth attract far more attention from medieval writers than deaths from old age or illness? That is, are we using the exceptional to create a false norm? The southern Italian evidence may provide some clues.

A woman might become a mother very early in her lifetime. Ages of majority for girls in legal texts hovered around the twelve mark in most parts of the Mediterranean. Whether this was an accurate reflection of the average age of menarche is unclear, but given the universal distaste in legal texts towards underage marriage, the age quoted must have carried some connotation of sexual maturity.[6] Lombard law set the age of marriage for girls at twelve. There is evidence to suggest that younger girls were being married off, however, from Liutprand's law of 729, reiterating that the twelfth year should be completed.[7]

We can rarely tell from charter evidence whether such young women were in fact being married off: the transfer of property, rather than the bride's age, was what mattered. However, a hagiographical text from the Amalfitan coast provides a fascinating insight into the moral attitudes that accompanied underage unions. The full text is given in Appendix I. In the translation and miracles of St Trophimena, it is related that 'in the time of the most pious prefect Pulchari', that is, the late ninth century, a girl named Theodonanda was married to a certain Mauro. Having consummated the union, she became close to death (*moribunda*), because she was not yet nubile (*quia necdum nubilis erat*). After four months, her relatives, in desperation, took her to a local, skilled doctor named Hieronymus, but he was unable to help, and advised instead that they pray to God, and the girl would 'either be saved or punished according to just judgement'. This recourse to the doctor, and his activities, will be discussed in more detail below. The parents then took the girl to Maiori (*Rheginna*) where she slept in front of the tomb of St Trophimena. There, she had a vision of the saint, and when she related it the

---

bridge, 1989), 180, quotes data showing higher numbers of old men than women, and puts this imbalance down to premature death in childbirth, again without any supporting evidence; see also S. Shahar, *Childhood in the Middle Ages* (London, 1990), 32-43.

[6] Atkinson, *Oldest Vocation*, p.39, criticises the age of 13 or 14 proposed by D. W. Amundsen, "The age of menarche in medieval Europe", *Human Biology*, 45 (1973) as 'improbably early', taking no account of class differences. Nevertheless, as an age of sexual activity it may be quite accurate.

[7] *The Lombard Laws*, ed. K. F. Drew (Philadelphia, 1973), Liutprand 112.

pavement of the church sweated holy oil. A nun named Agatha anointed her with this, and she was cured.[8]

There are several themes worth exploring in this text. The most obvious one is that, according to the doctor, if anyone was to be punished for the underage union, it was the girl herself, and only St Trophimena's intervention cures her. But the intriguing feature of the story is the nature of Theodonanda's vision, for it may provide a clue as to the cure she received. Having fallen asleep at the altar, she then (in a dream?) tiptoed out of the church, 'making for the river on her own, for the hollow/riverbed of the river had not yet hastened' (*flumen petebat sola; necdum enim fluminis alveus properaverat*). It is here that she has the vision of Trophimena. Does the river symbolise the girl's menstrual flow? Is this what Trophimena grants her as a cure? There seems to be a double image of lubrication and flowing in the text, as the holy oil is also used, and since the author attributes Theodonanda's original illness to her premature sexual activity, it seems likely that this is what is intended. The message is reinforced by the emphasis on the girl's 'tiny body' (*corpusculum*) when she is anointed; the whole tenor of the episode is that such marriages are to be avoided.

It is worth noting here that the distaste for underage marriage does not seem to have extended to boys. The Lombard king Liutprand's law 117 allows boys under eighteen to arrange a betrothal, even if consummation is not explicitly referred to. A much later document from Amalfi reveals at least one instance of a woman and her father-in-law acting for her underage (*qui est modo infra etate*) husband.[9]

Livi-Bacci describes the waves of population growth and contraction in the pre-industrial period: in the middle ages he recognises crisis in the late Roman and Justinianic era, marked by barbarian invasions and plague, and expansion in twelfth and thirteenth centuries.[10] One has only to read the vivid description of the Lombard historian Paul the Deacon to understand the miseries and the impact on population that the combination of the Gothic Wars and the plague had in the peninsula in the sixth century:

> Everywhere there was grief and everywhere tears ... dwellings were left deserted and the dogs only kept house. The flocks remained alone in the pastures with no shepherd at hand ... everything was in utter silence. Sons fled, leaving the corpses of their parents unburied ... You might see

---

[8] *Historia Inventionis ac Translationis et Miracula S. Trophimene*, in *Acta Sanctorum, v Julii*, p.240, chapters 35-37.
[9] *CDA*, doc. 209 (1182).
[10] Livi-Bacci, *Population and Nutrition*, p.1.

the world brought back to its ancient silence: no voice in the field, no whistling of shepherds, no lying in wait of wild beasts among the cattle ... the vineyard with its fallen leaves and its shining grapes remained undisturbed...[11]

An image of total desolation and virtual depopulation in the sixth century, then. How did the South recover? Significantly for our purposes, Livi-Bacci totally omits the seventh to eleventh centuries. Does his statement that mortality is not generally linked to nutrition stand examination from the sources of this period in southern Italy?

The Malthusian model suggests that population growth is determined by the availability of resources, in particular food, and that higher levels of production through technological innovations will only temporarily relieve the pressure on those resources. Marital restraint is seen as a far more effective way of checking population growth: if the land is not available to create a new household - the so-called 'niche' - then couples would be forced to delay marriage until they could support themselves economically.[12] Isolated examples from southern Italy reveal fathers allowing sons to take a portion of land to set up a new household,[13] but if property was scarce one answer was to make more land available by means of clearance and reclamation.

It follows, therefore, that with such rich documentary sources at our disposal in southern Italy, it may be possible, from an analysis of the patterns of land clearance, to suggest a rising population in at least some regions. Another indicator, although less reliable in that it may reflect population movement rather than growth, may be the enlarging of urban perimeters and the extension of houses.

The ages of pregnant women are never recorded in the charter evidence, so we cannot judge the average age a woman might expect her first child. On closer inspection of some medieval source material, we can detect a certain robustness in pregnant women that seems to have been overlooked by many historians. Just as the Roman matron Cornelia had borne twelve infants,[14] so later instances of large numbers of offspring are visible in Italian documents. Matrona, wife of Docibilis I, ruler of Gaeta in the late ninth century, bore him at least eight children. They survived to be documented, but it is extremely

---

[11] Paul the Deacon, *History of the Lombard People*, II.4, trans. W. Dudley Foulke (Philadelphia, 1907), p.57.

[12] Livi-Bacci, *Population and Nutrition*, pp.12, 16.

[13] For example, *CDB* V, doc. 109.

[14] Seneca, Letter to his Mother, quoted in E. Amt, *Women's Lives in Medieval Europe* (London, 1993), 32.

likely that they had siblings who did not survive into adulthood. Orania, the wife of Docibilis' eponymous grandson went one better; again, this number represents only the successful rearing of children, and hides the possibility of pregnancies not carried to full term, or infant deaths. The genealogy of the family as a whole between the ninth and twelfth centuries is testimony to the fecundity of its women.[15]

These women, however, may have been exceptional. Although the record is far from complete, since documents were not, for the most part, interested in counting children, some work can be done on the size of surviving families in southern Italy and the repercussions that this might have had on health. A survey of 65 eleventh-century documents (from areas outside Campania) revealed two women with five children, one with four, three with three, twelve with two and the remainder with one. Since the figures are derived from references to mothers and children in a number of contexts (including the use of matronyms), they may over-represent the single-child families.

The hardiness of women whilst pregnant can also be highlighted. A case in point is Willa, wife of Berengar of Ivrea, forced through her husband's flight from Italy to follow him, but told to take a different route through the Alps from the St Bernard pass which he had used. 'When she set out she was with child and very near her time, and yet she got across the Vogelberg. How she was able to cross that rough and pathless mountain on foot I cannot possibly comprehend,' comments Liutprand of Cremona.[16] Of course, Willa's journey was extraordinary enough to attract comment, but one wonders whether Berengar's order to her to follow him stemmed specifically from the fact that she was pregnant, that is carrying a possible heir of his whose value to his enemies was probably greater than that of his wife. Whatever the case, Berengar does not seem to have evinced much concern for her condition.

The southern Italian evidence does reveal at least some anxiety surrounding pregnancy. The safe delivery of a child was never, it appears, taken for granted. For example, in the *Vita* of the bishop of Naples, Athanasius, written in the tenth century, his mother Drosu promised that she would offer her second child, Athanasius, to the church, if he was born safely: *vovit Deo, ut de uteri sui fructum, si innesset proles, aequo assensu Christo traderent ad famulandum.*[17] In his gift of all his

---

[15] P. Skinner, *Family Power in Southern Italy* (Cambridge, 1995), 17, has the full genealogy.

[16] *Antapodosis*, chapter 10.

[17] *Vita Athanasii Episcopi Neapolitani*, in *MGH SRL*, pp.441-2.

lands to the Neapolitan monastery of SS Sergius and Bacchus in 970, perhaps prior to entering it, Basil Isabrus stipulated that his wife Eufimia was to have control of the estate until she died or remarried. He further promised that, if the child she was carrying was born alive, he would give an additional six *solidi* to the church.[18] This type of formula suggests that stillborn children, or at least children who died in very early infancy, were an accepted fact of life. Basil was, it seems, voluntarily giving up the possibility of having any more children if he was indeed entering the church: was his decision based purely on piety, or could his choice have been dictated by previous difficulties that he and Eufimia had had? We cannot tell, but the possibility that chaste marriage and/or the retirement of one of the partners to an ecclesiastical foundation was out of consideration for the other's health has, I believe, never received any serious attention from medievalists.[19]

In 1164, Xistus son of Petracca of Terlizzi took these precautions one step further. His wife, Delicia, was currently pregnant. The unborn child, whom Xistus feared would be born posthumously, was made his heir, but a further clause provided for the land to go to the cathedral of the city if the infant died.[20] As we shall see in the next chapter, the church's involvement in matters of health and wellbeing seems to have been assumed and accepted without question.

It is noteworthy that neither of these examples appear to display any concern for the fate of the respective wives. This reflects a wife's position in the southern Italian family and the nature of the documentation. She was merely the caretaker of the property mentioned; she was also the caretaker of the heir. Central to both Basil's and Xistus' concerns was the land being transferred. Less easy to understand is Basil's lack of interest in his unborn child to whom, apparently, he was leaving nothing. It is unclear what would happen when Eufimia died and the provision of the gift to the church was carried out. Perhaps Basil had not planned to become a father at this stage!

Christian sources do not reveal much worry on the part of mothers-to-be or their spouses. The tension surrounding pregnancy was, however, expressed in surviving material from the Cairo Genizah, and relating to the extremely mobile Jewish community of Fustat. It is worth noting because it provides us with an echo of women's own

---

[18] *RN*, doc. 185.

[19] Retirement to an monastery at a time of illness or imminent death, however, is a recognised phenomenon. The southern Italian evidence will be discussed below, chapter 5.

[20] *Magistrale* 2

fears, and has relevance for the Jewish communities in southern Italy. The archive includes several wills of pregnant women, who entrust the care of their unborn infants to their child's grandmother rather than to their own husbands. Husbands, it was assumed, would re-marry, and grandmotherly care was seen as preferable to that of a stepmother.[21]

The remarriage of widowers was a frequent occurrence in the southern Italian charters. Stepmothers are recorded far more often than stepfathers in our evidence. This may explain why, when anxi-ety is expressed by men about a pregnancy, it is the child's welfare that is paramount. A child represented the continuation of the family line, whilst its mother was simply an adjunct to the clan, with few rights or choices. She was also relatively easily replaceable to the extent that the wife, whilst mentioned in numerous male-authored documents, remains anonymous. Then, if she died, the provisions of the charter could equally well apply to the new spouse. The emphasis on a child's value is also revealed in the Lombard law codes. King Rothari decreed that a child killed in its mother's womb should be compensated for by payment of half the mother's *wergild*, even if the death was accidental.[22]

The fears surrounding childbirth carried on throughout the in-fancy of children. Several other wills from Terlizzi make provision for another heir should the child to whom property is left die. In 1149, Robert son of Peter left instructions should his young son Adam die before maturity.[23] A year later Gemma, who was ill when recording her wishes, made the same arrangement about property left to her young son Matthew.[24] In 1153, Bonadonnula left part of a house to her young son Maiurano, but this would go to the cathedral if he died underage.[25]

It may be argued that such a cluster of arrangements reflect a notarial tradition at Terlizzi rather than the actual experiences of the parties concerned. However, it is unlikely that such a discourse would have entered the legal tradition had not real fears existed about the fate of both the children and their property. In protecting the patri-mony, the documents also provide an insight into the worries of the owners.

---

[21] S. D. Goitein, *A Mediterranean Society III: the Family*, (Berkeley, 1978), p.232.
[22] Rothari, law 75 in *Lombard Laws*, trans. Drew, p.65.
[23] *CDB* III, doc. 62.
[24] *CDB* III, doc. 65.
[25] *CDB* III, doc. 70.

The possibility of infant death was a very real one in the middle ages. The Geniza material from Cairo provides a vivid example. A letter from Abu Said, living in Palermo but hoping to travel to Egypt in 1140, is full of the misfortunes he had so far encountered:

> I planned to arrive in Egypt this very year ... my misfortune forced me to spend 50 *murabiti dinars*, for the wife fell ill and also the two little ones, and God willed that one of them died, the baby, he was one and a half years old....[26]

We can only speculate what the money was spent on, but perhaps a little of it was on medicines, which seem to have been available in the city.[27] The death of Abu Said's young son, however, must have been a regular occurrence for many families in the medieval South.

The ages of children are rarely recorded, except in particular circumstances. A document from Benevento, dated 703/748, shows a couple and their newborn son.[28] However, they represented a commodity here in a sale between the widow Selberada and the church of Naples, and the child was presumably recorded as an asset in the same way that a young animal might be. That this was the case is suggested by other transactions in slave-girls, whose babies and young children are also recorded.[29] The Lombard law codes convey this sense. A clause in Rothari's code deals with the penalties paid for striking a pregnant female slave so that she miscarried. Compensation was to be paid for the child and, if she died, the slave as well. The clause follows exactly the same pattern as two immediately preceding ones on causing miscarriages in cows and mares, underlining the almost non-human status of the woman.[30]

The other context in which a child's age mattered was when it reached majority and was able to act on its own behalf (subject to legal restrictions on women's actions) in documented transactions. Thus the 'children' we see being represented by adults in documents are likely to have been under fourteen if boys and under twelve if girls.[31]

---

[26] Quoted from Goitein, *Letters*, p.325.

[27] See below, chapter 5.

[28] *RNAM*, doc. 1.

[29] For example: *CDB* IV, doc. 42 (1065): a slave-girl named Setanna and her son Nicolula. In medieval Spain, a nursing slave-girl and her child would be an expensive purchase, as double duty would be charged: Dillard, *Daughters*, 158.

[30] Rothari, law 334 on female slaves, 332 and 333 on cows and mares, all in *Lombard Laws*, trans. Drew.

[31] The definition of 'child' in medieval sources is discussed by John Boswell in *The Kindness of Strangers* (New York, 1988), p. 35.

Postnatal and infant care is not well-represented in the southern Italian evidence. Wetnurses, for example, are not well-documented: their use may have been patchy, and restricted to the very highest circles of society. Three separate documents record the property given to the wetnurse of king Roger's son Henry, by his first wife Elvira, as reward for her services.[32] The gifts, however, are dated 1136 (with a further confirmation in 1145); Elvira had died in February 1135. Adelina's nursing duties, therefore, were probably out of necessity rather than any custom for noblewomen to put their children out to nurse. Indeed, the illustrations in the *Carmen de Rebus Siculis* of Peter of Eboli include a depiction of Beatrice, the third wife of king Roger, breastfeeding his daughter, Constance.[33] Although this may be somewhat inaccurate (Beatrice died bearing Constance), it does perhaps represent the expectations of a court society in this area.

The rewards given to the Sicilian royal nurse, Adelina, are a reflection of the esteem in which nurses at this level were held, but they were also surrounded by restrictions. The ideas of Soranus of Ephesus (2nd century AD) regarding the ideal nurse were still influential in the middle ages. She should be of good health and lineage, possess an abundance of milk and even temperament, and even be good-looking.[34] But as Clarissa Atkinson points out, 'mothers did not read Aristotle or Soranus';[35] we have to accept that a large proportion of medieval peri- and post-natal carers had no access to these written sources for guidance. Given the taste for compilations of ancient medical sources in literate medieval circles, one might suspect that few innovative developments took place in the middle ages with regard to gynaecological or obstetric practice. But even if they did, the predominance of clerics over the preservation and transfer of knowledge would make it somewhat unlikely that they would record advances in female medical care.

Anecdotal evidence suggests that there was a very strong feeling that malformed babies indicated sin on the part of their parents, particularly some kind of sexual deviation.[36] Liutprand of Cremona's

---

[32] *Cusa*, doc. 50 (1136); *Garufi*, docs 12 (1136) and 21 (1145).

[33] Peter of Eboli, *De Rebus Siculis Carmen*, ed. E. Rota (RIS 31, Città di Castello, 1904), tav. II facing p.7. The same table also shows the burial of Roger's second wife, Sibyl, who had died in childbirth: *hic sepelitur Sebilia aborciens*.

[34] Dillard, *Daughters*, p. 156, illustrates how influential Soranus' ideas were on Avicenna and Maimonides in Spain, so that Spanish royal nurses were governed by such restrictions. They also received the same types of rewards.

[35] *Oldest Vocation*, p. 26.

[36] Sexual 'deviation' might simply be a case of having intercourse at times proscribed by penitentials: Sundays, during Lent, during the woman's menstrual period

picture of one pregnancy may, like other parts of his narra
intended to demonstrate the wicked doings of the parties invo
his view, the death of the mistress of pope John XII, who had
been the concubine of the pope's father and who had now co
by John, in 'an effusion of blood,' merely served to underline her
wickedness.[37] The *Chronicon Salernitanum* includes a similar story. A
woman who had conceived by a priest had a child without bones
showing, the chronicler notes smugly, that her repentance had not
been stiffened with true contrition.[38]

This 'intergenerational responsibility', as Christiane Klapisch
characterises it, must have been a burden both on the child and the
parents, particularly the unfortunate mother. As well as the obvious
problems involved in bringing up such a child, both parents would
also have to deal with the moral censure that the visible product of
their misdeeds would provoke. Since the father usually had the decision of life or death over a child, the newborn might be abandoned or
exposed rather than raised, particularly if it had a serious birth defect.[39]

There is some evidence to suggest, however, that not all physically
handicapped children met this fate. Sally Crawford has recently argued that medieval graves of adolescents with birth defects found in
England, and the discovery of a drinking vessel specially adapted for
a child with a cleft palate, reveal that some individuals survived and
were cared for.[40] Although medieval archaeology is less informative
in the Mediterranean, documentary references from southern Italy
and Sicily to adults nicknamed *surdo* (deaf)[41], *gardapedem* (looking at
feet)[42], *monoculum* (one-eyed) and *stultus* (mad),[43] and others certainly

---

or when she was nursing: Boswell, *Kindness*, p.260; see also James Brundage's delight-
ful flow-chart of 'the sexual decision-making process according to the penitentials' in
his *Law, Sex and Christian Society in Medieval Europe* (Chicago, 1987), fig. 4.2, p.162.
Atkinson, *Oldest Vocation*, p.91, highlights a tale of St Martin of Tours who cured a
severely deformed baby conceived on a Sunday. The narrator, Gregory of Tours,
places the blame squarely on the mother.

[37] *Antapodosis*, chapter 4.

[38] *ChronSal*, chapter 14.

[39] C. Klapisch, "Attitudes devant l'enfant", *Annales de Démographie Historique*, 1973,
p.65. See also D. Wilson, *Signs and Portents: Monstrous Births from the Middle Ages to the
Enlightenment*, (London, 1993), pp.1-28.

[40] S. Crawford, *Age Differentiation and Related Social Status: a Study of Anglo-Saxon Childhood*, (Oxford D. Phil. thesis, unpubl., 1991).

[41] *surdo* occurs as a nickname in three Neapolitan documents: *RN*, docs 98, 305
and 448.

[42] *CDA*, doc. 233.

[43] *Garufi*, docs 2 and 11 respectively. In this, as all the other cases, of course, it is
impossible to prove that they had had such disabilities from birth.

seem to indicate that here, too, physically disabled people functioned as part of the community.

Nevertheless, just as writers sometimes ascribed sickness to ill-doing on the part of the sufferer,[44] so physical deformity might also be used as a weapon of insult. In his illustrated chronicle of the civil war in southern Italy in the 1190s between emperor Henry VI of Germany and Tancred, the illegitimate grandson of king Roger II, Peter of Eboli, fiercely pro-Henrician, uses both text and pictures to dramatic effect when attacking the latter. Peter's portrayal of Tancred's birth, labelling the newborn as *abortivo* and drawing a picture of horror on the attendant woman's face as the midwife holds up the child (*hec viso abortivo stupet*), is clearly intended to show the reader of the chronicle that nothing good would come of the pretender's rule. A later folio portrays the adult Tancred as apelike, and again uses a label, *simia*, to reinforce the point.[45]

We cannot prove whether Tancred really did match up to Peter's description (and depiction) of him, but to do so is less important in this context than to stress that physical abnormality was seen as a useful tool for attacking political opponents. Indeed, Peter even adds a passage telling us that he consulted a certain *doctor*, Ursus, as to why Tancred was a *vir abortivus*. The doctor explained to Peter that to make a boy (*puer*), it was necessary for the seed of both parents to mix, but because he had been made from only his mother's seed, and she was not of noble blood, Tancred turned out a *dimidiatus homo*.[46] Thus, if Peter's description was basically accurate, and the king was born extremely small, his illegitimacy was held partly to blame for this state. It may say something about the levels of care available to the wealthy of southern Italy that he survived at all. The same may be true of a man living in Naples in the eleventh century, nicknamed *avorto*.[47] We shall return to the significance of nicknaming after physical characteristics in a later chapter.[48]

Peter's consultation with his friend the doctor is, of course, extremely interesting for the picture it provides of contemporary, that is, thirteenth-century, views of conception. Where had such an outlook of incorrectly mixed seed originated?

---

[44] See below, chapter 4.

[45] Peter of Eboli, *De Rebus Siculis*, tav. X. In an interesting parallel from northern Europe, abbot Guibert of Nogent tells us that at birth he was so small he was 'almost an abortion': *Self and Society in Medieval France: the Memoirs of Abbot Guibert of Nogent (1064?-c.1125)*, ed. J. F. Benton (New York, 1970), p.42.

[46] Peter of Eboli, *De Rebus Siculis Carmen*, pp.35-6. For the full text, see Appendix 2.

[47] *RN*, doc. 507.

[48] See below, chapter 4.

The class-conscious remarks of the doctor are illustrative of the more demarcated nature of twelfth- and thirteenth-century society, as individual self-consciousness of status and rank became more developed. But Ursus's understanding of conception, based on the mixing of both male and female seeds, reveals the continued influence of Hippocratic and Galenic theories at this time. Such theories held that a female seed existed, but was inferior to the male, in contrast to the Aristotelian model of the female contributing only nourishment to the man's seed.[49]

The inferior status accorded to females is often held to have led to efforts to limit female children, whether before or after birth. The level of care, for instance, might differ according to the sex of the baby. In his discussion of family limitation in the ancient and medieval worlds, Riddle suggests that, rather than out-and-out infanticide, it was perfectly possible to kill off a child simply through neglect.[50] Was there a preference for male children, as most authors seem to assert? We have already noted that king Roger's son, Henry, was put out to nurse whilst his half-sister was not. It is likely that this was due to the death of Henry's mother whilst he was still a baby, but it would be interesting to know whether the king's son would have received such special care anyway. If so, ironically, the practise of putting a child out to nurse might well have put it at higher risk of illness and death, the immunological properties of mother's milk being well-documented. However, if most children were breast-fed through their first year of life,[51] it would be at weaning-time that they were again at risk.

As well as levels of care, a family's whole treatment of its sons and daughters might be very different. An interesting feature noted by Goitein in the Cairo documents is the occurrence of very positive female names, translated as 'Good luck', 'Gain', 'Wish fulfilled' and 'the one hoped for.' He suggests that this represented a protest on the part of mothers against the prevailing desire for male children.[52] Positive names such as these also appear in some quantities in the southern Italian, Christian documentation, with names like Gemma and Bella finding particular favour alongside the ubiquitous Biblical appellations Maria and Anne. However, female names here are unlikely to represent protests as such—a daughter could be a significant asset to her family.

---

[49] J. M. Riddle, *Contraception and Abortion from the Ancient World to the Renaissance* (Harvard, 1992), p.141.

[50] Riddle, *Contraception and Abortion*, p.13.

[51] Livi-Bacci, *Population and Nutrition*, p.73.

[52] Goitein, *Mediterranean Society III*, p.318.

In Byzantine society, however, there may be some echoes of un-
wanted daughters. The eleventh-century *Peira*, a collection of judge-
ments on legal problems, contains evidence of the exposure of baby
girls.[53] This is supported by a revealing comment in Anna Comnena's
Alexiad. Having had Anna and her sister, Irene gave birth to a son:
'...not a trace of disappointment remained now that their desire was
fulfilled....'[54]

This chapter has, so far, only briefly touched upon whether having
children could be in any sense a choice rather than an inevitability.
Yet, as John Riddle demonstrates, knowledge of contraceptives and
abortifacients was available. By the sixth century, a Latin translation
existed of Dioscurides' *Materia Medica*, which included both forms of
family planning. It was probably made in Ravenna,[55] and may well
have reached other parts of the peninsula. A Greek version from the
seventh century certainly survives in Naples. Later on, Constantine
the African's translations of Arabic treatises in the eleventh century,
produced whilst he was a monk at Montecassino, also may have
included sections on contraception. The extant manuscripts, which
are copies, omit these sections, but this omission probably did not
originate with Constantine's work.[56] Again, however, we must make a
distinction between the survival of a medical text and the day-to-day
practices of the local population. Even if the substances recom-
mended in the many anonymous recipes were derived from local
observations (and this is by no means certain), there is no guarantee
that the recording of such methods indicated their infallibility.

Riddle's assumption that contraception was known and used presupposes a desire on the part of medieval families to limit their offspring; I would be cautious in applying this model to southern Italian
families. Contraception was, in any case, a haphazard way of pre-
venting conception, and there were, in any case, non-biological ways
of limiting the number of mouths to feed. I have already mentioned
Sergius Isabrus at Naples, who appears to have chosen to enter the
church despite (or perhaps because of?) his child's imminent birth.
Adoption was another means of reducing the number of children in
the home.

---

[53] G. Buckler, "Women in Byzantine law about 1100AD", *Byzantion*, XI (1936),
p.412.
[54] *[The] Alexiad [of Anna Comnena*, trans. E. R. A. Sewter, (Harmondsworth, 1969)],
VI, viii.
[55] Riddle, *Contraception and Abortion*, p.90.
[56] M. Green, 'Constantinus Africanus and the conflct between religion and science', in *The Human Embryo: Aristotle and the Arabic and European Traditions*, ed. G. R.
Dunstan (Exeter, 1990), pp.47-69 at 52.

Children from poor families, in particular, might not grow up in their parents' household. 'Those in debt eased their indebtedness through the sale of children or young people into indentured servitude.'[57] Whilst emotionally painful in the short term, such sales might ensure the survival of both the child and his or her family. Examples of these sales survive from southern Italy, and the phenomenon seems to have been far more common in the Mediterranean than further north.[58]

The centrality of children to family life had as its inevitable result the devaluing of childless couples. Women seem to have faced childlessness in two ways. Some ensured that their property would instead benefit young nephews and nieces, or would leave gifts for their servants. Others stated starkly that their sterility left them with little choice and gave their property to the church.[59] This action has a logic to it, for if women could not gain immortality through the children they had left, then spiritual immortality through pious gifts might have been the next best thing. Thus in a document from Vieste in 1031, the local *turmarch* and his wife made a donation to the abbot of St Maria in Tremiti since they had no sons or daughters.[60] Similarly, in Bari in 1067, 'the childless couple' Piper and Grisa are recorded as having endowed and handed over a church to a priest to care for it.[61] In the same city, Formosa, the wife of Caropisi, master pelterer, willed all her property to the church of St Nicolas in 1168, since she had no children.[62]

Like the example of St Trophimena's miracle for the underage girl discussed above, however, hagiography encouraged childless women to have faith in God. Perhaps this explains the prevalence of gifts to the church over gifts to other members of the family in our charters. Were such donations made in the hope of a conception? No donor gives this as a reason, but having seen the pious donations surrounding pregnancies, we must not discount the possibility. Belief in a supernatural intervention was perhaps encouraged by miraculous stories. The life of St Christopher, father of the tenth-century Sicilian

---

[57] *Hunger in History*, p.117.

[58] Skinner, "Light of my eyes". Frankish children were definitely being sold in Italy in the eighth century, and seventh-century Italy is taken as the setting for a much later literary tale of a child sale, Gautier d'Arras' *Eracle*, exploiting the fact that here Roman law allowed such transactions: Boswell, *Kindness*, pp.215 and 381-2 respectively.

[59] E.g. *PC*, doc. 89.

[60] *Tremiti*, doc. 12.

[61] *CDB* I, doc. 26.

[62] *CDB* V, frammenti 21-22.

saint Sabas the Younger, features an episode where an illustrious citizen of Rossano brought his wife to Christopher to be cured of her sterility. After the standard show of modesty—Christopher denied that he had such powers—the saint agreed on account of the man's faith and blessed the woman, who subsequently had a son.[63] (The fact that the child was male is itself testimony to the saint's miraculous powers—one wonders whether a daughter would have been welcomed after such efforts!)

In the absence of miraculous interventions, it appears that it was precisely childless couples such as these or Piper and Grisa, mentioned above, who might have been recipients in a process of child adoption. Although the cases we have of children going to new homes does not specify whether their new parents already had offspring (although an example from Naples may include other siblings), the initial characterisation of the child as servant does appear to have been tempered by the fact that he or she stood to benefit through a small emancipation gift or inheritance from their new home.

Because early life was so precarious, it was quite possible for a parent to die without living offspring, despite the evidence of remarriage to produce further heirs.[64] The absence of grandparents, too, is noticeable in the charter evidence, although this may owe more to the manner of recording identity than actual circumstances.[65] As we shall see in a later chapter, the population of southern Italy may have enjoyed a higher than average lifespan. But even if the perils of childhood disease and the risks of childbirth were overcome, sickness could still inflict havoc on family numbers. In the following chapter, I shall examine the disease and disabilities visible in the documents, and the effects these had.

---

[63] G. da Costa-Louillet, "Saints de Sicile et de l'Italie méridionale aux VIII, IX, et X siècles", *Byzantion*, **XXIX-XXX** (1959-60), pp.89-173, at p.141.

[64] We have several charters revealing death without heirs, although whether the parties concerned were married is often unclear. Thus prince Guaimarius of Salerno made a gift of land previously owned by the heirless Ademarius and Benenatus to the church of St Maximus in 886: *CodCav*, I, doc. 101.

[65] Only occasionally do we see three live generations of the same family, as, for example, John, his daughter Gemma and her son Stephen, authors of a document at Salerno in 1030: *CodCav*, V, doc. 831.

PART TWO

MENTALITIES AND HEALTHCARE

CHAPTER FOUR

SICKNESS IN THE COMMUNITY

Sickness in the community could have two levels of impact. One was the catastrophic decimation brought by pandemics such as plague; the other was more localised—an individual becoming ill. The medieval community's response to these two levels of illness, and whether differing susceptibility was due to class, form the subject of this chapter.

The first problem which must be overcome is that of deciding what ill-health meant to the medieval population. As Helen Bush and Marek Zvelebil recently commented, 'the concept of health itself is a problematic and culture-specific notion',[1] that is, what the modern author might categorise as sickness may not have been viewed as such in the middle ages. Aaron Gurevich castigates historians who 'imagined that people of the past understood meanings as we have done and behaved accordingly.'[2] Illness as a concept may have changed radically over the millennium separating the historian from the source material. Work on other areas in the middle ages, and contemporary anthropological studies, remind us that illness is not always constructed as a bad thing.[3] For example, mental illness could be interpreted as an evil possession or as a gift from God, depending on the observer.[4] The 'holy fool' is now a relatively well-documented phenomenon in both Islamic and east Mediterranean medieval history, and the medieval saint's healing power, whilst the saint him/herself suffers serious ailments, has strong parallels with the experi-

---

[1] Bush and Zvelebil, "Pathology and health", in *Health in Past Societies*, p.6.

[2] A. Gurevich, "Approaches of the 'Annales School' from the history of mentalities to historical synthesis", *Scandia*, LVIII (1992), pp.141-50, at p.143.

[3] For example, Roberta Gilchrist, "Christian bodies and souls: the archaeology of life and death in late medieval hospitals", in *Death in Towns: Urban Responses to the Dying and the Dead, 100-1600*, ed. S. R. Bassett (Leicester, 1992), p.114, discusses differing perceptions of leprosy.

[4] Cf. Robert Chartier's statement on the same phenomenon: "Madness, medicine and the state are not categories that can be conceptualized in terms of universals; every age makes their content unique." R. Chartier, *Cultural History*, trans. L. Cochrane (Oxford, 1988), p.46.

ences of the modern shaman, whose authority rests partly on having the strength to bear such torments.[5]

Conversely, what may seem a trivial complaint in the twentieth century West could have had devastating consequences in less developed societies, a phenomenon illustrated by the wiping out of entire populations in the New World in the early modern age of discovery.[6] In her survey of medieval medical care, Katherine Park stresses the hazards of influenza, tuberculosis, malaria, typhus and diarrhoea.[7] Physical disability, too, may have had different consequences: 'Myopia is presumably a grave disadvantage to a Stone Age hunter, but of little importance to modern man.'[8]

But, crucially, we rarely hear of such afflictions from the medieval sources themselves. More often than not, as we shall see in the examples cited in this chapter, charter and narrative evidence described the symptoms of the illness rather than identifying it. Does this mean that medieval authors were, for the most part, uninterested in the causes of disease, or simply that they were ill-equipped to explain them? And were certain diseases and disabilities so prevalent that they were not thought worth recording? This last question will become ever more pressing as archaeology reveals how common certain complaints, which leave evidence on skeletal remains, were. Arthritic joints, for instance, do not feature as a cause for comment in written sources. There may a problem of recording some illnesses or minor ailments either because they were just not seen as serious, or because their sufferers, even if not seriously ill, may never have met up with an institution or situation in which their suffering was recorded.

Another issue is the collective perception of the sick individual. How was he or she viewed by the rest of the community? 'In the middle ages, physical infirmity was regarded as a punishment from God and here, as with sickness and the sick, we come up against the ambivalence of social attitudes: compassion was mixed with scorn or horror.'[9] We shall examine the equation of sin with sickness in more

---

[5] See the comments and references in P. Horden, "Responses to possession and insanity in the earlier Byzantine world", *Social History of Medicine*, VI (1993), pp.177-194, at 192; I. M. Lewis, *Ecstatic Religion*, (Harmondsworth, 1971), pp.32-33., stresses the privileged position of the possessed person in relation to his or her superiors, but underlines the danger that such possession can also result in accusations of malevolent acts.

[6] See the discussion by Ann Carmichael, "Infection and hidden hunger", in *Hunger and History*, pp.56-61, and associated bibliography.

[7] Park, "Medicine and society", in *Medicine in Society*, p.62.

[8] R. J. Berry, "The genetics of death—mortal, morbid and selfish genes", in *Mortality and Immortality*, p.69.

[9] B. Geremek, *The Margins of Society in Late Medieval Paris* (Cambridge, 1987), p.301.

detail later in this chapter and in the next. Jacques de Vitry gives us a snapshot of the inhabitants of the French hospitals of the early thirteenth century: 'the poor, the infirm, the pusillanimous, the weak, the wretched, those who cry and those who are hungry and the lepers.'[10] His attitude, however, was one of horror: it needed the courage of a martyr, he wrote, to overcome one's repugnance at the filth and unbearable odours of the sick.[11] Modern historiography about the medieval sick seems to confirm this ambivalence, suggesting that they were both part of and marginalised from the society in which they lived, in 'internal exile'. Having nowhere to go, they crowded the streets and churches, but at the same time could play no effective part in a world of *oratores*, *bellatores* and *laboratores*.[12] However, this opinion tends to be based on narrative or prescriptive sources, or extrapolated from unusually expressive ones such as Jacques himself; rarely are the experiences of the sick themselves documented. The wealth of evidence available from earlier centuries in southern Italy might, therefore, offer a rather different perspective on being ill in the medieval community.

The prescriptive sources relevant to the lives of the inhabitants of southern Italy are explicit in their discrimination against certain types of ill or infirm people. They also convey some of the horror felt about certain maladies. A title of the emperor Justinian's *Institutes* is typical, listing those who were not allowed to make their own will: lunatics, deaf-mutes, and the blind were classed with the unfree, heretics, minors and spendthrifts.[13] Particular illnesses might attract particular censure, or be ascribed to the sins of the person afflicted. Two chapters of the Lombard king Rothari's lawcode, promulgated in the early seventh century but with equal weight for later southern Lombard populations, are illuminating:

> 176. On lepers. If anyone is afflicted with leprosy and the truth of the matter is recognised by the judge or by the people and the leper is expelled from the district or from his house so that he lives alone, he shall not have the right to alienate his property or give it to anyone. Because on the day that he is expelled from his home, it is as if he died. Nevertheless, while he lives he should be nourished on the income from that which remains.[14]

---

[10] My translation from M. Mollat, "Hospitalité et assistance au début du XIIIe siècle", in *Poverty in the Middle Ages*, p.37.

[11] My translation from Mollat, "Hospitalité", p.38.

[12] Their position is discussed in J. Agrimi and C. Crisciani, *Medicina del Corpo e Medicina dell'Anima: note sul sapere del medico fino all'inizio del secolo XIII* (Milan, 1978), pp.5-8.

[13] S. Epstein, *Wills and Wealth in Medieval Genoa, 1150-1250*, (London, 1984), p.9.

[14] Rothari, law 176, in *Lombard Laws*, trans. Drew, p.83.

A further law states:-

> 180. Concerning the girl who becomes a leper after her betrothal. If it happens that after a girl or woman has been betrothed she becomes leprous or mad or blind in both eyes, then her betrothed husband shall receive back his property and he shall not be required to take her to wife against his will. And he shall not be guilty in this event because it did not occur on account of his neglect *but on account of her weighty sins and resulting illness* [my italics].[15]

Now it is important to remember that in both these cases the thing with which the king is concerned is the transfer of property, not the afflicted person. It is also striking that no provision is recorded for the woman whose betrothed shows the same symptoms. This raises some important questions about the purity of a wife's body. For leprosy was commonly associated with sexual sin. Even if the law is more of a reflection of Rothari's desire to be seen as a legislator in the Roman mould, the message in this particular clause was clear: women were to be free of all taint whereas men's sexuality was not scrutinised in the same way. What is interesting here is that physical and visible illness was highlighted as a sign of misdemeanour on the part of the hapless bride. We have already noted the guilt attached to the woman in the case of malformed births. This emphasis on the visible perhaps begins to underline why certain sorts of affliction were re-corded.

Leprosy as treated in the Lombard laws was therefore considered the victim's own fault, and that it was customary to expel him or her from the community.[16] Since *lepra* seems to have 'encompassed a variety of conditions producing lesions of the skin',[17] the person afflicted might have been unjustly excluded from the community. 'In a period when even the most aristocratic lived in filth and bathed irregularly, infection and disfiguring skin conditions were common-

---

[15] Drew's translation, *Lombard Laws*, pp.84-5.

[16] Jean-Marc Bienvenu links the difficult famine conditions in Anjou at the end of the twelfth century to the rise of disease, and points up the connection that poverty could indirectly have with sickness: the rise in the level of prostitution there, he suggests, was accompanied by a concomitant spread in leprosy in that area: J.-M. Bienvenu, "Préhistoire du Franciscanisme", in *Poverty in the Middle Ages*, ed. D. Flood, (Werl, Westfalia, 1975), p.29. However, his sources may give a false impression here, for leprosy was seen as the result of sexual sin, and the link may have been made as much for moral reasons as medical ones.

[17] Siraisi, *Medieval and Early Renaissance Medicine*, p.130: she adds that secure knowledge that leprosy existed in medieval Europe comes from archaeological, not documentary, evidence.

place, and as a result so were diagnoses of leprosy.'[18] This is most vividly demonstrated by the stock representation of leprosy in contemporary art, the victim—as for example the emperor Constantine in a painting from the church of SS Quattri Coronati in Rome (plate 2)—being covered in red blotches.

Leprosy as a sign of guilt was not simply a Christian phenomenon. In Islamic society, references to the disease in the literature are comparatively rare, but nevertheless it was still regarded as a punishment by God for immorality. It is interesting to note that Maliki law allows either partner to dissolve a marriage on account of leprosy, in contrast to the one-sided provision in Christian, Lombard law related above.[19]

Madness too is mentioned as a cause for not going through with a marriage, and in a later clause from Rothari's code its connection with sin is restated, the victim having gone mad 'because of his weighty sins'.[20] An interesting contrast arises between Christian and Islamic cultures in their recorded attitudes to mental illness. A document from Sicily, dated 1137, is rich in material for the present study. It refers to the two underage children of 'the daughter of Iusef Alkisi' (Moslem society, rather like contemporary Jewish practice, preferring not to name women). One is described as an imbecile, and is represented by his mother in a sale of property.[21] No similar record survives of any mentally disabled individual living with his or her family in the Christian community of Sicily or southern Italy. Indeed, monastic records across Europe, recording the receipt of children as oblates, constantly complain about the number of mentally and physically defective children coming into their houses.[22] Again what I think is happening here is the Christian emphasis on the visible, with the object of guilt, in this case the child, being hidden away rather than remaining associated with its family.

Peregrine Horden points up the difference in attitudes between Byzantine (Christian) society and its Moslem neighbours towards mental disorder, which may explain this contrast. The former attributed madness to demonic possession, the latter to disease. To Mos-

---

[18] S. N. Brody, *Disease of the Soul: Leprosy in Medieval Literature*, (Ithaca, NY, 1974), p.59.

[19] M. Dols, "The leper in medieval Islamic society", *Speculum*, LVIII (1983), pp.891-916, esp. pp.895-7.

[20] *Lombard Laws*, Rothari 323.

[21] *Cusa*, doc. 54. However Dols, "Leper", p.915, points out that 'familial medical care goes back to antiquity ... and never died out in the Middle East.'

[22] J. Boswell, "*Expositio* and *oblatio*: the abandonment of children and the ancient and medieval family", *American Historical Review* LXXXIX (1984), p.21.

lems, mental disorder could be cured, whilst in the Christian mind
only exorcism would release the unfortunate individual.[23] The *Vita* of
St Nilus of Rossano features just such an episode, where a boy is freed
of the demons causing his madness.[24] It may be proximity to the
Moslem community in Sicily, however. that gives rise to a passing
reference in the *Vita* of St Nilus to a secular cure for madmen. Given
that this is hagiography, which would surely have stressed the demonic aspect of madness (and, indeed, did so when Nilus himself
cured the possessed boy), the saint's statement that 'it is good for
raging madmen to have their liberty restricted and food prescribed by
doctors' has a very Arabic sound to it.[25] His attitude may derive from
the fact that the Byzantine world had a slightly different outlook,
closer to the Islamic model, than the Latin West. In Byzantine and
Islamic societies a madman or woman might potentially be viewed as
a saint, or a 'holy fool', or as a dangerous lunatic, and was treated as
such.[26]

This differentiation between Christian and Moslem attitudes to
mental illness underscores the general difference between the two
societies in their perspectives on illness as a whole. William Jones has
recently summarised the contrast between Islamic measures to help
the sick, which were essentially philanthropic and secular in nature,
and Christian institutions, which were invariably attached to
churches.[27]

In addition to the contrast between Christian and Moslem, we
might also suppose that the rich and poor had rather differing experiences of illness. If Alan Goodman's assertion is correct, and modern
ethnographical data do indeed suggest that 'poor health is invariably
tracked back to poverty',[28] does the same correlation hold true for the
medieval period? Whilst we have seen that malnutrition and environmental conditions might have more impact on the poor, their suffering of disease is rarely recorded. A wealthy person might be able to
call upon more varieties of care, for example calling in paid physicians. The poor sick suffered a double impact, however: their earning

---

[23] P. Horden, "Possession without exorcism: the response to demons and insanity
in the earlier Byzantine middle East", in *Maladie et Société*, pp.1-19, especially p.15.
See also Horden, "Responses to possession".

[24] *Vita di San Nilo*, VIII, 58.

[25] *Vita di San Nilo*, X, 69.

[26] M. Dols, "Insanity in Byzantine and Islamic medicine", in *Symposium on Byzantine
Medicine*, p.136.

[27] W. R. Jones, "The clinic in three medieval societies", *Diogenes*, CXXII (1983),
pp.86-97.

[28] A. Goodman, "Health adaptation and maladaptation in past societies", in
Health in Past Societies, p.35.

potential was curtailed and they could not purchase care. Of course, the time they spent in bed might adversely affect their economic situation. Small wonder, then, that poverty and sickness were often bracketed together. Those without the ability to work, or without family members able to support them, had little option but to seek out charity from religious houses or beg on the streets. For the most part, sickness was seen as an admissible excuse for the latter activity in the early middle ages: only later, when alternative means of support were available, did begging become a less acceptable activity. Just as the church was a refuge from the consequences of criminal acts, by removing the perpetrator from the jurisdiction of the secular authorities, so it became a closed-off space for the sick, drawing them off the streets and enclosing them until they were able once more to function as members of the community. We shall return to the issue of places of care in a later chapter.

With these thoughts in mind, what evidence survives of illness in our region?

Pandemics

It is possible to find traces of major pandemics fairly easily in the medieval narrative source material. Their effects were so disastrous that no chroniclers worth their salt would have left them out. One might argue that the earliest signs of interest in medical history in Italy come from antiquaries' investigations and systematic listing of such occurrences. Such a work was that of A. Corradi, who gleaned a wide variety of material accessible at that time to survey Italian epidemics right up to his own day.[29] His findings for southern Italy are set out fully in Appendix 3, but some comments are desirable.

The risk of plague was ever present in an area whose communications by sea were so frequent. Ships arriving in ports might bring with them more than the cargo expected. This was a particular concern for those ports, such as Naples, Amalfi and the Apulian coastal towns, which all had varying degrees of exchange with the Byzantine East and/or North Africa throughout our period. But contemporary sources do not seek the reasons for such pandemics from these external sources, as we shall see.

Plague hit southern Italy on several occasions in the early middle ages. As well as the episode in Rome in 599/600, there was a further

---

[29] A. Corradi, *Annali delle Epidemie Occorse in Italia dalle Prime Memorie fino al 1850*, 2 vols (Bologna, 1863, repr. 1972).

outbreak in the city in 654. The far South and Sicily were affected by a serious outbreak in 748, and the whole of Naples and southern Italy were hit in 767.[30] Unfortunately, this is precisely the period when Neapolitan documents are at their scarcest, and we cannot gauge what effect this had on the population. Neverthless, the chronicle of the bishops of Naples, the source of our information on this outbreak, reveals that the people's response to alleviate their suffering was to turn to prayer.[31]

Pope Gregory the Great had claimed the sixth-century plague outbreaks in Italy were due to communal sin, and similarly had arranged penitential exercises to alleviate it.[32] Marie-Hélène Congourdeau has recently illustrated the way in which prayer was seen as a reasonable response to epidemics of plague in Byzantium in the sixth and fourteenth centuries,[33] and we have already seen that the response of the population of Salerno to the documented tenth-century outbreak in their territory was much the same.[34]

One of the most prevalent problems for the inhabitants of southern Italy may have been frequent bouts of malaria, but these are not recorded in the documents. It may well be that it was such a common problem that it was not worth recording beyond noting a 'fever', and indeed an accurate diagnosis of the illness was, like the plague, unlikely. Environmental factors were paramount in the occurrence of the disease, for it occurred most in swampy, wet areas. Franco Bonelli's study of the disease in the eighteenth and nineteenth centuries reveals how, in fleeing to areas of higher ground, people contributed to the spread of malaria by progressively de-foresting the mountain slope and thereby aggravating the run-off of water down to the plains, resulting in ever-larger marshes.[35]

---

[30] J.-N. Biraben and J. Le Goff, "La peste dans le haut moyen age", *Annales ESC*, XXIV (1969), pp.1484-1510.

[31] *Chronicon Episcoporum S. Neapolitanae Ecclesiae*, in *Monumenta*, ed. B. Capasso, I, chapter 199.

[32] Gregory of Tours, *History of the Franks*, trans. L. Thorpe (London, 1974), book X, chapter 1, relates his deacon Agiulf's eyewitness account of the procession. See also H.-H. Mollaret and J. Brossollet, "La procession de Saint Grégoire et la peste à Rome en l'an 590", *Médecine de France*, CIC (1969).

[33] M.-H. Congourdeau, "La société byzantine face aux grandes pandémies", in *Maladie et Société*, pp.21-41.

[34] See above, chapter 1.

[35] F. Bonelli, "La malaria nella storia demografica ed economica d'Italia: primi lineamenti di una ricerca", *Studi Storici*, VII (1966), p.676. Bonelli's article was primarily seeking to explain the economic retardation of the modern Mezzogiorno, and exploring the possibility that mortality through a higher level of malaria could be a contributory factor to the low population of the South.

Bonelli's findings are extremely relevant to a discussion of the early middle ages, for even then we can detect this movement away from the plains to higher ground. For example, already by late antiquity the Roman settlement of Minturno on the banks of the Garigliano river in Lazio had moved onto a nearby hill to become the town of Traetto.[36] In much the same way, the ancient settlement of Paestum on the Sele plain in Campania shifted to higher ground to become Caputaquis ('the river's head'—a vivid description of the change). The excavators of the medieval site attribute this shift to the population's desire to flee the Saracens at Agropoli in the late ninth century and to the spread of malarial conditions on the plain as the ancient canalisation system began to decay. Of course, the abandonment of the lowland site only exacerbated the situation, as the marshes were left to advance with little attempt to maintain the drainage channels.[37] The ecological disaster of deforestation and land clearance served only to aggravate the problem of flooding and the advance of marshy land.[38] A key point to note, therefore, is the impact of political conditions on the health of the population. The progressive degradation of marsh management techniques, practised under the Romans, was partially attributable to the lack of political will (or, possibly, the technical knowledge) of local leaders. A much easier solution to the problem, particularly when coupled with hostile attacks, was to move to higher ground. This created further problems which only modern drainage techniques have managed to bring under control.

In any discussion of pandemics, the overriding concern seems to have been with episodes associated with plague. This may reflect the preoccupation of many writers, all clerics, with spiritual health above physical. The issue of where the plague had come from is never addressed. Instead, its Biblical associations clearly influence the ways in which individuals and communities reacted to it. None of the southern Italian sources sought to explain plague in any way except as a judgement of God; this reflected the overriding tendency for these sources to be descriptive and introverted in their concerns rather than attempting any diagnostic statements. The effects of such

---

[36] It is interesting to note that the new settlement retained a riverine name, with its meaning of 'ferry': the modern settlement has reverted to the name Minturno.

[37] P. Delogu, "Storia del sito", in P. Delogu, G. Maetzke, P. Natella, P. Peduto, E. Tabaczynska and S. Tabaczynski, *Caputaquis Medievale*, I (Salerno, 1973), p.23. P. Peduto, "Aspetti urbanistici e caratteri architettonici di Capaccio Vecchia", p.35 of the same volume, highlights the fact that the abandonment of Paestum also contributed to the deterioration of conditions on the plain.

[38] Fumagalli, *Landscapes*, pp.88 and 105.

a perspective on the reliability of such sources for medical history will
be discussed presently.

Local and Individual

Illness at an individual level is very rarely referred to in any detail in
the southern Italian *corpus*. The most common context in which ill-
health is mentioned is in documents recording gifts or wills. In an age
when even mild sickness could be fatal, the impulse to arrange one's
affairs before succumbing was strong.

Thus in Salerno in 837, Radipertus, whilst ill 'but still able to
speak', made a gift to Arnipertus.[39] Urso, of the same city, states that
he was ill in bed when he made a gift in 872 to Ermipertus.[40] In 903,
the ordering of the affairs of Angelus, abbot of St Maximus in
Salerno, is recorded, again while he was sick.[41] At Conversano in
965, Lupo the cleric handed over some land to the monastery of St
Benedict in the same town.[42] In 1012, Disidio son of Manso, an
Amalfitan, made his will whilst ill in Salerno.[43] At Canne near
Barletta in 1030, Risandus, being ill, made an offering to the episcopal church there.[44]

Other, similar examples of this type of gift could be cited,[45] but
more complex documents could arise from ill-health. One can only
pity the plight of Walfa, daughter of Walfusi of Salerno, in 872.
Whilst widowed and ill in bed, she had to contend with the fact that
her brothers were captives of the Saracens, and that the city was
under siege. Faced with these calamities, she offered all her goods to

---

[39] *Cod Cav* I, doc. 17. The reference to the ability to speak became something of a
formulaic feature of wills, but has striking parallels with modern cross-cultural research among the Kabyle people, for whom the loss of speech is a sign of approach-
ing death, leading to a new status of dying person: S. C. Humphreys, "Death and
time", in *Mortality and Immortality*, p.264.

[40] *Cod Cav*, I, doc. 71.

[41] *Cod Cav*, I, doc. 117.

[42] *PC*, doc. 18.

[43] *CodCav*, IV, doc. 646.

[44] *CDB*, VIII, doc. 7.

[45] Documents following a similar pattern include *SGA*, doc. 4 (937, Naples);
RNAM, doc. 194 (982, Capua); *CDB*, IX, doc. 10 (1081, Corato); *PC*, doc. nos 50
(1089), 78 (1128) and 138 (1188, all Conversano); *PAVAR* I, doc. 39 (1143, Ravello)
and *Théristes*, doc. 42 (1197/8, Calabria). Wills made whilst ill include a group preserved in the archive of the abbey of Le Trinità, Cava: *Arca* XVI, doc. nos 99 and
100, *Arca* XVIII, doc. nos 92 and 97, *Arca* XX, doc. 31; also *CDB*, I, doc. 41 (1120,
Bari); *CDB*, V, doc. 100 (1146, Palermo); *CDB*, III, doc. nos 92 (1164, Terlizzi) and
96, (1167, Bitonto).

the church of St Maximus, on condition that she and her mother be supported for their lifetimes.[46] Ianiportus of Ciciano, in the territory of Salerno, used a his illness as a pretext for returning land that he had disputed with the monastery of St Sebastian in Naples.[47] John the cleric, from Salerno, made his will whilst unwell in 996.[48] In 1023 the illness of Iaquintus son of Peter of Caputaquis caused him to sell a portion of his lands, stipulating that the buyer should make a division with Iaquintus' son.[49] In 1035 illness prompted Atenolf son of Balsamus to acknowledge the existence of a natural daughter, and to make provision for her.[50] The gift of land by the ill Sariano of Devia, made in 1053, was in addition to the provisions of his will in favour of his infant daughter.[51]

However, in 959 Dumnella of Conversano made a gift to the monastery of St. Benedict while she was 'infirm';[52] and in 1007 Cosmas, the abbot or *hegoumen* of the monastery of St. Anastasius at Carbone in Calabria/Lucania, set out his wishes 'now that I am weak.'[53] Such infirmity could also be caused by old age, but this can only be inferred in the documentary record.[54] For example, the frailty of John the priest is cited as the reason for his transfer of a church in his care to Nicholas the priest at Bari in 1067.[55] However, a clause setting out what should happen if John outlives Nicholas casts doubt on whether John is ill or aged. This is a problem which can seriously affect the interpretation of such transactions.

Another problem is to determine whether the person concerned in the transaction died after making it. A note of caution should be induced by the example of Ugo, brother of duke Leo II of Gaeta. In 1023, 'whilst ill', he handed over all of his lands to the abbey of Montecassino, presumably anticipating his own death.[56] In fact he lived on for at least another seventeen years, and repeated part of his gift in 1040.[57] Less ambiguous are two mid-eleventh century dona-

---

[46] *CodCav*, I, doc. 75.
[47] *RNAM*, doc. 81 (951).
[48] *CodCav*, III, doc. 491.
[49] *CodCav*, V, doc. 754.
[50] *CDB*, VIII, doc. 12; I discuss this case further in "Women, wills and wealth".
[51] *Tremiti*, doc. 48.
[52] *PC*, doc. 13.
[53] *Carbone*, doc. 1.
[54] For a discussion of the difficulty of establishing 'old age' as a concept in medieval sources, although rather later, S. Shahar, "Who were old in the middle ages?", *Social History of Medicine*, VI (1993), pp.313-341.
[55] *CDB*, I, doc. 26.
[56] *CDC*, I, doc. 142.
[57] *CDC*, I, doc. 173.

tions preserved in the Tremiti archives, in which each of the authors is described as being on his deathbed.[58] However, even these may reflect only the prognosis on the donors at the time of the documents, rather than their subsequent fate. Could such gifts during a period of infirmity have performed a dual function, representing not only insurance for the hereafter, but also a donation made in the hope of a miraculous cure? The latter issue will be discussed more fully below.

Sickness might prompt other transactions than gifts. In a rare direct reference to the type of ailment being suffered, John Gititio of Naples sold off a piece of land which his parents had bought from a sick aunt, who at the time of the original sale had been gravely ill *de infirmitate paralisis*.[59]

The uncertainties of sickness seem to be summed up in a very interesting document from Salerno, dated 1028. It records an unresolved dispute over an earlier will of one Iaquintus, who had five children by two women, Cara and Sica. His and Cara's daughter, Dibitia, was ill at the time of the will. Iaquintus stated that, if she did not marry, his three sons were to support her with 6 *tertiaria* of grain, 1 of vegetables, 4 *saume* of wine and a *quartarium* of salt annually and, every three years, two pairs of shoes. He made provision for his other daughter to receive a normal dowry from his son Peter, Sica's son. This suggests that it was Dibitia's unspecified illness that was likely to prevent her from marrying. Perhaps unsurprisingly, Peter was now challenging the will against his two half-sisters' mother.[60]

A similar case occurs in a will from Ravello, dated 1170. Again, a daughter of the testator, Ursus Rogadeo, named Ambrosia, was provided for in a specific clause. If she was to recover, her brothers were instructed to marry her off 'honourably'. If, on the other hand, she did not regain her health, she was to be given 300 *solidi* over fifteen years to support herself, and allowed to stay in Ursus' house with a bed and clothing.[61]

Illness seems often to have been sympathetically viewed and, real or feigned, may have functioned as a face-saver in difficult situations. For example, during a dispute over property before the court of Eustathius Skepides, *strategos* of Lucania, in 1042, the decision turned

---

[58] *Tremiti*, doc. nos 41 (?1049) and 72 (1059-62).

[59] *RN*, doc. 502.

[60] *CodCav*, V, doc. 797. Compare with the provisions of this will with those in an almost contemporary Anglo-Saxon will, that of Wulfric Spott (c.1002/4), in which he made provision for his 'poor daughter' so long as her life lasted: *English Historical Documents*, I, ed. D. Whitelock (2nd ed. London, 1979), p.586.

[61] *PAVAR*, II, doc. 73.

on the affirmation of the man who had written charters supporting one side's case. He, crucially, was ill and unable to come to court, but sent a written statement which was accepted as evidence by the *strategos* and won the case.[62] A court in Amalfi accepted that a woman could not attend on account of her illness.[63] In Giovinazzo, the co-executor of a will had to be represented by others at the sale of part of the estate, since he was ill in bed.[64] Finally, in 1176, again in a courtcase, a notary called as a witness had to send his son to court to represent him, and this again seems to have been acceptable.[65]

Some general comments are possible about all of these transactions. Being sick met with the expectation that the individual would not wish to, or could not, participate in public life. This non-participation does not appear to have resulted in censure of any kind, nor in any expression of regret or apology from the sick person. Furthermore, there is no hint of any attribution of illness to some kind of ill-doing on the part of the unfortunate person. But what if the inclusion of illness in the preamble to many of these documents was in fact a formulaic precursor to that individual being allowed to make a will? If illness was a pretext for such actions, could it also function as a way of relaxing rigid social rules? Suspicion is heightened by the fact that only a tiny minority of those citing illness as a reason for their actions actually provide any detail of their complaint, and the survival of some testators for several years after their wills are made merely reinforce the impression that it was necessary to preface an arrangement of one's affairs with a suitable excuse.

In the face of this apparently sympathetic attitude towards the sick, and in support of this argument, we find that feigned illness could also provide a convenient way to save face in a potentially awkward or embarrassing situation. The *Chronicon Salernitanum* illustrates this well. There are several instances where illness is affected or pleaded with varying levels of success. During the reign of Grimoald IV of Benevento, one Sico tries to avoid coming into the prince's presence by feigning sickness. Grimoald does not believe him. In the same chapter, however, the prince is able to use exactly the same excuse to withdraw from a fruitless attack on Sico.[66] In doing so, he is able to avoid the possible humiliation of an unsuccessful foray. Later, prince Sicard (817-39) refuses to believe Nannigone's plea of illness when

---

[62] *Donnoso*, doc. 3.
[63] *CDA*, doc. 104.
[64] *CDB*, V, doc. 114 (1157).
[65] *Mileto*, doc. 21.
[66] *ChronSal* chapter 44.

ordering the latter to go as an envoy to Africa. This would have foiled
Sicard's plan to rape Nannigone's wife.[67]

Looking further afield, it is clear that sickness was a valid excuse
for absence from public events. At a synod held in Rome before
emperor Otto I Ingelfred, patriarch of Aquileia, was represented by
his deacon, having been seized by a sudden sickness.[68] At a subsequent meeting, the absence of the disgraced pope, John XII, was
condemned because he had not sent messengers to provide an adequate excuse, 'illness or some such insuperable difficulty.'[69]

The source of this information, Liutprand, bishop of Cremona,
unfortunately did not meet with such sympathy. On his embassy to
Constantinople, of which he has left us a personal, and venomous,
record, he was repeatedly called to the court of the emperor
Nicephorus despite being seriously ill.[70] This treatment must be read
in the context of Liutprand's invective against the Byzantine emperor, but there is little doubt that it further reinforced his prejudices.
Towards the end of his stay he leaves a verbal portrait of himself, put
into the mouths of the Byzantines, in order to emphasise his suffering:
'The pallor of your face, the emaciation of your whole body, the
unusual length of your hair and beard, all reveal the immense pain
that is in your heart...'[71] It is interesting to speculate that the treatment of Liutprand points up a difference in attitude between East
and West towards sickness: if we believe the bishop of Cremona, his
illness was not considered a valid excuse for absence from the Byzantine court. But we have to read his account in the light of the fact that
he was on an ambassadorial mission and so more than in any other
circumstance was required to attend on Nicephorus. As we have seen,
in day-to-day Byzantine administration in southern Italy, absence
through illness was noted but not forbidden.

Besides being a valid excuse for non-participation in public events,
illness had other functions in medieval narrative sources. Liutprand
delights in describing the sickness of those whom he accuses of
crimes. Thus, he says king Arnulf of Italy 'died of a disgusting
malady. He was cruel tormented by the tiny worms that are called

---

[67] *ChronSal*, chapter 65. On the rape, see above, chapter 2.
[68] Liutprand of Cremona, *A Chronicle of Otto's Reign*, chapter 9.
[69] *Chronicle of Otto's Reign*, chapter 14.
[70] Liutprand of Cremona, *The Embassy to Constantinople*, chapter 13: he and his
companions fall ill from 'indignation as well as heat and thirst' on account of the
brackish water they were drinking instead of wine; in subsequent chapters, 19, 21,
23, and 25, Liutprand stresses that he is commanded to attend the emperor and to
dine, despite his sickness.
[71] *Embassy to Constantinople*, chapter 50.

lice and expired in agony. It is said that these worms bred so fast that no doctor's care could diminish their number.'[72] The bishop leaves open the question as to whether this was punishment for letting the Hungarians loose in Italy, but his disapproval is apparent. In another description, concerning Henry, the rebellious brother of Otto I of Germany, Liutprand relates the after-effects of an injury in battle, when 'Henry was struck heavily on the arm.... the cruel force of the blow turned the skin completely black. In spite of all his doctors' care the bruise never healed and caused him every year excruciating pain. Indeed it was acknowledged that his death many years later was due to this injury.'[73] Finally, of pope John XII, Liutprand says that he died after 'disporting himself with some man's wife outside Rome, the devil dealt him such a violent blow on the temples that he died of the injury within a week.'[74]

The anonymous author of the tenth-century *Chronicon Salernitanum* also provides a great deal of anecdotal evidence about illness, and echoes Liutprand's attitude that sins brought retribution in the form of illness to the perpetrators. A case in point is the tale, already discussed in chapter 3 above, of the woman who gave birth to a child without bones. Whilst this type of tale is not much use to us medically, it underlines the association that the chronicler was making between wrongdoing and illness.

There are further episodes in the chronicle of unfaithful subjects or traitors being punished with illness or injury. During the reign of Sico and Sicard of Benevento (817-39) Agelmond, murderer of Grimoald, has a vision of his victim. The apparition cuts him with a sword between his shoulder blades, and he begins to vomit blood. Having recounted the tale to his companions, (and thereby ensuring its survival for posterity), Agelmond dies three days later of his mortal wound.[75] In the same period one Roffred, having obtained the death of abbot Alfanus, is struck with paralysis in one leg which never heals.[76]

The tone of the chronicle is echoed by the *Vita* of St Nilus of Rossano. This text is liberally sprinkled with those whose pride and other sins led them to ignore the saint's advice, and who were, as a result, struck down with ill-health. For example, during Nilus' sojourn in the principate of Salerno, a 'tyrant', who boasted that he had ten

---

[72] *Antapodosis*, chapter 36.
[73] *Antapodosis*, chapter 24.
[74] *Chronicle of Otto's Reign*, chapter 20.
[75] *ChronSal* chapter 56.
[76] *ChronSal* chapter 71.

years of his life left, and that he intended to spend eight of them
gratifying his every desire before repenting in the final two, was struck
down with illness and died within ten days, not years.[77] Similarly, a
domesticus, Leo, was struck down with a pain in his head after fooling
around with a monk's cowl, and died soon after Nilus' remon-
strance.[78]

The most detailed episode of this type concerns the imperial judge
Eufrasius. Arriving in southern Italy in 968, he was incensed that
Nilus did not come out to fete him as the rest of the population had.
His threats against the saint, however, were punished with a grave
illness, gangrene of his genitals. This, relates the *Vita* with relish,
'resisted the doctors' care, and punished in him the organs of disso-
luteness, with which he had intemperately violated the laws of nature.' Nilus, having ignored the man's pleas to visit him, left the judge
in this state for three years, until his genitals were eaten away. Then,
as the affliction threatened to affect the judge's internal organs and
kill him, Nilus, the 'spiritual doctor', went to his bedside.

In a passage reminiscent of the much later testimony of Jacques de
Vitry, the judge describes the bitter pain and intolerable smell that
the disease had caused, which neither unguents nor seven changes of
clothing a day had alleviated. Nilus was persuaded to tonsure the
unhappy man, who found some relief from wearing the poor clothes
of a monk, before dying three days later.[79] An almost contemporary
life of a southern Italian saint, Fantinus, also features episodes of this
type, with an unmerciful duke struck down by a fever and only cured
when the saint forgave him.[80]

Both chronicle and hagiographical sources in southern Italy thus
appear to present birth defects and illness as the result of sin. This
type of association derived from the patristic writings of the first six
centuries of the Christian era, which connected sickness with the Fall
and with men's sins.[81] The tendency to view the equation of sickness
with sin as part of the medieval *habitus*, however, must be modified in
the light of investigations by Kroll and Bachrach. In their survey of a
wide range of chronicles and hagiography from the early middle ages,
they found that such an association was more often a rhetorical device used to condemn the writer's adversaries than a reflection of

---

[77] *Vita di San Nilo*, II,9.
[78] *Vita di San Nilo*, VII, 52.
[79] *Vita di San Nilo*, VIII, 54-6.
[80] *Vita di San Fantino il Giovane*, ed. E. Follieri (Brussels, 1993); this difficult text is
discussed further below, chapter 5.
[81] Siraisi, *Medieval and Early Renaissance Medicine*, p.8.

actual beliefs about illness. Whilst sin was an important part of explanations of illness, it was not the primary part except in this specific context of general animosity.[82]

Although Bachrach and Kroll did not examine many Italian sources, the pattern displayed by Liutprand, the Salernitan chronicle and southern Italian hagiography appears to support their argument. It is also reinforced by earlier accounts, for example the *Historia Langobardorum* of Paul the Deacon, written at Montecassino towards the end of the eighth century, and replete with incidents of this type.

However, some passing references in the narrative material can be taken not simply as rhetorical devices, but perhaps as evidence of the writer's own knowledge of particular ailments. Liutprand, for example, makes allusions suggesting that the points he was making would have been familiar to his readers. Thus, for example, he characterises lovers of learning as being like 'men sick of the dropsy: as these thirst the more ardently the more water they drink, so students, the more they read, the more eagerly seek after new knowledge.'[83] The passing references in the Salernitan chronicle also reveal substantial knowledge of complaints and drug administration. During the reign of Arechis II, for example, a woman is said to have strangled her husband and claimed his death was due to an apoplectic fit.[84] To feign illness, a man took a purgative.[85] The chronicler gives a fairly detailed image of the last days of prince Siconolf of Benevento (840-9): taken ill, he felt very hot and oppressed in all his limbs, and burnt with fever. Having handed on power to Sico, he died.[86] In the late ninth century, the plotters against Radelchis of Benevento had to carry him to the church where they imprisoned him, because he suffered from gout (*podagra*).[87]

The chronicler is also fascinated by physical abnormalities in those he describes. He tells us about Dauferius the mute, so-called because of voice defect,[88] and a pretty girl with an eye defect.[89] The chronicler is at his best, however, when relating the Saracen siege of Salerno in the late ninth century. The Saracen king Abimelec, he says, was brave and astute in human affairs, *for all that he was a eunuch* [my

---

[82] J. Kroll and B. Bachrach, "Sin and the etiology of disease in pre-crusade Europe", *Journal of the History of Medicine and Allied Sciences*, XLI (1986), pp.395-414.
[83] Liutprand of Cremona, *Antapodosis*, chapter 1.
[84] *ChronSal* chapter 15.
[85] *ChronSal* chapter 66.
[86] *ChronSal* chapter 92.
[87] *ChronSal* chapter 154.
[88] *ChronSal* chapter 76.
[89] *ChronSal* chapter 96.

italics].[90] As if to compensate, his next chapter tells of a famous Saracen with three testicles.[91]

Physical deformity, however, did not always attract attention for frivolous reasons. It could be used as a way of identifying someone in a document when the use of surnames was inconsistent. In an environment where surnames were only beginning to be used, nicknames are often recorded to identify an individual in a document. We have already considered some of these, relating to deafness, possible spine deformity and the lack of an eye, in chapter 3. In addition, the surname *pumillo* suggests that dwarfism also occurred in the South, and again appears not to have carried any stigma.[92] Even if 'any physical oddity, any disconcerting physical shortcoming or disagreeable trait, was mercilessly highlighted',[93] it did not lead to the individual's exclusion from his or her community. Indeed, many nicknames highlighted physical features without referring to deformities, for example *buccalata* (big mouth) and *boccapiczula* (small mouth), from Neapolitan and Salernitan documents.[94]

This is an important point to bear in mind when we consider the picture presented by other types of source material from southern Italy. The charter evidence, in particular, gives no hint that illness was interpreted as some form of divine punishment. People drawing up gifts and wills when they were ill might include, in the formulaic preamble to the document, an awareness of the fragility of human life and the importance of pious works in order to achieve a reward after death, but they do not make any statement linking their present illness to their way of life. Nor, as we have seen, did others make that judgement when an individual could not perform some public duty because of illness. The chroniclers might attribute some misdeeds, but the gatherings recorded in charter evidence did not. Of course, we have to be careful in our use of any kind of evidence. Even if the charters appear more 'real', because they deal with the mundane concerns of landowners and families, they nevertheless followed fairly uniform frameworks of formula and layout. They functioned as a record of a transaction, not of the feelings of those present. Yet private documents do sometimes include emotional and/or judgemental statements, and their presence proves that it was quite possible to express an opinion. Thus the fact that we have a relatively large sample featuring illness but no derogatory comment suggests that

---

[90] *ChronSal* chapter 112.
[91] *ChronSal* chapter 113.
[92] In a Neapolitan document: *SGA*, doc. 13 (1020).
[93] Fumagalli, *Landscapes*, 182.
[94] *SGA*, doc. 1 (911) and *CodCav*, V, doc. 712 (1018) respectively.

communities were largely sympathetic, or at worst neutral, in their dealings with the sick or, as I have suggested above, that the mention of illness was a mere pretext to allow the transaction to go ahead.

The illness of some individuals, however, might provoke more than sympathy. The *Vita* of St Nilus of Rossano introduces the saint's own afflictions at particular points in the narrative to herald significant episodes in his life. For example, his initial conversion to the religious life is precipitated by a bout of fever which leads him to leave his wife and young daughter.[95]

His biographer repeatedly notes the effects on Nilus' health of the ascetic diet that he follows,[96] but the saint, too, is aware of its drawbacks. Having abstained from liquids, he decides not to continue, 'fearing that the excessive dryness of his lungs might prejudice his health.'[97] Most of the attacks of illness, however, are framed in terms of spiritual tests. Alone in his cave hermitage, Nilus is assailed by demons who attack his body.[98] More seriously, the devil sends a tumour which affects Nilus' vocal chords, striking him dumb and rendering him unable to take anything but liquids. The saint's patience in bearing this is rewarded by God, who opens the tumour and allows the festering to drain away.[99] The devil then hits Nilus on the head, causing the side of his face and eye to swell, and paralysing his arm (perhaps a stroke?). In this discomfort he spends a year, refusing the care of doctors because he knows that 'injuries inflicted by demons cannot be cured by human hands'.[100] His condition is relieved by prayer, as is a wound to his leg caused by slipping on ice.[101] Only on his deathbed is the saint attended by a doctor, Michael, and this only to check whether he is dead or not (he feels the saint's pulse, and confirms that Nilus still lives, as 'he has no fever or sign of death').[102] Soon after, the saint dies at the age of ninety-five.

I have dwelt at some length on St Nilus and his ills. It is difficult to decide what element of realism there is in the episodes recounted, but the function of the saint's illness is perhaps more significant. For it was by being sick, and repeatedly cured, as well as by his asceticism, that Nilus was marked out as 'saintly'. His contemporaries knew this:

---

[95] *Vita di San Nilo*, I, 3.
[96] E.g. *Vita San Nilo*, VI, 40; XIII, 87 (including the fact that the saint never ate meat nor used a bath).
[97] *Vita di San Nilo*, III, 17.
[98] *Vita di San Nilo*, III, 18.
[99] *Vita di San Nilo*, III, 21 and IV, 22. See also below, chapter 5, the episode of Constantine of Fondi.
[100] *Vita di San Nilo*, IV, 23.
[101] *Vita di San Nilo* IX, 63.
[102] *Vita di San Nilo*, XIV, 98.

several local political leaders clearly hoped that he would die in their jurisdiction, so that they would have custody of a saint's relics.[103]

Nilus' initial illness, forcing him to leave his family, has parallels in modern anthropological study of the 'searing experiences, which typically herald the onset of the shamanistic vocation.'[104] Like the saint, who is reluctant to be recognised as such, the shaman's vocational experience is often, in the form of an illness, not a welcome calling. Having overcome the invading demons, the shaman is seen as their master, and thus acquires authority. In the medieval period, Nilus' recovery from two life-threatening illnesses and several other less serious ailments, not to mention his long life thereafter, must have contributed to the awe in which he was held. Vito Fumagalli highlights the coincidence between a spell of illness and life-changing decisions, such as conversion or withdrawal from the world, in medieval biographies. He suggests that such illnesses may well have been psychosomatic, or depressive, and that the period of introspection forced by illness and inactivity might lead to such decisions being made.[105] This correlation is most visible in our region in the life of St Elias Speleotis. His withdrawal from the world is attributed by his biographer to a childhood accident and subsequent poor medical care, which led to the saint losing the fingers of his left hand.[106] We shall return to the care itself in the next chapter.

An all-too-rare comparative saint's life survives from the Lombard part of southern Italy. The *Vita S. Barbati*, a ninth-century life of a seventh-century bishop of Benevento, despite its brevity, contains some interesting imagery associated with medical terms. God is called *hic piissimus medicus*, but apart from one chapter, miraculous healing is not included as a major feature. Even that chapter is not about physical healing, as such, but uses the medical metaphors to describe Barbatus' preaching to the Arian Lombards: '...the holy man tried with divine cures to clean them to health from the fevers of their sins and from their innermost flowing squalor and .... he strengthened with wonderful signs the words of his preaching; so that, if not by words, then they might be bent to health having seen the miracles.'[107]

---

[103] On the tussle surrounding Nilus' death, see below, chapter 6.
[104] Lewis, *Ecstatic Religion*, p.187.
[105] Fumagalli, *Landscapes*, p.62.
[106] da Costa-Louillet, "Saints de Sicile", p.114.
[107] '...eos sanctissimus vir divinis medicaminibus conabatur a peccatorum febribus et ex intimis squalida profluente sanie emundare ... etiam mirabilibus signis suae predicationis verba firmaret; ut, si non verbis, ad suam salutem visis miraculis flecterentur':*Vita Sancti Barbati Episcopi*, in *MGH, Scriptores Rerum Langobardorum et Italicarum*, ed. G. Waitz (Hanover, 1878), pp.557-63, chapter 3.

Thus the southern Italian hagiography presents sickness as a result of sin, but also sin described as a sickness. These associations, it must be presumed, filtered through into the preaching of clerics to their local communities, which only served to reinforce the association.

Conclusions

The medieval southern Italian source material contains many different depictions of illness. Some are sparse references, others give detailed descriptions of the symptoms, and others still use a specific or unnamed illness as a metaphor for other shortcomings or afflictions. Common to all, however, is a complete lack of any diagnostic or etiological discussion beyond the depiction by the narrative sources of disease as a judgement. The causes of illness were either ignored or unknown to medieval authors. Some illness might even have been used as a pretext in the charter sources to enable land transactions which might otherwise not have gone ahead. After all, it was perfectly reasonable to argue that an ailment *could* be fatal, even if subsequently it proved not to be. In the meantime, the principle of disposing of a piece of property to a certain person had been established in writing, and might prove hard to challenge later.

How, though, do we reconcile this picture of illness as a spiritual test or sickness, and the opinion of legislators, hagiographers and chroniclers that the sick were the victims of their own, sinful life, with the apparent indifference in charter material to the spiritual health of the sick person?

Before generalising too far, it is worth stating that leprosy may have been a special case. Depicted as particularly a result of sexual deviance, it was believed to be highly contagious and, of course, had a horrifyingly visible effect on the sufferer. The southern Italian attitude to leprosy is vividly exemplified in a passage from the life of saint Nilus of Rossano: warning his disciple that they should set themselves apart from the world, St Nilus compares them to 'lepers and other foul beings'.[108] If the leper did not live in a house away from the community, he or she might enter a *leprosarium* or leper-house. Given the fear which the disease generated, such isolation may well have acted as a protection as much as a confinement. There are, however, no recorded examples of leper-houses in the southern Italian documentation.

---

[108] *Vita di San Nilo*, V, 33.

It is unlikely that any of the people whose charters we have discussed were sufferers of this disease. But nevertheless, the narrative
and prescriptive sources associate other illnesses with sin as well. I
would suggest that our answer lies in examining why such a construction of illness existed. If illness was God's punishment, then only God
could cure it—a view expressed by the mass prayers in the face of
plague outbreaks. But what if there was competition to heal people
from other sources? Then, the message that there was only one cure
might have to be restated by discussing the causes of illness. Whether
the chronicler's enemy, as Bachrach and Kroll suggest, or a simple
sinner, a sick individual had to be guided to the right sort of cure. As
we shall see in the next chapter, such guidance was extremely necessary in medieval southern Italy.

CHAPTER FIVE

DOCTORS, HOSPITALS AND CURES

I suggested at the end of the previous chapter that the association of illness with sin in some narrative and legislative sources derived from an overwhelming need to establish God (via the Church) as the only source of cure and care. That argument rests, however, on the existence of alternatives to prayer. In this chapter, I shall attempt to outline what evidence survives for the existence of medical care in southern Italy. It should be noted at the outset that, as in the case of illness, what constituted care in the medieval community may differ considerably from our notion. Valerie Flint underlines the choice of care in early medieval Francia: a sick person might consult a *medicus*, a saint, or an enchanter, or all three, in search of a cure.[1] These are only the documented choices; we must also suppose the existence of others who offered help including, it has been argued, many female practitioners. What care was available to the southern Italian sick?

Doctors

Doctors make an early appearance in the lawcodes of the Lombard kings, dating from the seventh and eighth centuries.[2] Particularly notable is a series of laws issued within the earliest code, that of king Rothari, ordering that the compensation to be paid for causing injuries should include payment of the doctor's fee.[3] Furthermore, the assailant is charged with calling the doctor for his (or her) victim.[4] This approach, even if somewhat idealistic, may at least be proof that doctors were available to be called. Fischer Drew is somewhat dubi-

---

[1] V. J. Flint. "The early medieval *medicus*, the saint—and the enchanter", *Social History of Medicine*, II (1989), pp. 127-45. See also her discussion of the wide variety of practitioners in early medieval Europe in V. J. Flint, *The Rise of Magic in Early Medieval Europe* (Oxford, 1991), pp.61-79.

[2] An accessible translation of these is *The Lombard Laws*, ed. K. Fischer Drew, (Pennsylvania, 1973). Citations are by king and law number in this edition.

[3] Rothari 78, 79, 82-4, 87, 89, 94, 101-3, 106-7, 110-2, 118 in *Lombard Laws*. It is striking that the Salic law current in Francia and almost contemporary with the Lombard codes also includes such a provision: J.-L. Goglin, *Les Misérables dans l'Occident Médiéval* (Paris, 1976), 26. It is likely that both derive from a Roman origin.

[4] Rothari 128

ous about their function, since 'the histories of science and medicine do not refer to any physicians or doctors in Lombard Italy.' This does not seem to be a reason to limit their role solely to 'the treatment of wounds', as she does.[5]

Nevertheless, there may be a problem in taking Rothari's measures at face value. It has been suggested that the king's measures on leprosy, discussed in the previous chapter, were not prompted by any upturn in the disease, but were simply the continuation of a Roman tradition of legislation about it.[6] The laws including the calling of a doctor may be similarly derivative. However, as we shall see, the Lombard law codes were often closely followed by the heirs of the Lombard kings, the inhabitants of the southern principalities of Benevento, Salerno and Capua, some three or four centuries later. In their later context, they may actually have had more relevance to the realities of southern Italian life than they had had earlier in the kingdom. In the South, paid doctors may well have been available to be called upon to tend to the victims of injury.

In support of this view is the evidence of the later narratives of Liutprand from northern Italy, the *Chronicon Salernitanum*, and in the southern Italian documents. A survey of the occurrence of the term *medicus*, 'a general term that could be applied to anyone who practised medicine or surgery',[7] reveals a wide distribution of the term throughout southern Italian sources. For the purposes of this discussion, it is probably safe to define a *medicus* as a medical practitioner and to translate it as 'doctor', but at this date it is unwise to load the term with any sense of professional regulation. This, I would suggest, came later, towards the twelfth and thirteenth centuries, when the terms doctor and surgeon, the latter not appearing until the twelfth century, begin to indicate some regulation of function.

The presence of *medici* is in fact recorded in Salerno from a relatively early date. Delogu highlights the presence in the ninth-century *Translatio Sanctae Trophimenis* of a certain Hieronymus *archiater*, whose 'huge books' are also referred to. Because of his title, Delogu hypothesises that Salerno at this time must already have had a functioning hierarchy of medics.[8] I rather think that the conferring of such a title merely illustrates the respect in which this particular medic was held, for there is little other evidence to support Delogu's assertion. However, the reference to Hieronymus' books certainly supports Piero

⁵ *Lombard Laws*, p.242, note 26.
⁶ R. I. Moore, *The Formation of a Persecuting Society* (Oxford, 1987), p.48.
⁷ Siraisi, *Medieval and Early Renaissance Medicine*, p.21
⁸ P. Delogu, *Mito di una Città Meridionale* (Naples, 1977), p.153, n.5.

Morpurgo's impression of an active book market in the city later on.[9]

Unfortunately, reflecting the concerns of the documentation, all the medics in the Salernitan charters are shown in their roles as landowners rather than their medical function. The earliest reference occurs in 849. In that year, Iosep *medicus* bought vineyards in *Malianu* (Magliano Vetere) next to property he already owned.[10] Seven years later, he added to his holding here, buying from the same vendor.[11] Both properties were located in the southern part of the principality, in Lucania near the river Calore (called the Lirino in the documents), along which in 855 Iosep bought another piece of vineyard.[12] Finally, in 865, he is recorded as having built a mill on the river.[13]

Iosep has already received attention in general histories of southern Italy. Barbara Kreutz locates him in the Jewish community on the basis of his name and the fact that he made a gift to St Maximus and that 'a Jew (or converted Jew) might particularly have considered such a gift politic.'[14] Given that the document she cites does not appear to show such a gift (and that a donation to a powerful ecclesiastical institution was a desirable action by any Christian), it is really only Iosep's name which supports this view. However, her statement that 'by the late tenth century Jewish doctors were unquestionably practising at Salerno' is backed up by the appearance of one Judex (or Judah) the Jew, son of Jude *medici* in a charter of 1004.[15]

The strong tradition of Jewish medicine present in Muslim Spain,[16] therefore, may have a less well-known parallel in southern Italy, as Jews in the latter area undoubtedly also had contact with Muslim communities both in Egypt and in Sicily. The Jewish community had a long and continuous history in southern Italy, of which the surviving evidence from Christian archives, for example the sixth-century letters of pope Gregory I or the later charter material, only provides glimpses. One of the most valuable sources of evidence for a Jewish presence is the relatively large number of grave inscriptions that have survived. These will be discussed in a later chapter but, in his study of the Jewish communities of the South, Ferorelli notes the

---

[9] P. Morpurgo, "L'ingresso dell'Aristotele latino a Salerno", in *Rencontres de Cultures*, p.273. On the circulation of texts, see below, chapter 7.

[10] *CodCav* I, doc. 29.

[11] *CodCav* I, doc. 47.

[12] *CodCav* I, doc. 40.

[13] *CodCav* I, doc. 61.

[14] B. Kreutz, *Before the Normans*, (Philadelphia, 1991), p.206, note 43.

[15] *Before the Normans*, p.145, and further discussion on the medical practitioners of Salerno pp.145-147; *CodCav* IV, doc. 567.

[16] Siraisi, *Medieval and Early Renaissance Medicine*, p.29

early reversion to Hebrew in the surviving Pugliese examples, which he ascribes to the greater possibility of contact with other groups in the Mediterranean.[17]

One Pugliese Jew has left us evidence of his work. Shabbetai Donnolo (913-post 982) lived and worked in Oria, and wrote a herbal of over a hundred recipes. Significantly, he addressed it to Jewish doctors, suggesting that there was a considerable number practising in the South in the tenth century. The head of the Jewish community in nearby Bari was also a doctor, documented in 944.[18] An isolated reference to one Ahanael *medicus* at Amalfi, in Benjamin of Tudela's itinerary of 1165, is our only other evidence of Jewish medical practice.[19] Only in the later middle ages do Jewish practitioners become widely visible in southern Italy and Sicily, when licensing became the norm.[20]

Owing to their skills, the doctors at Salerno are likely to have commanded a certain amount of respect, particularly if they were familiar faces in their local community and built up a circle of associates. A closer examination of the documents featuring Iosep reveals a quite tightly-knit group of people. We know that he bought land twice from the same man, Lupo son of Maio. Witness to all three purchases made by Iosep was another man, Leocardo son of Lupi; four other men appeared in two of the three documents. This suggests that Iosep had a close circle of associates in the local community around Magliano—one might suggest that he was the main source of medical care in this district. The intensely local nature of the documents is reinforced when we trace other people featured in Iosep's documents: a group of four appear together in a charter, a couple in another, and a couple in a third. All three charters relate to land around *Iovi*, modern Gioi near Magliano.[21] Further references to individuals found in Iosep's charters are found in a cluster of documents relating to Nocera and San Severino, much closer to the city, but Iosep himself appears to have concentrated his transactions further South. There is little indication that he associated with the higher strata of Salernitan society, preferring perhaps to maintain his status by his local activities.

One means of expressing the respect in which they were held was for medics to act as witnesses (thereby conferring authority) on other

---

[17] N. Ferorelli, *Gli Ebrei nell'Italia Meridionale dall'Età Romana al Secolo XVIII* (Bologna, 1966), p.29.

[18] A. Sharf, *The Universe of Shabbetai Donnolo*, (Warminster, 1976), p.109.

[19] Ferorelli, *Gli Ebrei*, p.39.

[20] Siraisi, *Medieval and Early Renaissance Medicine*, p.31.

[21] *CodCav* I, documents 42, 43, 48.

people's charters. This is illustrated by a document of 977, when Lotherius 'cleric and medic' signed as witness to a copy.[22] Such activity might lead to elevated status. The *Chronicon Salernitanum* tells us of one Peter, a cleric and able medic, who was very dear to prince Gisolf (943-78), and later became bishop of Salerno.[23] In a similar vein, the Salernitan princess Sikelgaita, wife of Robert Guiscard, may have had her own man. In a document of 1086, probably written at Bari and certainly conserved there,[24] one Peter Borda, *nostro medico*, is mentioned. Given Sikelgaita's origins and the existence of at least a tradition of medical practice in her home city, it is highly likely that he was Salernitan. However, it is apparent that Peter's function here was again not medical but rather more mundane - he was responsible for writing the document which Sikelgaita had authorised.

Peter's surname does not otherwise appear in the Barese *corpus*, but further investigation into the archive from Cava reveals a document of 1071 in which Peter *qui dicitur Borda* sold land near Vietri to a Peter Astone.[25] Unfortunately, the document appears only in paraphrase in Peter Astone's subsequent disposal of the land, but the striking thing to note is that if this is the same Peter Borda he is not identified by his medical activities in the earlier document. Nevertheless, the likelihood of it being the same man is strengthened by another Cava document of 1087, when Landolf Borda, son of Peter, guarantees a gift by Landoarius the monk son of Lambert the count of one sixth of the church of St Nicolas di Gallucanta to the abbey at Cava.[26] For we know that this church and Landoarius did have medical connections in the late eleventh century.[27]

More medics appear in later documents relating to Salerno and its territory. In 1081 Gemma, daughter of Peter, cleric and medic, borrowed money from Cava.[28] A gift made to the abbey in 1086 was for the soul of John, cleric and medic.[29] One John *lebita*, son of Peter, cleric and medic, was present at a sale in Salerno in the following year.[30] In 1092, another sale there was guaranteed by Peter, son of Philip, *medicus Chartaginensis*, that is, from Carthage.[31] In the same

---

[22] *CodCav* II, doc. 298.
[23] *ChronSal*, chapter 163.
[24] *CDB* I, doc. 30.
[25] *CodCav*, IX, doc. 115.
[26] Cava, *Arca* XIV, doc. 78.
[27] See below, chapter 7.
[28] Cava, *Arca* XIII, doc. 105.
[29] Cava, *Arca* XIV, 53.
[30] Cava, *Arca* XIV, 75.
[31] Cava, *Arca* XV, 26.

year, one Scolarius son of Peter *siculi et medici* acted as the guarantor of another sale.[32] The intriguing references to these two outsiders, one from North Africa, the other from Sicily, underline the liveliness of exchange between the Campanian city and other parts of the Mediterranean by the late eleventh century. Such exchange might be attributed to the existence of the Salernitan 'medical school' or, conversely, might have acted as a catalyst in its formation.[33]

It is clear that medics in Salerno and its environs were predominantly members of the clergy. This tendency continued in the twelfth century. In 1102, one Peter cleric, son of Peter, cleric and medic, received a guarantee about a house in which he was living.[34] Three years later, Iaquintus, cleric and medic made a gift to Cava.[35] Yet another Peter, cleric and medic, son of Urso, acted as the guarantor of a gift to Cava in 1118.[36] In 1138, John, cleric and medic, son of Peter Lombardus, was among the guarantors of a dispute settlement.[37] In 1139, more rarely, we have direct evidence for a monk and medic, Malfred, representing Cava in a gift to the abbey.[38]

Medici are to be found elsewhere in Campania as well. They are frequently recorded in the documents from Naples.[39] There is even a reference to one Anna, *medica de Balusano*, a district of Naples,[40] although she, like the other medics recorded, is unfortunately not seen in a practising context.

It is striking that one of the main functions in which *medici* or their relatives are recorded at Naples is that of witnessing charters for the city's inhabitants. Christopher son of Mauro *medicus* signed four in the first half of the tenth century,[41] and John *medicus* appears in four from the second half.[42] Their action suggests that here, as in Salerno, *medici* were respected members of the community: Tiberius *medicus*, whose heirs appear in a boundary clause of 946, had the title of prefect as well.[43] Nancy Siraisi highlights the tasks, besides medical practice, 'that could have been performed by any educated, reliable subordi-

---

[32] Cava, *Arca* XV, 49.
[33] The 'medical school' at Salerno will be discussed below in chapter 7.
[34] Cava, *Arca* XVII, 30.
[35] Cava, *Arca* XVIII, 8.
[36] Cava, *Arca* XX, 107.
[37] Cava, *Arca* XXIV, 39 and 40.
[38] Cava, *Arca* XXIV, 83.
[39] Apart from those referred to in the following text and notes, there is *RN*, doc. 14 (927): Scauracio *medicus* son of Gregory who co-owns church.
[40] *RN*, doc. 23 (923).
[41] *RN*, docs 26 (934), 34 (936), 42 (939) and 45 (941).
[42] *RN*, docs 115 (960), 190 (971), 197 (973) and 200 (973).
[43] *RN*, doc. 57.

nate', and with which late medieval physicians might be entrusted, and thereby underlines the special place of respect that these men held.[44]

In the case of Christopher, son of Mauro *medicus*, at least, we can go a step further. Certainly his witnessing activities attest to the prestige which he enjoyed (either through his own achievements or those of his father), but with whom is he associated? A closer examination of his co-witnesses and the named individuals in the four documents reveal a network of contacts which place Christopher in the very highest circles of Neapolitan society.

For example, he is twice witness to documents recording gifts to the church of St Severus in the *vicus* Radia Solis in the city. The priest, Mauro, may have been a member of Christopher's family, since his name is uncommon in Neapolitan documents. Moreover, the church itself was subject to the jurisdiction of the Basilian, that is Greek, monastery of SS Sergius and Bacchus in the city. Christopher also witnessed a document of exchange between the *igumenos* or abbot of the monastery and a member of the Isabri family in 936. This direct link with both a Greek monastery and a family who, I have argued elsewhere,[45] may have had eastern origins suggests strongly that Christopher's father had access to Greek knowledge and texts, even if his son chose to sign his name in Latin. Significantly, John *medicus* also appears as a witness to a charter of SS Sergius and Bacchus later in the century.[46] And a further, obscure piece of evidence may support the notion that SS Sergius and Bacchus was an important focal point for medical activity or knowledge in the city. In a boundary clause of a piece of the monastery's land outside Naples at S. Pietro a Paterno in 993 we find 'the *medici*' listed as proprietors.[47]

Christopher may have been elevated by his father's reflected prestige, but this also brought him into contact, as a co-witness, with one Kampulus son of John. Independent evidence suggests that Kampulus was a member of a cadet branch of the Neapolitan ducal

---

[44] Siraisi, *Medieval and Early Renaissance Medicine*, p.36: for example, the transport of the iron crown of Lombardy in 1311 entrusted by Henry VII to his physician.

[45] P. Skinner, "Urban communities in tenth-century Naples", *Papers of the British School at Rome*, LXII (1994), pp.279-299.

[46] *RN*, doc. 190: it is far less easy, however, to place him in any one social circle. His witnessing activities for a group of Gaetans in 960 and for one Gregory son of John 'Surrentini', whose name may indicate his origins, suggest that John moved in a rather different sphere. This is supported by his appearance in a document featuring the smiths of Naples, who similarly did not mix with higher social classes: Skinner, "Urban communities".

[47] *RN*, doc. 278. This does not, however, indicate any formal association of medics in the city: consortia of property-owners were by no means unusual at this date.

dynasty.[48] Thus, just as in Salerno, there is the likelihood that the rulers of Naples included medics in their court circle. Finally, the properties involved in Christopher's witnessing activities suggest that he lived in the northern part of the city, near *vicus* Radia Solis and the neighbouring *vicus* Virginum. The latter was where Kampulus' family concentrated its property.

Naples appears to have been a centre of learning and literacy from a relatively early date, and the association of medical practitioners, all laymen, with the ability to write may, even if signing their names was no guarantee of literacy, suggest that they were able to read the documents they signed. Evidence for an actual medical text, however, occurs only in an ecclesiastical setting. Among the possessions of the church of St Euthimius in the city of Naples, perhaps founded and certainly controlled by Gregory, priest and medic and monk,[49] was a 'book of the arts of medicine.'[50]

It is possible that the John *laudibilis medicus*, son of Gregory *clarissimi medici*, documented in 1037 buying some land,[51] was the son of this same Gregory of the church of St Euthimius. Whether he was or not, his existence is proof that fathers handed on their skills to their sons. In 1070, the same man is documented, this time making a gift of a small house and some land to the convent of St Gregory Armeno in Naples.[52] Intriguingly, he had bought the house from another John *medicus*, 'uncle of Gregory *medici*', and the land from a group including John and Maria Marenda, son and daughter of Gregory *laudibilis medici*. Thus there seem to have been a number of men known by the title in Naples in the eleventh century, and their common Christian names make secure identification of each individual difficult. Indeed, it might be argued that *medicus* was a surname of a family rather than an occupation, particularly given the earlier occurrence of a group of *medici* in a boundary clause.. If so, it must surely have retained its occupational significance, for it is not applied to all the individuals with links to the family.[53] The documents also reveal a clustering of these individuals around the *platea Nustriana*, closer to the centre of the city, but also explicable given that they seem to have had close links with the convent of St Gregory Armeno. Again, strikingly, we see

---

[48] Skinner, *Family Power*, pp.43-5.
[49] *RN*, doc. 162 (967).
[50] *RN*, doc. 179 (970).
[51] *RN*, doc. 461.
[52] *RN*, doc. 505.
[53] I have argued a similar line for the better-documented smiths of Naples: "Urban communities".

medics associated with an eastern foundation: St Gregory had been founded by nuns fleeing iconoclasm in Byzantium.[54]

The evidence from Naples casts doubt on the common assumption (expressed, for example, even by a recent historian of Naples[55]), that medical practice was a skill limited to ecclesiastics. But the city does appear to be exceptional. Why does medical practice here appear to have been carried out almost exclusively by laymen? One answer lies in the picture of Neapolitan society presented by the charter evidence. This was the largest city in medieval southern Italy, with a lively artisanate whose activities are well-documented. Since many were identified by their trade, it is perhaps inevitable that *medici* should show up. This does not explain the almost total lack of clerics, however. Although it is impossible to link any lay *medicus* to a medical text in Naples, the issue of literacy may have been crucial in this city. If the usual pattern of dissemination of medical knowledge through texts was that it occurred via communication between ecclesiastical houses, then the clergy might be expected to predominate as practitioners. In Naples, however, literacy and text production were quite clearly not the preserve of the church. We have definite evidence that tenth-century rulers of Naples were interested in, could read, and patronised the translation of Greek texts, brought from Constantinople, into Latin. Even if these were not medical texts, their interest demonstrates that anyone with access to the extremely stable Neapolitan court might also be able to follow literary interests of their own. The explicit reference to translation work in the city also opens up the possibility that medical texts might have entered southern Italy via this route. Only the paucity of ducal documents from the city prevents further analysis of the role laymen had to play in this process.

Evidence from elsewhere reveals a predominance of clerical practitioners. The only reference to a medic in Amalfi is to the deceased John, cleric and medic, whose widow, Theodonanda, handed over property and movables to the church of St Stephen *de Mare* in 1095. Intriguingly, she stated that her husband's previous document, which does not survive, was now annulled. The goods handed over included books, but no details are given as to their contents.[56] More overt is a document from Atrani recording the bequest of John the priest in 1007 to the monastery of St Maria there: a 'flores evangeliorum cum

---

[54] Arthur, *Naples in the Dark Ages*, ms p.117.
[55] G. Cassandro. "Il ducato bizantino", in *Storia di Napoli*, II, i (Naples, 1969/73), p.237.
[56] *PAVAR* I, doc. 26.

aliquanta antidota scripta'.[57] Thus, like the church of St Euthimius in Naples, discussed earlier, even small foundations had rudiments of written medical knowledge.

Medics were present in Apulia and Sicily too. In Apulia they once more fulfil a prominent role in validating documents as witnesses. Earliest is John, deacon, notary and *medicus*, documented in Trani in 1075.[58] Paganus *medicus* (surely there is significance in his name) signed two charters from Vico in 1145 and 1151, and Grifo *medicus* witnessed the will of Bisantius the notary in 1180.[59] In 1196, Suriana, the widow of Peter *medicus*, gave a small house in the city of Corato to the church of St Maria there.[60] More doctors can be found on the island of Sicily in the twelfth century, perhaps reflecting the status of the island as the chosen location of the Norman court. Yet again, however, their activities as landowners and respected witnesses are privileged over those as medical practitioners in the documents. Petronus Johannis *medicus* owned a mill near Messina in 1196,[61] and Bartuchus *medicus* signed a sale to the church of St Maria Latina in 1177.[62]

Female Medical Practice

The appearance of Anna, *medica de Balusano*, in the Neapolitan documents reminds us that women were active in the healing profession as well. Their visibility is, at best, patchy. If medicine was to be practised by a certain privileged group of people, then 'women were, almost by definition, the wrong sort of person, and medical texts are filled with diatribes against "the ladies" who were evidently a very real threat to learned medical practice'.[63] Such a sweeping generalisation is fairly typical of much historiography on female practitioners. In his survey of the Cairo Genizah documents, Goitein records that many occupations undertaken by women of the Jewish community there revolved around female life itself: bride-combers, midwives, wetnurses and female doctors. The latter group are frequently attested to, but were not qualified.[64]

---

[57] Beccaria, *Codici di Medicina*, p.84.

[58] *Trani*, doc. 19.

[59] *SLS*, docs 22 and 30, *CDB* V, doc. 144 respectively.

[60] *CDB* IX, doc. 75.

[61] *SMML*, doc. 9 (1196).

[62] *Garufi*, doc. 66.

[63] F. M. Getz, "Introduction", in *Health, Disease and Healing*, xv.

[64] S. D. Goitein, *A Mediterranean Society, I: Economic Foundations*, (Berkeley, 1967), pp.127-8.

The Egyptian evidence may provide a model for the functions that women were usually to be found performing, but we should not automatically limit their horizons to these roles. The predominance of male, literate medics we have encountered occur in the documents of the landed elite. Further down the social scale there may have been numerous skilled, local medical practitioners, male and female, whose activities never reached the written record. The charter evidence provides useful references to build up a rough distribution of care, but does not give the whole picture nor comment on its quality. The best example of such patchiness is the fact that despite the immense archive of documents surviving from twelfth-century Salerno, none feature the city's most famous practitioner, Trota, now proven to be the author of at least one of the texts attributed to her under the name 'Trotula' (plate 3).[65] Her case also belies the tendency on the part of historians to relegate female medical practice to the category of illiterate and unlearned.

Anecdotal evidence from other parts of Europe also seems to support the notion that female medical practitioners were associated with Salerno. Orderic Vitalis, the chronicler of the Norman monastery of St Evroul, includes in Book III of his 'family saga'[66] of the Giroie, Grandmesnil and Bellême clans the story of Ralph 'Ill-tonsured', son of Giroie. This monk of Marmoutier, who had acquired his nickname through his frivolity, was clearly well-educated, having been schooled in grammar, dialectic, astronomy and music in both Gaul and Italy. He was so learned in physic and science that when he went to Salerno he found no-one as knowledgeable as himself except *quandam sapientem matronam* [a certain wise matron].[67] Whilst we must be aware that Orderic is here relating events from before he was born, nevertheless it is significant that Salerno features so prominently as *the* place to test out one's knowledge. As for the wise matron, she may belong to a tradition of learned medicine exemplified by Trota's work, or may have had more practical skills. Ralph's intellectual background and comparison with her would suggest the former choice. There is no definitive evidence, apart from Orderic's report, that Ralph even visited Salerno: the city may function already by the twelfth century, the date of Orderic's work, as a rhetorical benchmark for an author

---

[65] Monica Green is presently editing this text for publication: its history and background are described in M. Green, "Estraendo Trota dal *Trotula*: ricerche su testi medievali di medicina Salernitana", *Rassegna Storica Salernitana*, n.s. XII (1995), pp.31-53.

[66] *Ecclesiastical History of Orderic Vitalis*, ed. M. Chibnall, II (Oxford, 1968), xxix.

[67] *Ecclesiastical History of Orderic Vitalis*, II, 29, 75-77.

wishing to convey the extent of the subject's medical skills. But Ralph's family's history of southern Italian enterprises makes the story likely. Orderic clearly derives some satisfaction that this Norman monk's learning was already far ahead of that of the Salernitans.

It has frequently been argued that female medical practitioners are very much under-represented in the medieval source material. Their practical skills, it is suggested, meant that they did not or could not participate in literate medicine and so they remain invisible.[68] But the southern Italian evidence is I think full enough to question these assumptions. We have a variety of sources at our disposal, and yet only two confirmed female practitioners, Anna and Trota. It might be argued that this is because women's skills did not qualify them to be called *medicae*, but the example of Anna, in Naples, seems to refute that line.

Another argument in favour of an invisible army of female medical practitioners might be that women did not, for the most part, gain access to literacy skills, and so their contribution to medical practice would be through oral transmission and practical remedies which do not show up in written records. Is Trota therefore an exception? If we look again at the function in which many male *medici* are recorded, it is as witnesses, adding their prestige to a document. Women, although in a tiny minority, do appear as witnesses to charters in southern Italy, and I have argued elsewhere that the level of lay literacy among women may have been quite high in this area;[69] it might be expected, therefore, that if a local woman gained respect for her medical skills, she might be called upon to act as a signatory. Yet we have no examples of this happening.

Finally, it could be argued that the regulation of later medieval medical practice excluded women, explaining their invisibility from official documents. But the kingdom of Naples was one of the few areas where regulation allowed women to practise.

---

[68] A view most recently expressed by V. Nutton: 'The number of known female practitioners is small.... and may be distorted by biases inherent in the sources': "Medicine in medieval western Europe", in L. Conrad, M. Neve, V. Nutton, R. Porter and A. Wear, *The Western Medical Tradition, 800B.C. to A.D.1800* (Cambridge, 1995), p.170. Cf. N. Siraisi, *Medieval and Early Renaissance Medicine*, p.27: 'It is probable that many more women may have engaged in midwifery and healing arts without leaving any trace of their activities in written records.'

[69] P. Skinner, "Women, literacy and invisibility in medieval southern Italy", in *Women, the Book and the Worldly*, ed. J. Taylor and L. Smith (Woodbridge, 1995), pp.1-11. At the time of writing this paper, I had not found evidence of female witnesses; my subsequent discovery of several examples fortunately supports my general argument.

It must be concluded, therefore, that, even taking into account the dangers of arguing from silence, early medieval southern Italy probably did not have very many female medical practitioners. This is not to say that women did not have medical skills: a mother's traditional role in caring for her family must have included some knowledge of common remedies. But the number of women who made their living from such skills was probably extremely small. In an area such as Naples, where artisanal and professional skills show up very clearly in people's nomenclature, we find only one *medica*. It is extremely dangerous, in my view, to blame the pattern of evidence for hiding large numbers of women practising, when in fact medical skills are highlighted as worthy of record. If medieval evidence is guilty of distorting the historical record in favour of men's concerns, as is often suggested in histories of medieval women, then to try to restore the balance by arguing for a hidden presence may produce equally distorted history.

Charter material can only provide a part of the story. The documents tell us where some, but not all, medics were to be found and sometimes a little about their social status. The importance of medics in their local communities is underlined by their special status as witnesses,[70] although their role in the social hierarchy is not fixed by their position in the lists of witnesses we have. That is, a *medicus* was as likely to sign last as first, and no strong order of rank appears to be expressed in the southern Italian witness lists. The documents tell us nothing about what those medics did to earn their title. There are, however, numerous attestations of medical practice in another type of source material—that describing supernatural cures.

Saints

Overt references to cures occur far more frequently when they are performed by saints rather than the secular medics. Recourse to secular healing had carried no religious stigma in the ancient world, but the arrival of Christianity seems to have changed attitudes to medical knowledge, as Nancy Siraisi points out.[71] Recent research has demonstrated a more lenient attitude on the part of the Church Fathers towards the role of medical practitioners: they might be consulted so

---

[70] This phenomenon is not limited to southern Italy: one Teuzo *medicus* appears signing in a relatively competent hand in two documents from the archive of the monastery of SS Cosmas and Damian (the healing saints *par excellence*) in Rome in the early eleventh century: A. Petrucci and C. Romeo, *"Scriptores in Urbibus": Alfabetismo e Cultura Scritta nell'Italia Altomedievale* (Bologna, 1992), p.130.

[71] *Medieval and Early Renaissance Medicine*, p.7

long as the patient did not place absolute faith entirely in their skills.[72] Just as some narrative sources associated sickness with sin, as we saw in the previous chapter, so physical healing might be associated with spiritual health, and this union is reflected in later evidence from southern Italy.

This raises the difficult issue of Christian belief and hagiography as a source for sickness and cures. The faith of the medieval population in miraculous healing, and the ascribing of illness to divine will, was a mechanism for coping with disease when medical practitioners seemed unable to perform effective cures. Valerie Flint argues that in order to render the powers of the saint credible, the account of the doctors' failure had to be technically accurate, and that therefore hagiography can be informative about contemporary medical practice.[73] This assertion must be treated with caution: the average consumer of didactic *Vitae* probably did not have such an in-depth knowledge to appreciate such subtleties and, moreover, most hagiography is not as detailed in its description of treatment as Flint's Frankish material. It is also clear that much of the average saint's life as written down derived from set models of the genre. As Patrick Geary acutely puts it: 'We should not pretend that Jacques Derrida has revealed something radically new to us: that hagiography reproduces hagiography rather than some putative reality. Hippolyte Delahaye pointed this out in 1905 ... although because he wrote in plain, comprehensible language his message was perhaps not as clear as that of Derrida.'[74]

Nevertheless, we must not dismiss out of hand the records of miraculous cures in hagiography: they may or may not tell us about the physical condition of the afflicted person, but they are invaluable testimony to the mentalities surrounding illness.[75]

Given the generic purpose of medieval hagiography, to inspire belief and awe in the presence of divine works, it is perhaps no surprise to find the common *topos* of a failure by a secular practitioner preceding a miraculous cure by a saint. 'The criticisms of medical practitioners ... sprang less from dissatisfaction with medicine's limited effectiveness than from religious tradition, with its powerful themes linking healing with religious charity and miraculous interven-

[72] Amundsen, "Medicine", p.341.
[73] "Early medieval *medicus*", p. 136.
[74] P. Geary, "Saints, scholars and society", in his *Living with the Dead in the Middle Ages*, p.17.
[75] See the article by Susan Ashbrook Harvey, outlining ways of using Byzantine hagiography to gain information about illness, "Physicians and ascetics in John of Ephesus: an expedient alliance", in *Symposium on Byzantine Medicine*, ed. J. Scarborough, (*Dumbarton Oaks Papers* XXXVIII, 1984), pp.87-91.

tion, and its assertion of the priority of the healing of the soul over the healing of the body.'[76] For example, in a later medieval context, some 10% of the 3000 recorded miracles at seven English and two French shrines had been preceded by a visit to an unsuccessful medical practitioner.[77] Commissioners enquiring into the sanctity and healing miracles of Chiara of Montefalco (d.1308) actually sought evidence of a prior visit to a medical practitioner.[78] This merely demonstrates the tension that might be felt between clerics and medical practitioners in an age when neither were able to overcome entirely the afflictions of their communities.

Do southern Italian saints' lives exhibit similar patterns? One of the most detailed to survive is that of St Nilus of Rossano (910-1004). Nilus takes on the attributes of a healing saint relatively late in his *Vita*, which focuses more on his own spiritual development but he was, predictably, reluctant to acknowledge his gift or to win fame by it. Thus, having freed a possessed young boy,[79] this aspect of his life is not heavily stressed.

The tension between clerics and medics is, however, far more explicitly featured. Whilst Nilus is in Rossano, a Jewish doctor, Domnolus, offers to prescribe a drug to alleviate the saint's recurrent illness and keep him from falling sick throughout his life. The saint indignantly refuses this offer, saying that God is his doctor, that he has no need of the doctor's drugs, and that furthermore he is not going to boost Domnolus' business by allowing the doctor to boast that he has treated the holy man![80] Of course, this tale is edifying both in its promotion of faith in God, but has added impact in that the person at fault is also Jewish. Domnolus is mentioned later as the medic who had failed to cure the imperial judge Eufrasius. For our purposes, it provides another piece of anecdotal evidence to support the impression that many of southern Italy's medical practitioners in the tenth century were Jewish.[81] To an audience of the *Vita*, at least, this must have been a reasonable association.

---

[76] Siraisi, *Medieval and Early Renaissance Medicine*, p.43.
[77] Siraisi, *Medieval and Early Renaissance Medicine*, p.22.
[78] Siraisi, *Medieval and Early Renaissance Medicine*, p.40.
[79] *Vita di San Nilo*, VIII, 58.
[80] *Vita di San Nilo*, VII, 50.
[81] Sharf, *Universe*, pp.115-6, equates this Domnulus with Shabbetai Donnolo of Oria. It is hard, beyond the double occurrence of the name, to find any evidence for this assertion. Nilus' *Vita* states that he had known Domnulus of Rossano for a long time, making it unlikely, as Sharf suggests, that Shabbetai somehow fled here from the persecution of Jews at Otranto. An alternative reading of this episode may be that Shabbetai's fame had reached Calabria, and that Nilus' biographer included the medic to emphasise Nilus' authority.

Alexander Kazhdan focuses on the southern Italian hagiography to support his assertion that hostility towards physicians in Byzantine hagiography reached a peak towards the end of the tenth century, before softening to the more common accommodation of them, discussed already in the case of patristic texts, in the eleventh and twelfth centuries. As well as the episode between Domnulus and Nilus, he cites the description in the *Vita* of St Elias Speleotis of 'an ignorant and inexperienced *iatros*' to support his case.[82] However, given that Kazhdan offers no explanation as to why such sharpness should be specific to the tenth century, I think we can read both texts in a slightly different way. Nilus' hostility may not be to Domnulus as doctor, but to Domnulus as fee-charger, as the text to some extent makes clear. An almost contemporary source from northern Italy reflects this view: Ratherius of Verona thought that doctors should help the poor free of charge.[83] Even though this is a Christian, didactic text, the hostility shown by Nilus is unlikely to have derived from the fact that Domnulus was Jewish: Jews suffered some discrimination in this region, but there is little evidence of overt anti-Semitism.[84] In the case of St Elias, the criticism seems to be more of an individual letting down an otherwise respected tradition of medical practitioners, rather than condemning *iatroi* as a group. And we must remember that the victim of the ignorant doctor was the saint himself, whose crushed fingers, the result of a childhood fall, were placed in a wooden box and then tied so tightly that they fell off. Whether the doctor intended this to happen is unclear, but the result of his care was that the boy decided to retreat from the world.[85]

Why was the church so keen to stress the message that God, via the saints, was the most effective healer? And was its message convincing? The answer to the first question appears to lie in Valerie Flint's concept of a choice of healers: in fact, her model for early medieval Francia may be even more applicable to the rich evidence from southern Italy. For here, as we have seen, there were lay medics in Naples, clerical ones elsewhere, Jewish scholars and practitioners and, if the passage in St Nilus' life is derived from observation,[86]

---

[82] A. Kazhdan, "The image of the medical doctor in Byzantine literature of the tenth to twelfth centuries", in *Symposium on Byzantine Medicine*, p. 48.

[83] Goglin, *Misérables*, p. 42.

[84] This attitude of tolerance, broken only by a shortlived persecution in Apulia under the Byzantine emperor Romanus, appears to have diminished later on. Jews were expelled from Benevento in 1063: Moore, *Formation*, p.32.

[85] See above, chapter 4, for further discussion of this issue of illness and withdrawal.

[86] See above, p. 62.

medical practice within the largely invisible Moslem community of
Sicily as well. In addition, as I have suggested, there were probably
many more practitioners who do not make it into the written record.
With so many people offering cures, ecclesiastics had to strengthen
their contention that only God was a true healer. Kazhdan used the
lives of tenth-century southern Italian saints to stress the particular
hostility of the church to secular healers in that period. But the hostility might also be read as a response to a uniquely skilled body of local
medical practitioners, that is, the sharpness noted by Kazhdan might
be regional, not temporal.[87]

Another tenth-century saint's life, however, presents problem in
simply ascribing the sharpness to local conditions. The *Vita* of St
Fantinus, only recently edited as a single text, appears to have been
written soon after Fantinus' death in Thessaloniki in c.975. The pecu-
liarity of his life lies in the fact that there are two manuscript traditions, one eastern and relating to a certain Fantinus *senior*, the other a
western saint of the same name. A recently-discovered, tenth- or eleventh-century manuscript in Moscow, however, links these two traditions closely into one life; that is, it appears that at the age of sixty
Fantinus, a native of Calabria, travelled to Greece and died there
some fifteen years later.[88]

The value of this text lies in the fact that it presents two different
periods in the saint's life in two different areas, for all that it is written
from a Greek perspective. The difference in describing episodes of
illness and cures between the western and eastern sojourns is marked.
Whilst the saint is still in Calabria, sickness and/or miraculous cures
do not feature heavily in his biographer's priorities. Thus we are told
that Fantinus released a madman from demons, and that everyone
who came to him was treated either with words, medicines (*farmaka*)
or deeds.[89] The majority of his miracles in Calabria, however, feature
natural events, as the editor of the life points out, including dissuading
a bear from eating his monastery's honey-bees and providing water
for some monks searching for stray mules.

When Fantinus moves East, however, his *Vita* takes on a strong
theme of the failure of doctors, and the saint is inundated with people
seeking cures. 'What type of free hospital was now at their [the peo-

---

[87] It is worth noting that this sharpness is expressed in another region with large
numbers of skilled medics. Taking into account his obvious antagonism against his
hosts, Liutprand of Cremona ascribes his survival of illness in Constantinople to a
vision of the Virgin Mary: *Embassy to Constantinople*, chapter 24.

[88] *Vita di San Fantino il Giovane*, ed. E. Follieri (Brussels, 1993); the manuscript
tradition is discussed in pp.4-10.

[89] *Vita di San Fantino*, chapters 22-23.

ple's] disposal, both before and after his [the saint's] death?' asks the
biographer rhetorically. And, sure enough, Fantinus dispenses cures
to all who present themselves, despite their having been first to doctors. For example, a man with a head and ear complaint is cured by
massage, and his elderly mother, 'having returned from consulting
the doctors (*iatroi*) without result', rejoices at her son's recovery.[90]
Another man suffering from head problems and toothache, 'having
placed all hope in the medics', which only resulted in the pain wors-
ening, is nevertheless cured by the saint with a blow to the head.[91]
Other miraculous cures are also described in detail.

What are we to make of this sudden quickening of saintly activity
with regard to cures? The first, and most obvious solution, is that we
are here reading two conflated lives, albeit rendered into a whole as
early as this *Vita* and surviving in an almost contemporary manuscript. But the editor's arguments for one complete life are strengthened by the appearance of other, documented, tenth-century figures
in both halves of the *Vita*: St Nilus makes an appearance in the
Calabrian half, St Athanasius the Athonite in the Greek.

The answer may simply lie in the origins of the author, who appears to have been a monk with Fantinus in Thessaloniki. His knowledge of southern Italy is sketchy, although this is the only eastern life
featuring a pilgrimage to the shrine of the Archangel Michael at
Monte Gargano. The author is also writing, as most biographers did,
to establish the cult of Fantinus at his final resting place, that is,
Thessaloniki. Thus there was little need, even if the reports had
reached him, to record in detail the saint's southern Italian miracles.
What was required was ample evidence of his curative powers in the
local community. Thus detailed accounts of the saint curing those in
Byzantium whom the doctors had failed, and a catalogue of local, *post
mortem*, miracles performed at his tomb and in patients' homes, form
the latter part of the incomplete *Vita*. The *topoi* used, however, fitted
neatly into the Byzantine tradition of hagiographic texts. Doctors
would be available in a large city like Thessaloniki, thus their efforts
had to be discredited.

The life of St Fantinus does not, however, compromise my assertion that the particular sharpness of tone against doctors was a purely
regional phenomenon. Indeed, it supports my contention. For if, as
Kazhdan argues, the tenth century was the century *par excellence* for
Byzantine hagiography to heap disparagements on doctors, then

---

[90] *Vita di San Fantino*, chapter 38.
[91] *Vita di San Fantino*, chapter 44: it is tempting to speculate that the blow removed
the offending tooth.

Fantinus' tenth-century life lets them off very lightly indeed. Other contemporary southern Italian hagiography appears to use the failure of doctors as a stock literary device: the study of da Costa-Louillet on the saints of the region underlines the repeated use of the theme.[92]

Returning, then, to southern Italy, was the church's message successful? Charter evidence from the South, whilst not, as I have stressed, mentioning any guilt associated with the sick person's ailment, nevertheless illustrates the faith of ordinary people in the power of divine healing. For example, a gift to the monastery of SS Sergius and Bacchus from John son of Theodore was made in return for the healing that he had received.[93] Risus, son of Maraldus of Terlizzi, promised in 1182 that if he recovered from his present (unspecified) illness, he would give all his property to and enter the church of St Angelus.[94]

More informative still is the case of Constantine son of Leo, of Fondi in Lazio. In 1039 he records that whilst at the house of his father-in-law at Terracina he fell ill and could neither drink nor speak. A miracle of the cross in the local church allowed him to make a will. Then John, the bishop of Terracina, came with holy water for Constantine to drink. The 'wound' in his throat broke and he vomited *fracidume* and spoke, vowing to make an offering to the church in thanks for his cure. After a period at home convalescing he returned to Terracina and made the gift, the occasion for the record to be made.[95]

Whilst we may not believe the miracle that occurred to cure Constantine, some comments on his document are possible. The notable absentee in the entire proceedings is any kind of medical care, despite the fact that the illness sounds extremely serious. Perhaps we should not expect to see such care, since the document is about Constantine's gratitude to his healer. He perhaps had already consulted doctors in vain before the events he describes.

The key issue to note about all three documents is, of course, the fact that despite the church's condemnation of medics who took fees, it was still perfectly willing to accept significant offerings of property

---

[92] The theme of failure by doctors who had been well-paid for their services also appears in the lives of St Leo of Catania, St Elias Speleotis and St Vitalis of Sicily: G. da Costa-Louillet, "Saints de Sicile et de l'Italie méridionale aux VIII, IX et X siècles", *Byzantion*, XXIX-XXX (1959/60), pp.89-173, at pp.94, 120 and 128 respectively.

[93] *RN*, doc. 155.

[94] *CDB* III, doc. 134.

[95] *CDC* I, doc. 172. Compare this episode with that of St Nilus, recounted in chapter 4, where the saint, too, had a wound in his throat.

from people who believed their cure had or would come from the local saint.[96] Of course, our picture is derived from the pattern of charter preservation: the documents were kept by the institution which had benefited from the gift. Nevertheless, the evidence we have suggests that supernatural cures remained a viable alternative to what was, in this region, an exceptional network of medical practitioners.

Places of Care

One aspect of illness that is important in this context is the fact that those afflicted might withdraw from secular life and seek repose or care in a religious house. Liutprand of Cremona's father, returning from a diplomatic mission in Byzantium, was taken ill and did just this. Within two weeks of taking the habit, he had died.[97]

Southern Italian archives contain many instances of entry into a religious house, accompanied in most cases by the donation of the author's entire fortune and the stipulation that they are henceforth to be supported by the monastery or convent. Again, this must have significantly increased the wealth of the institutions in which the sick person was housed. The earliest case concerns prince Guaiferius of Salerno (*fl.*861-880). Having become a monk, he was struck by a grave illness, and asked to be transported to the monastery of St Benedict to finish his life.[98]

Only a few donation charters, however, can be connected directly to illness. The sons of Angerius testified in 1099 that their father, when he was ill and had entered the monastery at Cava, had left certain property to the house.[99] Similarly, Alfanus son of Ademarius the count had been ill in the monastery of St Archangel in the Cilento, a house under Cava's control. His will in favour of Cava was noted in 1120.[100] In a document of 1115, the illness of John, son of Constantine Siculi, is directly cited as the reason for his retirement to Cava and will in favour of the monastery and his family.[101] A document from Molfetta, dated 1173, records the retirement of the author's father, Laurence, to Cava, and the will he made there. The author, Garzianon, was disputing the testament, protesting at losing

---

[96] The same pattern is seen in gifts in the hope of, or thanks for, a safely-delivered pregnancy: see above, chapter 3.

[97] *Antapodosis*, III, 24.

[98] *ChronSal*, chapter 128.

[99] Cava, *Arca* XVI, 99.

[100] Cava, *Arca* XVIII, 92.

[101] Cava, *Arca* XX, 31.

an entire piece of land which the monastery had received, and succeeded in recovering half.[102]

Elsewhere, in 1124, Grimoald the priest of Conversano retired to the monastery of St Benedict there, giving it all his property, when he was in danger of death.[103] In 1180, John the notary of Mondragone recorded the arrangements he had made when ill. Initially he had made his will, and left property to the monastery of St Maria there. Then, 'continuing to be ill', he became a monk in the same monastery. This seems clear evidence that he expected to die there. The 1180 document recorded a division of property with the heir of John's late wife.[104] Ten years later, Godelferius, count of Monopoli, recorded his retirement to the monastery of St Pantaleo there, citing as the reason his infirmity.[105] Given the quite high number of gifts to ecclesiastical institutions during illness, it is reasonable to suppose that the donors looked as much for care as for spiritual inspiration.

Such retirements appear to encapsulate the mentality of the southern Italian population with regard to illness. Apart from Naples, we have seen that much of the medical care available on the peninsula was provided by clerics. Thus a donation accompanying retirement might assure the health of the donor's soul, might also have been made in the hope of a cure, but most of all brought the donor into a place where medical care, too, was on offer.

It is noticeable that most of the references to retirements occur relatively late in the documentation. This suggests that ecclesiastical foundations, both male and female, perhaps in response to the demands placed on them, only began to allocate some of their buildings to hospitals or infirmaries for both inmates and outsiders in the eleventh century or even later. Yet we know that some kind of ecclesiastical care had been available some centuries previously. John of Ephesus names two types of institutions for the care of the sick in Byzantium. Hospitals were purely church institutions where the clergy tended the ill; diaconates were serviced by lay *philoponoi*. Some diaconates were especially set aside as women's hospitals.[106] We know that diaconates also existed in Naples from an early date.[107] Gaeta,

---

[102] *CDB* VII, doc. 51.

[103] *PC*, doc. 76

[104] "Elenco delle pergamene già appartenenti alla famiglia Fusco ed ora acquistate dalla Società Napoletana di Storia Patria", *ASPN* (1883), pp. 775-787 at 783 (doc. 45).

[105] *PC*, doc. 141.

[106] H. J. Magoulias, "The lives of the saints as sources of data for the history of Byzantine medicine in the sixth and seventh centuries", *Byzantinische Zeitschrift*, LVII (1964), pp.127-150, at 135.

[107] See above, p. 34.

too, had a diaconate early in its history,[108] but the upheavals caused
by Arabic attacks and political change in the late ninth century appear to have disrupted its activities, as it does not reappear after-
wards.

The testimony of Luke, abbot of the monastery of St Anastasius at
Carbone in Lucania, illuminates the circumstances under which a
place of care might be set up. Stating in 1059 that he was about to go
on pilgrimage to Jerusalem, he handed over control of the abbey and
its houses to his successor, Blasius. They included the oratory of SS
Luke and Blasius, which he had built for the sick. Although he gives
us no further details of the running of the oratory, the cause of its
construction may be hinted at, for Luke says that he had also 'suffered the pest', that is, the plague.[109] It is entirely possible that this
episode of plague does not show up in the chronicle evidence, but it
is worth noting that Luke also complains that he had suffered robbery
as well. Might his woes have been caused by the twin disasters of
plague and Saracen invasion which had occurred in Calabria in
1005-7, as noted by Corradi? This would mean that Luke had
reached an advanced age by the date of his document, but a pilgrimage to Jerusalem at the end of a long career makes sense.

Unfortunately, we have no other documents as explicit as Luke's,
and must rely instead on fleeting references to hospitals. Another
institution which provided an infirmary was the convent of St
Gregory Armeno in Naples: the infirmary is frequently referred to in
the twelfth-century documents from that house's archive.[110]
Frustratingly, it is the infirmary's property that is recorded rather
than its work. The fact that such property was designated separately,
however, suggests that the abbess of St Gregory in this period,
Gemma, was concerned that its work should be suitably supported.
In a similar vein, the less well-documented infirmary of the convent
of St George in Salerno was also well-endowed with property, benefiting, as did St Gregory's, from pious gifts.[111]

We know virtually nothing of the running of such infirmaries, but
may perhaps draw parallels from the Byzantine world. Catia
Galatariotou's study of the *typika* or foundation charters of a number
of Byzantine convents reveals that the convent doctor, where men-

---

[108] One Eustratius, *pater diaconiae*, appears as a witness to a charter of the bishop of
Formia in c.830: *CDC* I, doc.2.

[109] *Carbone*, doc. 7.

[110] Naples, Archivio di Stato, Sezione Politico-Diplomatica, *Monasteri Soppressi* 3437,
documents 391 (1142), 319 (1153), 321 (1162/1171), 139 (1180), 322 (1183), 300
(1167/1183), 554 (1186).

[111] See, for example, a gift by Leo the deacon in 1038, *SG*, doc. 1.

tioned at all, was almost always male.[112] This piece of information underlines Byzantine preconceptions about the people skilled enough to provide medical care, that is, that they would be male rather than female. It seems not to credit the female monastics with any ability to help the sick, either from within or outside the convent.

Those who did not wish to embrace the monastic life could patronise it instead, and the care of the needy and sick became a favourite target. To patronise hospitals was seen as a pious duty, and even empress Constance did so in Palermo in 1196.[113] Such donations are extremely useful, of course, for their records provide evidence of the existence of the institutions themselves. A series of documents reveals that the church of St Nicolas at Bari had a hospital by the early twelfth century.[114] A charter of 1134 informs us that it had its own prior, Urso, who in that year joined the abbot of the main church in a dispute over three men.[115] The hospital won, and was successful again in a dispute in 1164, held at Trani.[116]

Inland, the church of St Lucia at Terlizzi seems to have had a hospital by 1160: in that year its property is recorded in a sale.[117] Up the coast, the church of St Jacob at Molfetta had begun building a hospital in the 1170s: in 1173 it received a donation of all the market dues of the market of Molfetta, to aid the building work, from count Robert of Loritello and Conversano.[118] In 1180, revealingly, Robert referred to 'his' hospital of St Jacob as the setting for a document recording a confirmation of the abbey of Cava's property in Molfetta.[119] By 1187 another hospital, that of St John in Barletta, is also recorded.[120] Another Apulian hospital was that of St Thomas at Barletta. No records survive of its activities, but in 1197 it was given by emperor Henry VI to the Teutonic hospital in Jerusalem.[121]

The other major Hospitaller order, that of St John, had received another church, that of St Stephen outside the gate of Melfi, from

---

[112] C. Galatariotou, "Byzantine women's monastic communities: the evidence of the *typika*", Jahrbuch der Österreichischen Byzantinistik, XXXVIII (1988), p. 287. It is unclear how many of the convents studied, if any, had infirmaries.

[113] *NSK*, doc. 44.

[114] It received a number of gifts: records exist from 1101 (*CDB* V, doc. 34), 1135 (*CDB* V, doc. 85) and 1137 (*CDB* V, doc. 90). The hospital also bought properties, as in 1155 (*CDB* V, doc. 110), and owned lands just outside the city (*CDB* V, doc. 86, 1135).

[115] *CDB* V, doc. 81.

[116] *CDB* V, doc. 121.

[117] *CDB* III, doc. 85.

[118] *CDB* VIII, doc. 119.

[119] *CDB* VII, doc. 62.

[120] *CDB* VIII, doc. 152.

[121] *CDB* X, doc. 37.

that city's bishop in 1149. The knights were instructed to care for the poor there.[122] The location of the building suggests that Stephen's choice was carefully made. Being extramural, its inmates were kept away from the city, if only symbolically. In addition, the foundation lay next to the bath. The document does not say whether this was still functioning, but if it was it would have been a valuable aid to the care of the sick.

The existence of so many hospitals in a relatively confined corner of Italy is perhaps not surprising, given that southern Italy provided an embarkation point for travellers to the crusader states of the East. The direct connection with the two orders of Hospitallers in the mid- to late-twelfth century is probably only the tip of their activities in the Apulian towns.[123]

What did the foundation of a hospital entail in this period? We have no information about the organisation of places of care. Abbot Luke of Carbone's eleventh-century testimony would suggest that his oratory for the sick was a separate building among several at the Carbone monastery, but no other document makes any reference to a hospital's location in relation to other monastic buildings. Certainly the management of its property appears to have been handled separately, but this simply implies that there was a member of the community, such as the prior at St Nicolas in Bari, with specific responsibility for the running of the hospital's functions. We do not even know whether the places designated as infirmaries and hospitals admitted outsiders, although there is an interesting gender distinction between the terms, with infirmaries appearing in the records of female houses and hospitals, with their implied welcome of strangers, in those of male houses.

A striking feature of the evidence recording lay entry into monastic houses during a time of sickness is that all of the individuals doing so are male. Did convents admit lay people to their infirmaries? It is probable that, as in other parts of Europe, women might retire to a convent at certain times in their lives, for example when widowed. But we have no evidence that such retirements were to benefit from the care provided by the infirmaries of those houses, which may have

---

[122] A. Mercati, 'Le pergamene di Melfi all'Archivio Secreto Vaticano', *Miscellanea Giovanni Mercati* V (Vatican City, 1946), 263-323, document 3 at 276.

[123] The Hospitallers and Teutons were the leading orders in caring for the sick: A. Forey, *The Military Orders from the Twelfth to the Early Fourteenth Centuries* (London, 1992), p.126. See also T. S. Miller, "The Knights of St John and the hospitals of the Latin West", *Speculum*, LIII (1978), pp.709-733 at 719: 'king Roger had specified in 1137 that the Knights treated the infirm in the houses of his kingdom.'

performed a rather different function from that of their male counterparts.

Hospitals attached to monasteries are difficult to assign a purely medical function to, for they fulfilled a number of functions in helping the poor, sick and needy. When Urso, the archbishop of Agrigento in Sicily, gave a church in Caltanissetta to a certain brother Gregory in 1199, the building was to be used simply as a 'hospital for poor pilgrims'.[124] However, it would seem that the monastery of Cava's hospital really did treat the sick, for it is referred to in a document of 1129 as a *nosocomium* rather than the more common *hospitalium*. Whilst the latter word has a much wider sense of hospitality and lodging, the former is a Latin version of the Greek term *nosokomion*, whose etymology is much more tightly related to disease (*nosos*). In the West, the term *hospital* and it Greek equivalent, *xenodochium*, were used interchangeably. The word *nosocomium*, on the other hand, emerged in the East to denote places dedicated to the sick.[125] The fact that the term occurs in a Lombard part of southern Italy, where Latin was the usual language of documents, suggests that a specialised function was being recognised at Cava. The location of the monastery, in the mountains above Salerno, may also have contributed to its perception as a medical centre. Again, the document records a gift made specifically to the hospital, suggesting that care was assigned special resources.[126] This was true of another foundation, whose function of healing is explicitly stated. In 1194 Benedict, the bishop of Cefalu in Sicily, assigned the offerings made to the major chapel of the cathedral to the infirmary there. They would be used to buy food and *medele* for the sick inmates.[127]

Our survey of the recorded places of care in medieval southern Italy has revealed that they appear in the documentation rather later than many medical practitioners. The exception to this statement is the provision of *diaconiae* in early medieval Naples, but these cannot be proven to have had any medical function beyond the nourishment of the hungry. The rise of institutional healthcare in the later eleventh century suggests that the church was acutely aware of the economic benefits to be gained from offering shelter and care to members of the local community. Those whose charters survive were landed and wealthy, not the poor sick who might be expected to receive charity

---

[124] *Le Più Antiche Carte dell'Archivio Capitolare di Agrigento (1092-1282)*, ed. P. Collura (Palermo, 1961), doc. 42.
[125] Miller, "Knights", p. 714.
[126] Cava, *Arca* XXII, 92.
[127] *Garufi*, doc. 109.

from these institutions. The care available in a monastic house might conceivably be based on the knowledge gleaned from medical texts, whose preservation will be discussed in a later chapter, or on practical solutions. Given that many of the lay inmates who took the habit late in life appear to have expected imminent death, the function of monastic carers was perhaps only to provide a restful environment. Another important point to note from the evidence is the apparent gender divide in the function of monastic places of care. The male hospitals may have welcomed laypeople far more freely than convent infirmaries, whose responsibility may have extended only to the care of sick nuns.

The rise of ecclesiastical institutions may signal the final triumph of the church over the management of medical practice. Even though lay medics continue to be documented in the twelfth century, they never appear to have visited and worked in the hospitals of southern Italy. We therefore have at least two separate traditions of medical practice in the peninsula, but because the survival of documentation is largely dictated by its preservation in ecclesiastical archives, the provisions of the church loom rather larger than the efforts of individuals whose skills may have been considerable.

Medicines

This raises the question of the use of drugs as cures, and here an interesting gender specificity arises. Whenever a drug or potion was needed, it seems to have been women who were perceived as having the skill necessary to produce it. This derives in part from another context, in which women are portrayed in medieval texts as gaining the advantage over their enemies not through military strength, but via the more subtle means of drugs and poisons. This perhaps is a product of the common medieval motif of women as deceitful and underhand in their dealings, but does provide some evidence of the types of concoction that they were believed to be capable of producing. King Arnulf of Italy, it was reported by Liutprand, was rendered 'devoid of understanding' by a draught prepared by the wife of an enemy.[128]

The Lombard law codes provide evidence about poisoning as well, but without the definite role for women. Rothari makes a distinction between the man or woman that mixes the draught and those that

---

[128] *Antapodosis*, I, 32.

administer it, adding a further refinement of the penalty depending on whether the intended victim dies or not.[129] At least one instance of poisoning is recorded in the *Chronicon Salernitanum*, but the person preparing the draught is not identified.[130]

That the care that a sick person received might be directly related to the wealth he or she had has been highlighted in discussions of the care available in monastic houses and in the availability of nourishing foodstuffs. Copho, a physician at Salerno in the twelfth century, extends this privilege into the realms of the medicines they might receive. He explicitly advised his colleagues to make up rich people's mixtures from expensive spices, and those of other people from ordinary herbs.[131]

The types of ingredient needed might have derived their elevated value from the fact that they needed to be imported. Southern Italy was, in fact perfectly positioned to benefit from the lively trade in spices and other luxury goods from the East. A valuable source of information for trade is the *Honorantie Civitatis Papie*, an eleventh-century compilation of tenth-century dues to be paid by merchants entering the city of Pavia. The Venetians, we learn, paid to the treasurer of Pavia one pound of pepper, one of cinnamon, one of *galanga* and one of ginger. In the next chapter, the men of Salerno, Gaeta and Amalfi are recorded as giving the same spices.[132] The source of these goods can only be guessed at, although a ninth-century Arabic source, the *Book of the Routes and the Kingdoms*, explicitly credits the multilingual Jews with bringing musk, aloe wood, camphor and cinnamon back from China to the West.[133] There is relatively little evidence of this trade in the southern Italian charters. However, one document from Gaeta records an undertaking made in 1012 by one Ramfus son of Christopher to provide luxury goods including pepper to Ubertus of Rome.[134]

It is not the purpose of this study to try to correlate the ingredients available to southern Italians with the recipes prescribed in the sur-

---

[129] Rothari 139-142, in *Lombard Laws*.

[130] *ChronSal*, chapter 105.

[131] Henisch, *Fast and Feast*, p.103: whether the more expensive spices were any more effective, however, is open to question.

[132] *Honorantie Civitatis Papie*, ed. C.-R. Brühl and C. Violante (Köln-Wien, 1983), chapters 4 and 5.

[133] R. Lopez and I. Raymond, *Medieval Trade in the Mediterranean World* (Oxford, 1955), p.31.

[134] *CDC* I, doc. 123/4.

viving medical texts.[135] Nevertheless, the collection of such recipes
formed a large proportion of text production in the region. Because
southern Italy had such a diverse population and lively commercial
cities, certain people here may have enjoyed far greater access to rare
remedies than in other parts of Europe. The role of the Jews in the
transmission of ingredients has been suggested, and it is striking that
a Jew compiled one of the most comprehensive herbals to survive.
Intriguingly, it is from the Arab community of the South that the only
recorded specialist in remedies originates. Ali b. Abulkasem b.
Abdallah the druggist occurs in a document from Sicily in 1137,[136]
but little can be said about his practice. Given the transmission of
much medical knowledge from the ancient world via the Arab countries, it is perhaps to be expected that Sicily would be something of a
centre of that knowledge. A letter from the Cairo Geniza, dated
1153, from Perahya b. Joseph to his father, is proof of the remedies
available: he reiterates a medical prescription which he had previously sent from Palermo to his mother in Egypt, and thereby confirms the strong link between Jewish transmission and a possibly Arabic source of the drug.[137]

Conclusions: science and the supernatural

In describing the sources of care and cure in this chapter, it is important to bear in mind the positivist nature of the evidence. The charters record gifts in thanks for beneficial outcomes as well as for cures
hoped for. A miraculous intervention by a saint almost always has a
happy ending. But the types of illness cured are extremely formulaic,
based on a Christological model.[138] We never hear of a saint repair-

---

[135] A leading practitioner of this line of inquiry is John Riddle, whose numerous
studies include *Contraception and Abortion from the Ancient World to the Renaissance*
(Harvard, 1992) (with a selection of Riddle's earlier bibliography); and "Ancient and
medieval chemotherapy for cancer", *Isis*, LXXVI (1985), pp.319-330.
[136] *Cusa*, doc. 54.
[137] Goitein, *Letters*, p.330.
[138] A survey of cures performed by southern Italian saints reveals:-

	Nilus	*Fantinus*	*Elias*
possession	yes	yes	yes
others unspec		yes	
head & ears		yes*	
paralysed/withered hand		yes*+	yes
tumours		yes*+	
cripple		yes*+	

ing broken bones, for example, even though these might be just as debilitating and possibly life-threatening.

The belief and faith in the supernatural, however, surely underlines the hopelessness of most serious illness. But such strength of belief might also aid in recovery. M. L. Cameron argues this point in a study of the Anglo-Saxon texts *Bald's Leechbook* and *Lacnunga*. Whilst pointing out that many of the so-called magical parts of these texts were in fact perfectly rational cures, the study acknowledges that the charms used may well have had a powerfully positive effect on the patient's chances of recovery, simply by giving the patient confidence in the powers of the physician.[139] Thus, in the discussion above of belief in saints' miraculous cures, at least some recoveries may have been the result of the powerful psychological boost that the authority of the saint conveyed.[140] The power of such belief was acknowledged as early as the sixth century: Alexander of Tralles included the use of magic and amulets in his writings because the patients believed in their efficacy. "We are apt to connect such phenomena more to the lower classes, but this work warns us against underestimating the role of so-called popular beliefs in the upper strata, where Alexander and his patients belong."[141]

A significant proportion of those who fell ill might, however, expect to die, as their wills illustrate. Again, the redaction of their last testament, including such phrases as "on my death bed", is likely to have been formulaic, but such formulae did not enter scribal tradition without some good reason. The following chapter, therefore, turns away from health care to examine attitudes towards death and its impact on family and community.

	Nilus	*Fantinus*	*Elias*
mute		yes*+	yes+
retention of urine		yes*+	
paralysis		yes*+	yes+
dropsy		yes*+	
scrofula		yes*	
toothache		yes*	yes

*in Byzantium +post mortem cures

[139] M. L. Cameron, "Anglo-Saxon medicine and magic", *Anglo-Saxon England*, XVII (1988), p.210.

[140] The sincerity of belief in supernatural occurrences is illustrated in another context in a document from Salerno: in 935 a group of men declared that they were going to build a church in honour of St Severinus because they had had a vision of the saint: *CodCav*, I, doc. 157.

[141] J. Duffy, "Byzantine medicine in the sixth and seventh centuries: aspects of teaching and practice", in *Symposium on Byzantine Medicine*, p.26.

CHAPTER SIX

RECORDING THE DEAD

Whilst a disease might strike any level of society, the level of mortality might well show a class divide, as the poor could not eat well, suffered the worst living conditions and spent all their energy on manual labour or simply finding enough to eat. Thus they were more vulnerable in the face of infection, and would die in greater proportions.[1]

Death is presented to us in a variety of ways in the medieval record.[2] As Vito Fumagalli points out, 'the dead met with the living everywhere' — tombs, churches and houses could all signify their presence. Deserted ancient sites were often chosen for new monastic foundations (which in their turn attracted other habitation); the existence of an earlier community on a site meant that graves were likely to be present as well.[3] Also, the dying requested prayers for their souls from the living, maintaining a constant contact. Our evidence about death comes from charter material, which often records such requests and the sum paid to have them carried out. This chapter will first examine the tangible remains of the dead, and then consider the dialogue between living, sick, and dead.

We have already touched upon the information to be derived about sickness from skeletal remains. The major problem surrounding such remains is that we can never be sure whether the record of serious illness left on the bones was the actual cause of that person's death. The difficulty of gleaning information from cemetery sites is compounded by the fact that cremation was often used rather than burial to dispose of the dead. For example, the *Chronicon Salernitanum* records that when, during the reign of Gisolf I (943-78), one Landenolf of Capua died on his marriage procession from Trani to

---

[1] M. S. Mazzi, *Salute e Società nel Medioevo*, (Florence, 1978), p.7. In the same discussion, p.13, Mazzi makes the valid point that, faced with a period of poverty and disease, the community might well abandon its weakest members — the old, the poor, babies and women.

[2] As well as P.Ariès' classic, *L'Homme devant la Mort*, see also the recent discussion in P. Vovelle, "L'histoire des hommes au miroir de la mort", in *Death in the Middle Ages*, ed. H. Braet and W. Verbeke (Leuven, 1983), pp.1-18. Vovelle examines the ways in which the discourse of death has changed over time.

[3] V. Fumagalli, "Il paesaggio dei morti: luoghi d'incontro tra i morti e i vivi sulla terra nel medioevo", *Quaderni Storici*, XVII.ii (1982), pp.411-23, at 413-4.

Salerno, it was his urn (*salma*) which was brought to Salerno.[4] We know that the earliest Lombard settlers of the peninsula had buried their dead with grave goods, but that this practice had dwindled in the seventh century.[5] It is possible that after this date cremation became the preferred method of disposal, although later inhumations also survive. A fragmentary document of 1069 records the gift by duke Robert Guiscard of a church to the abbey of the Holy Trinity, Venosa, on the occasion of the transfer of its [the church's] brothers' ashes to the abbey.[6] It is conceivable that these two examples could represent exceptional cases of cremation. The need to move corpses in each instance might suggest that the transfer was the reason for cremation, allowing simple transport across what was, in one case, a long distance. They are also testimony to the desire in both cases to see the dead deposited in the right place. Landenolf was brought home, and the removal of the brothers' ashes to Holy Trinity was a potent symbol of their integration into the new community. The merging of communities is the theme in a document from Naples, dated 1041, which decreed that those in the monastic community of SS Marcellinus and Peter who knew their Greek letters were to be buried in the monastery of St Sebastian.[7] The importance of the dead in the lives of the living forms a major theme in medieval history in this period.

The poor, whether urban or rural, probably could not afford a memorial when they died. Richer Christians have left us their wills as memorials to their lives and wealth, but remarkably few pieces of epigraphic evidence survive as testaments to their deaths. The Jewish community, in contrast, is relatively well-documented in the epigraphic record. We have a significant number of epitaphs dating from the ninth century and surviving in various parts of southern Italy. One cluster survives in the fabric of the unfinished church of the Holy Trinity at Venosa. Published some sixty years ago,[8] they provide an insight into the life of a community which is hardly represented in the surviving documentary evidence. Their information has hardly ever been exploited, and it is worth listing the pertinent details of all of the fragments in order to bring them to wider attention (table 6.1).

---

[4] *ChronSal*, chapter 176.
[5] N. Christie, *The Lombards* (Oxford, 1995), p.126.
[6] *Ducs*, doc. 20.
[7] *RN*, doc. 473.
[8] U. Cassuto, "Nuove inscrizioni ebraiche di Venosa", *ASCL*, IV (1934), pp.1-9, and "Ancora nuove inscrizioni ebraiche di Venosa", *ASCL*, V (1935), pp.179-184.

Table 6.1: Jewish Inscriptions from Venosa

Date	Deceased	Age	Cassuto no.
814	SARA daughter of GEREMIA	5	1
821	rabbi ABRAHAM	37	2
822?	JOSEPH son of BENJAMIN	35	16
825	DAVID son of DANIEL	60	16
829	PAREGORIO son of TEODORO	63	3
829	REBECCA daughter of BONO	63	12
830	DINA daughter of JULIAN	30	13
834	unknown	unknown	4
838	AZRIEL son of LEVI	40	5
838	SAMUEL son of JOSEPH	50	6
838	unknown	30	7
850?	.. son of ELISEO	child	14
?	SAMUEL son of ..	70 or 90	8
?	DONNOLA daughter of AYYO	21	9
?	SADOQ son of ..	?	11

From this limited sample, it is perhaps hazardous to try to draw any conclusions, but two comments are possible. It seems apparent from an initial reading of this list that the Jewish community was very concerned to record age at death. The advanced age of most of the subjects is worthy of note. Of the thirteen whose age at death is known, almost half had reached forty years or considerably more. Of these, however, only one was a woman, and the other recorded females seem to have died young. The other striking feature is the care with which children were buried and recorded. Indeed, the fragmentary headstone of Eliseo's son, whose name we do not know, does more than simply record his age at death. It also gives a eulogy of the child's life. He was: 'the child../..school, kind../.. his readings, and was skilled in everything../'.

Another smaller group of five Jewish gravestones, dating from between the ninth and thirteenth centuries, was discovered at Bari in 1933. Only two, however, the epitaphs of David son of Menassah, and Mosheh son of Taddeus, give the ages at death of the deceased, forty-five years and six years, three months respectively.[9] Once again

---

[9] U. Cassuto, "Iscrizioni ebraiche a Bari", *Rivista degli Studi Orientali*, XV (1935), pp.320-1.

we can note the relatively advanced age of David, and the care with which the child was recorded.

This is in distinct contrast to a recent archaeological discovery in Naples. The risks of urban life for children are summed up in the discovery of at least seven infant skeletons in the early medieval strata of the Carminiello ai Mannesi excavation in the centre of Naples. All were between four months and four years old, and had apparently died at the same time, probably from an epidemic or the plague.[10] Further disconnected human remains were found amongst the refuse dumped on this site, and their unusual location may say something about the circumstances in which they had died.[11] But the striking fact to note is that the children, perhaps because the epidemic made swift burial necessary, do not seem to have merited purpose-made graves. Alternatively, it may have been their infancy which determined their indifferent disposal: the youngest child among the Jewish epitaphs was already five years old.

There are many methodological problems associated with the use of epigraphic information like the Jewish gravestones. The major one is in deciding how representative of the wider community the information of such limited samples might be. Even if ages at death are recorded, can we assume that these are in any way 'normal'?[12] Such an assumption can only be made if other information is available about the living conditions of the community, its relative wealth and the status of those afforded a memorial stone. The possibility of variation in burial practices within a community may mean that even an entire cemetery may not reflect the population using it.[13]

The average life expectancy in classical times and the middle ages has been estimated at twenty-five to thirty years.[14] This provides a measure against which to make some kind of calculation for southern Italians in the ninth to twelfth centuries, and suggests that those

---

[10] *Il Complesso Archeologico di Carminiello ai Mannesi (Scavi 1983-1984)*, ed. P. Arthur (Rome/Lecce, 1994), pp. 74-5.

[11] Umberto Albarella, in *Complesso Archeologico*, p.430, suggests their value in comprehending disease and epidemics: his implication seems to be that during such times of disaster formalised burial may have been dispensed with.

[12] Compare Shahar, "Who were old?", criticising the common assumptions about the limited longevity of medieval people.

[13] A point emphasised in a recent collection of essays on death and burial: *Mortality and Immortality: the Anthropology and Archaeology of Death*, ed. S. C. Humphreys and H. King (London, 1981), p.4. See also Neil Christie's pertinent comments on this problem from an Italian perspective in Christie, *Lombards*, p.157.

[14] Livi-Bacci, *Population and Nutrition*, p.20, figure 5, based on work by K. H. Weiss. Christie, *Lombards*, p.42, gives 30-35 as an average age from Lombard cemetery sites in Pannonia.

whose ages exceeded fifty or sixty were isolated cases. A very well-documented area, for example the duchy of Gaeta in Lazio, provides a sample of people who are recorded over a number of years. Assuming that they were at least twelve, the average age of legal competence, when they first appear, we can arrive at a minimum age for a number of individuals. This may in turn permit a comment on longevity, perhaps related to a good general state of health among the wealthy in this area, and the impact that the local environment may have had in this respect. Whilst it is always risky to generalise from a small sample, it is reasonable to assume that other small cities with rural territories would exhibit similar characteristics to Gaeta.

The full data from Gaeta, along with the criteria used for selection, are set out in Appendix 4. The nature of the sample means that we have no record of children's ages, but the pattern of adult ages is rather similar to that exhibited by the Jewish cemetery evidence, that is, the majority were in their twenties and thirties, but with isolated examples of extreme old age. This brings the mean age of the sample to somewhere between 37 and 38. The statistical validity of this information might be compromised by the survival of documents, but it is striking that an average age calculated for members of the ducal family comes out at some four years older. Obviously the *documentary* life of these individuals might be rather longer, considering that the Gaetan archive is almost unique in its detailed coverage of the ducal clan. But the value of the Gaetan evidence lies in its density, for all that it tells us only about the wealthy of this community.

The sample from Gaeta comprises only lay people. Clerics, the other well-documented group of inhabitants, are rather more difficult to age. In theory, the canonical ages governing when a man might become a priest, an abbot or a bishop, and so on,[15] should provide us with firm starting points to add to the man's documented career length, in order to reach a minimum age. However, it is by no means certain that these entry ages were adhered to in tenth- and eleventh-century southern Italy, and so no conclusions can be drawn as to whether the contemplative life or one spent at the top of the local church hierarchy contributed to relative longevity.

Another facet of death that can be traced fairly closely in the charter material centres around widowhood and remarriage. We have already touched upon the subject of female mortality in childbirth, and might expect therefore a number of second and third wives

---

[15] The minimum age laid down for entry to the priesthood, for example, was twenty-five: J. H. Lynch, *The Medieval Church: a Brief History* (London, 1992), p.241.

to occur in the documented sources. How is this borne out by the evidence?

A survey of the charter material from southern Italy reveals that remarriage was not uncommon. Both men and women are recorded with second or, exceptionally, third spouses; of 28 cases, however, twenty are remarried women (table 6.2). And the likelihood of their having divorced their first husbands is extremely remote in this period. The statistical evidence, therefore, suggests that husbands were more likely to die first. How can we explain this phenomenon? Taken at face value, the documents imply that husbands ran greater risks of dying prematurely than their wives. Given the fact that warfare was an endemic part of southern Italian political life throughout our pe-

Table 6.2: Remarried Women in Southern Italian Charters[16]

Date	Name	First Spouse
848	Wiseltruda wife of Ildeprand	Radeprand
853	Ermeperga wife of Ragenfrid	Dacipert
882	Orsa wife of John the notary	Walpert
912	Rimperghe wife of John the notary	Adelferi
954	Gemma wife of Mirandi	Richard
996	the widow of Marinus told to remarry	
999	Iaquinta the nun widow of John	Lictu
1001	Mira wife of Leo	?
1002	Matrona wife of John	Constantine
1003	Calomaria wife of Caloiohanne	Maio?
1006	Bigurita widow of Mari	John
1008	Maroccia wife of ?	John
1010	Leni wife of John	Martin
1013	Adelghisa wife of John	Brocconi
1029	Roma wife of Iaquinti	Maraldus
1034	Eufimia wife of Senioricti	Cesarius
1063	Maria wife of Aligerni	John
1068	Regalis wife of Mauro	Mauro
1090	Altruda wife of Maraldi	John Capuanus
1094	Malore wife of Laurence	Russ...?

[16] Documents cited are, respectively, *CodCav* I, docs 32, 37, 92, 129 and 185; III, docs 494 and 524; *RN*, doc. 315; *CDC* I, doc. 109; *CDB* IV, doc. 8; *CodCav* IV, doc. 591; *RN*, doc. 333; *CodCav* IV, docs 628 and 667; V, doc.819; *RN*, docs 450 and 495; *CP*, doc.48; *Troia*, doc. 24; and *CDB* X, doc. 3.

riod, the high death rate amongst husbands could be ascribed to this factor alone. And indeed it may well be a strong contributory cause, for if we examine the occurrence of remarried women chronologically, there is a lull in the tenth century, a period of relative peace.

However, remarried women recorded in the *Codex Cavensis* form a very high proportion of those cases. Is the picture presented by the evidence more reflective of differing documentary traditions than of the reality of husbands' mortality rate? It would appear so, for the women in these documents, issued in an area where Lombard law and custom prevailed, had to identify their previous husbands for a very specific reason: they held a quarter of their former husband's property as their marriage-gift or *morgengab*. Combined with the fact that they remained under the tutelage or *mundium* of their present husband in any future land transactions, the personal circumstances of these Lombard women were recorded in greater detail than almost anywhere else.[17]

The occurrences of remarried husbands, far fewer in number, are much more widely-scattered across the southern Italian evidence (table 6.3). A striking feature is the fact that we know the names of very few of these men's previous spouses. This again reflects the need of the documentation to record the pertinent facts. Given that she or her heirs might retain part of his property, a husband had to record his deceased wife's existence and continued hold on his life, but unless he was making a gift in remembrance of his deceased wife, there was little reason to give her name.

Records of deceased spouses, therefore, were prompted in both cases by property concerns; rarely was the dead person mentioned for emotional reasons. The pattern of male and female mortality cannot safely be determined from the statistical evidence we have, therefore, and so the question as to whether wives died earlier, say in childbirth, than husbands for other reasons must remain open.

It is clear, however, that the dead retained a place in the thoughts of the living, and their continued hold on property meant that they were often cited in the same way as living members of their family. This leads us back to the physical evidence of their presence: the family sepulchre.

---

[17] In addition to the evidence from the *Codex Cavensis*, three further documents in the cited sample about remarried women also come from areas of Lombard law, reinforcing my argument about documentary tradition.

Table 6.3: Remarried Men in Southern Italian Charters[18]

Doc	Name	First Spouse
973	John smith husband of Sassa	?
974	Peter husband of Maria	Sillitta
996	John cleric husband of Theodonanda	?
1028	Iaquintus husband of Cara	Sica
1029	Dauferius husband of Alzeiza	?
1031	John husband of Muscata	?
1034	Siolfo husband of Ranuise and Gervisa	
1089	Maurelianus husband of Gemma	Altruda

Burial sites had been strictly extramural during antiquity, but moved into towns in the early middle ages.[19] This tendency appears to be illustrated by the tenth-century chronicle of the bishops of Naples, in which several of the bishops of late antiquity were initially buried outside the city and later moved to the cathedral within the walls.[20] Cilento ascribes this wave of intramural translation to the growing confidence and autonomy of the Neapolitan see in the ninth century. Certainly the threat of Saracen or Lombard attacks contributed to the concern felt to protect holy relics buried outside the city walls, but the main function of their movement, he argues, was to reinforce the longstanding history of the bishopric of Naples *vis-à-vis* papal interference.[21] In such competitions, the dead could be just as strong allies as the living.

Several charters point to a concern on the part of individuals about their own burial. When John the deacon gave his church of St Salvator to the monastery of St Benedict in Conversano, he reserved the right to graves in the church, presumably for himself and his

---

[18] Documents cited are, respectively, *RN*, docs 195 and 202; *CodCav* III, doc. 491; V, doc. 797; *CDC* I, doc. 157; *RN*, doc. 432; *Tremiti*, doc. 15; and *CDB* V, doc. 12.

[19] On the dynamics of this shift, J. Harries, "Death and the dead in the late Roman West", in *Death in Towns*, pp. 56-65.

[20] *Chronicon Episcoporum S. Neapolitanae Ecclesiae*, in *Monumenta ad Neapolitani Ducatus Historiam Pertinentia*, ed. B. Capasso, I (Naples, 1881), pp.145-232. For example, p.163, the fourth-century bishop Fortunatus is reburied inside the walls *post longo tempore*.

[21] N. Cilento, "Il significativo della 'translatio' dei corpi dei vescovi napoletani dal cimitero di S. Gennaro 'extra moenia' nella basilica della Stefania", *Campania Sacra*, I (1970), pp.1-6.

family.[22] In 1052 Ursus made a donation to the church of the Apostles in Taranto, and bought himself a tomb in that church.[23]

The site of burial carried much significance to medieval people, especially those from important families who wished to preserve their high profile in death. Family burial does appear to be common, not surprising in an age and area where kin groups formed the main political power structures in any particular locality. Thus in 965 Andreas specified in a document that he and his heirs be buried at Gualdo near Avellino.[24]

Burial might also represent a family's continuing control over an ecclesiastical foundation or piece of land. For example, a gift to the convent of St Laurence at Amalfi, by Constantine and his sister Anna and Anna's son Maurus, all members of one of the city's noble families, was accompanied in 1059 by the specific instruction that only family members were to be buried in the tomb of their mother Boccia.[25] Similarly, when Iannaci of Atrani rebuilt his church of SS Mary and John, which had been destroyed by the Saracens, at Vietri, the archibishop of Salerno reconfirmed the Atranian's control over the activities of the church, including the burial of the dead.[26] The foundation of a church carried with it the right to bury there: in 1083 the archbishop of Bari freed the church of All Saints at Cuti into the control of its founder, Eustasius, acknowledging the latter's right to appoint priests and accept burials.[27] A similar instance occurred in 1086 at Bari: Pascal the priest offered a piece of land adjoining the church of St John the Apostle to that church, reserving a burial plot for himself and the children of his sister. It appears that Pascal had co-founded the church.[28] The recipient of the gift on behalf of the church, Passarus, later sold his half of the church and its tombs five years later to the archbishop of Bari.[29]

If a family did not own a private church or sepulchre, its members nevertheless still tried to maintain contact in death as in life. In 1094, Boccia, a widow from Amalfi, bought land next to the grave of her husband, presumably for her own burial. Since the heirs of duke Alberic were buried nearby, this plot may have been in a prestigious site. The vendor, Maurus bishop of Maiori, was able to charge 300

---

[22] *PC*, doc. 33 (1014).
[23] *Trinchera*, doc. 39.
[24] *CodCav* II, doc. 231.
[25] *CP*, doc. 75.
[26] *CodCav*, VI, document 898.
[27] *CDB* V, doc. 4.
[28] *CDB* V, doc. 6.
[29] *CDB* V, doc. 16.

solidi, a tremendous amount of money compared with contemporary land transactions, and illustrative of the premium placed on the plot.[30]

The value of graves is reiterated again and again in our documentary evidence, whether in terms of price, as in Boccia's case, or in other ways. In 1040, when two brothers sold all of their land in Matera in Apulia, the only property they retained was their three tomb sites.[31] In his will of 1071,[32] Sergius son of Kampulus, of Gaeta, left a tomb site to one Romana; the transaction clearly had some importance to him, but Romana's connection to him is unclear.

Illustrative of the problems of context is a particularly fine memorial, an inscribed sarcophagus, in the portico of Salerno cathedral. The inscription reads: *sepulchrum Sergii Capo Grassi et heredu masculini sexus* (plate 4). The inscription cannot securely be dated (the tomb itself being a reused Roman sarcophagus), nor is its original location securely identifiable. The limitation of the tomb to male heirs is unusual, but we cannot derive any information from the inscription alone. Only when we know more about the Capograssi from the documents can we ascribe any significance to the exclusion of females from the family sepulchre.[33]

Wills often provide information about burial sites and patterns of patronage. When Theodata the nun made her will in Naples in 968, she ordered that her house be sold and the price given for her soul, presumably to the monastery of SS Severinus and Sossus where she expressed a wish to be buried.[34] In 1024 Gregory *magnificus*, a member of a cadet branch of the ruling family in Gaeta, left a gift of silver to the monastery of St Angelus there, probably the family's favourite church of St Michael *ad Planciano*.[35] The implicit purchase of a tomb site with a donation is overtly expressed in Taranto in 1052: executing the will of Calus, Ursus gave land to the church of the Apostles *on condition that* Calus was buried in the church.[36]

The location of tombs was almost certainly a mark of social status. At Taranto in 1045, the children of the *domesticus* donated land to the

---

[30] *CDA*, doc. 93.
[31] *CDB* IV, doc. 29.
[32] *CDC* II, doc. 245.
[33] The only reference we have to this surname is from Naples in the tenth century when Bonus Isabrus Capograssa appears in a charter: *RN*, doc. 272. Given the descriptive etymology of the name, however, it would be unwise to speculate that he and Sergius were from the same family.
[34] *RN*, doc. 164.
[35] *CDC* I, doc. 143.
[36] *Trinchera*, doc. 39.

episcopal church in return for burial plots in the atrium of the church.[37] When the episcopal church was rebuilt in Gaeta in the eleventh century, donors to the building work were rewarded with extremely prominant tomb-sites. One such, Stephen son of John, received a site in 1052 from the bishop which directly adjoined the steps into the church and lay next to other tombs in the portico.[38] Nevertheless, the integrity of the ruling family's earlier burials on the site seems to have been preserved. In 1149, a gift of a tomb in the cathedral noted its position next to that of the *hypatus* and duke of Gaeta, Docibilis, at least two centuries old.[39] In a similar way, in 1068, the abbot of SS Theodore and Martin in the same city gave a burial plot within the cloister to a couple in return for their services to the monastery.[40] Both foundations demanded a gift of lighting oil for each body buried, thereby continuing the ongoing relationship with their benefactors.

The respect for previous burials may have varied according to social class and circumstances, however. Docibilis' tomb was that of a remembered and much-respected ruler, whose family may well have remained in the city long after their political demise in the mid-eleventh century. The respect shown for it also derived from the fact that, situated within the church, it was probably accompanied by monumental structures or, at the very least, an inscription.

The Lombard king, Rothari, had legislated in the seventh century against the disturbance of tombs. This may say more about the fact that valuable grave goods were still to be found by enterprising robbers at this date, but also indicates that the integrity of graves was not always respected.[41] Archaeological evidence from the hilltop cemetery at the monastery of St Vincent on the Volturno river, similarly, points to reuse and reopening of graves in what has been identified as the eighth- to ninth-century burial ground of the monastery's lay community. But in this case the mixed ages and sex of the individuals found in multi-occupancy graves appear to indicate that families were buried together.[42] This may have been the only occasion on which re-

---

[37] *Trinchera*, doc. 34. An earlier donation by the count of Taranto to the same church in 1040, *Trinchera*, doc. 32, had not specified the location of the tomb sites granted in exchange, but these are likely to have been equally prominant.

[38] *CDC* I, doc. 191.

[39] *CDC* II, doc. 340: the use of the title *hypatus* suggests that the tomb was that of Docibilis I (d. c.906), despite the fact that his grandson, Docibilis II (d. c.954), was the first recorded user of the ducal title.

[40] *CDC* II, doc. 236.

[41] Rothari, laws 15 and 16, in *Lombard Laws*, ed. Drew.

[42] C. M. Coutts, "The hilltop cemetery", in *San Vincenzo al Volturno 2*, ed. R. Hodges (London, 1995), pp.98-118 at 116.

opening a grave or built sepulchre was an acceptable practice.

The right to bury, however, was not always a matter of generations of the same family: when four men of Terlizzi gave olive trees to
the church of St Lucia there in 1065, they each received two tomb
plots, presumably for themselves and spouses. No ongoing arrangement was here intended.[43]

The continued use of family sepulchres could be interpreted as far
more than simple sentiment or political gesture, however. Valerie
Flint underlines that a strong belief persisted into the early middle
ages of the supernatural powers of the dead. The Roman *parentalia*,
when deceased members of the family had been commemorated by a
feast at the tomb, gave way to a more general remembrance of the
dead in late February; and the dead were held to be able to return to
use their supernatural powers, whether for good or evil.[44] The latter
theme is of course most vividly illustrated by medieval hagiography,
full of visions of long-dead saints, and by the regular pilgrimages to
the tombs of holy men and women. Indeed, anniversaries of martyrs'
deaths were regularly celebrated with a feast and liturgical celebra-
tion at the tomb.[45] The persistence of a form of the *parentalia* in
secular society, however, has attracted rather less attention. How
were the dead incorporated into the lives of the living?

Patrick Geary has recently discussed this question in a series of
essays, stressing the close links between the past, present and future
generations of a family through donations of property to a particular
church or the preservation of family names.[46] This model certainly
works for medieval southern Italy, where the continued use of a particular name persisted within noble families, especially down the male
line, and where family churches were common even in the face of
ecclesiastical reform. Families lived close together and participated in
a variety of communal activities, centred in our evidence around
property transactions. These, via the church as mediator, included
the deceased members of the family, commemorated in charters with
gifts for their souls and written into church diptychs as a means of
remembrance.

The formulaic gift for the soul of the donor was an early and
common feature of southern Italian documents. The gift had a variety of purposes. In one of the earliest examples, dated 831 and con-

---

[43] *CDB* III, doc. 9.
[44] Flint, *Rise of Magic*, pp.213-4.
[45] Flint, *Rise of Magic*, p.269.
[46] P. Geary, "Exchange and interaction between the living and the dead in early
medieval society", in *Living with the Dead*, pp. 77-92.

sisting of a donation in the will of the bishop of Formia of his clothes, a directly charitable intention is visible; it is likely that the garments would be distributed to those in need.[47] A more frequent act was to designate some item or piece of land to be sold, and the proceeds to be donated. Rather rarer in such donations was an accompanying request that the donor's name be written down. Table 6.4 lists these examples.

Table 6.4: Donors Requesting Commemoration[48]

Date	Name	Action requested
964	Anna Pacifica	name written in diptych
966	Maria widow of Leo	" "
1030	Eupraxia daughter Cesari	" "
1036	Marinus count & wife	" "
1072	Bisantia widow	prayers and masses
1073	Bona	name in 3 *chartulae*
1105	Robert the deacon	prayers and masses

Several comments are possible about this list. The prevalence of women requesting commemoration must have some significance. In an age when remarriage was common, were the actions of Anna, Maria, Eupraxia, Bisantia and Bona a means of ensuring that their lives were remembered even if their families or husbands forgot about them? Men did not have to state that they had previously been married (unless they had a claim to some of their deceased wife's property—which is how we find out about widowers in our evidence), whereas a deceased husband's name was continuously remembered when his widow, as almost all women, declared her marital status. Only further investigation into more documentary evidence of this type from other parts of medieval Europe would indicate whether women were in the majority in having their names commemorated in ecclesiastical lists and services.

We have several extant examples of the type of church diptych which preserved the names and memory of members of the community. The most famous from this region is the extensive necrology and *liber confratrum* of the church of St Matthew in Salerno. The necrology,

---

[47] *CDC* I, doc. 4.
[48] Documents cited are, respectively, *RN*, docs 137, 159, 425, 458; *Trani*, doc. 18; *RN*, doc. 514; *Venosa*, doc. 6.

arranged as a list of days in the year and containing columns dating from the eleventh century onwards, provides valuable evidence for inhabitants of the city who do not otherwise appear in the charters. Records earlier than the twelfth century are relatively sparse and confined largely to the clergy, but the twelfth century itself sees a fascinating cross section of Salernitan society, including one Matheus de Paolo *doctor in phisica* (recorded as having died October 18, 1142). There is also a certain Alaire wife of Alfani and Marotte *nutricis sue* listed under June 29 1156; if Marotta is to be understood as Alaire's nurse (the term might also be interpreted as 'mother'), then her association with her ward was fittingly commemorated.[49]

The *Liber Confratrum*, on the other hand, is far less informative. The oldest part derives from a *liber vitae* or *diptychon* of the late tenth century, copied in the eleventh, but this is simply a list of names of benefactors of St Matthew's, with no patronyms or occupations except for the clergy. Later parts of the *Liber*, recording twelfth-century donors, are again a little more detailed, and include another medic, Cicero *clericus et medicus*.[50]

What function did such commemorative lists perform? If the diptych was really intended to record a noted benefactor, why were only personal names listed, without any identifying features, earlier on? And why did the entries become more fulsome in the later parts of the *Liber* and the necrology?

It could be said that death held less fear in the earlier period, when the community itself was smaller and family and kin memories were sufficient to keep their deceased member 'alive'. The dead were included in family activities, and their names and memories lived on. As Fumagalli suggested, they remained close and part of the early medieval community. They might also, in this earlier period, be commemorated in a small *liber* in the family church or *eigenkirche*.

This has implications for our perception of healthcare in the area under examination. We have already seen that, despite the relatively widespread availability of medical practitioners in urban centres, many cures were still sought from supernatural sources in church. Might this be related to the presence of friendly family spirits there as well as to aggressive marketing on the part of the clergy?[51] What

---

[49] *Necrologio del Liber Confratrum di S. Matteo di Salerno*, ed. C. A. Garufi (Fonti per la Storia d'Italia 56, Rome, 1922), pp.162 and 88 respectively.

[50] *Necrologio del Liber Confratrum*, p.276.

[51] Even between different churches and resident saints there could be keen competiton: 'they were no doubt concerned with their own loss of prestige and, perhaps, revenue': P. Geary, "The ninth-century relic trade: a response to popular piety?" in *Living with the Dead*, pp.177-93 at 187.

happened when papal reformers began to inveigh against such personal churches? With a move to clerical control, did the family to a certain extent become detached from its foundation? At the same time, did the increased hostility of clerics to secular medicine in the twelfth century provoke a greater sense of personal salvation, which rendered death a more frightening prospect? If so, the more detailed entries in necrologies of the twelfth century could be both a reflection of this greater focus on the individual and his or her wish to have their good works recorded at greater length? At the same time, more detail would be needed if the *Liber* had to function in lieu of the kin group in preserving the memory of that individual.[52]

One person who remained uppermost in the minds of his or her neighbours when they died was, of course, the local saint. Tombs might quickly become the sites of reported miracles and, just as we saw that the populace made offerings along with their prayers of hope and thanks, so the tomb was a focus of still more revenue for the church. Local lay rulers benefited too: the presence of a celebrated saint's corpse added prestige to their cities. Several hagiographic texts from southern Italy illustrate the lengths that local clerics and rulers were willing to go to to obtain such benefits. When the body of St Sossus was moved into Naples from Misenum, it was pointed out that the Lombard prince, Sicard, had already tried to take the saint's remains back to his city but had been unable to find them.[53] The *Life* and *Translatio* of bishop Athanasius of Naples reveal that his body was at first buried at Montecassino, and then, fifty years later, tranferred to the church of St Ianuarius at Naples. At both sites, miraculous cures had occurred, explaining the reluctance of abbot Bertarius and the Cassinese monks to release the corpse: the *Translatio* relates the quarrel that broke out, and the Benedictines' vain request that at least part of the body be left at Cassino![54]

Illustrative of lay interest in saints' tomb sites is the chapter dealing with St Nilus' choice of resting place. Having lost his companion, the blessed Stephen, Nilus ordered that two tombs be built (the saint was

---

[52] Other *libri* follow a similar pattern. See the survey of surviving southern Italian examples by Hubert Houben, *Il "Libro del Capitolo" del Monastero della SS Trinità di Venosa (Cod. Casin. 334)* (Bari, 1984), pp.13-20. The potential of this type of text for social historians has given rise to several studies of southern Italian examples in recent years: *Monachesimo e Mondo dei Laici nel Mezzogiorno Medievale: Il Necrologio di Montevergine*, ed. M. Villani (Altavilla Salentina, 1990) and *Monasteri Femminili e Nobiltà a Napoli tra Medioevo ed Età Moderna: Il Necrologio di S. Patrizia (secc.XII-XVI)*, ed. A. Facchiano (Altavilla Salentina, 1992).

[53] *Translatio Sancti Sosii*, chapter 25.

[54] *Vita Athanasii Episcopi Neapolitani*, chapters 8-10, and *Translatio Sancti Athanasii Episcopi Neapolitani*, chapter 1, in *MGH SRL*, pp.449-50.

currently at Serperi near Gaeta). However, duke John III of Gaeta who, with his wife, Emilia, had previously visited the saint, was clearly alive to the benefits that a dead saint could bring. Having heard the reason for the double tomb, he exclaimed [according to the hagiographer's account]: 'What? If the Father dies am I to leave him here? Am I not to carry him into my city and deposit him there as the strongest tower of its defence?' Nilus, however, heard of John's intention, and fled the duchy, 'preferring to die miserably than be thought a saint by any man'.[55] Duke John's loss was Gregory of Tuscolo's temporary gain, as the saint took up residence there instead. But when Nilus died, his body was placed in 'the destined place, as the most holy father had decided', that is his double tomb, which became the centre of the new foundation of Grottaferrata.[56]

Notable by their absence, however, as in his lifetime, are any *post mortem* miracles at Nilus' grave. The miracles surrounding the tomb of the southern Italian saint, Fantinus, in Thessaloniki, have already been touched upon in the previous chapter. The saint, as might be expected, was buried rather than cremated. Cures then ensued through use of the oil from the lamps on the tomb, from sleeping near to it and having a dream of the saint, and from the saint's own instructions to drink lamp oil mixed with wine. To add impact to these events, the biographer underlined that even when dead, the saint could still cure those who had 'taken great pains to run from doctor to doctor, without obtaining a cure'.[57]

The continued stress on the inefficacy of doctors' care even compared to saints' burial places reinforces my argument that much of the church's hostility to medical practitioners was born out of the competition for revenue between the two. An incomplete chapter of the *Translatio Sancti Severini* suggests that a cleric seized by fever, 'who had already spent all his money on doctors', would receive a cure at that saint's tomb.[58]

A saint's death, therefore, seems to have added only potency to his miracles. This may explain why the *Translatio Sancti Severini* begins with a fairly lengthy *excursus* on the Saracens' ill-treatment of

---

[55] *Vita di San Nilo*, chapter 95. Cf. the very similar scenario in the *Translatio* of St Severinus from the castle of Lucullum outside Naples. When the abbot of St Severinus in the city petitioned for the saint's body to be removed to his care, the consul of Naples, Gregory, pointed out that the saint already had a resting place in the tomb constructed by Barbaria, *illustris femina*, at Lucullum. The abbot's prayers, however, prevailed: *Translatio Sancti Severini*, chapter 5, in *MGH SRL*, p.455.

[56] *Vita di San Nilo*, XIV, 96-100.

[57] *Vita di San Fantino*, chapters 56-58.

[58] *Translatio Sancti Severini*, chapter 9.

Procopius, bishop of Taormina. His resistance to the pagan king has all the hallmarks of a good martyrology, but his body, when he was finally killed, was burnt.[59] The use of this tale is probably intended to underline the good fortune of the Neapolitans in having a saintly protector to exhume: it is likely that the Arab king was equally well aware of the potency of relics in Christian cult. An almost contemporary hagiographical text from Calabria, the *Vita* of St Elia Speleotis, supports this view: the Saracen raiders who attacked the tomb of the saint's master, Arsenios, in the church of St Eustratius in Reggio are also said to have tried to burn the corpse, but in this case such a fate would not have served any hagiographical purpose (Procopius gained martyrdom) and so their attempts were in vain.[60]

To conclude, death is represented in a number of ways in our documentary evidence. The number of wills surviving suggests that people who fell sick expected death to follow, and arranged their affairs accordingly. The cause of an individual's death is, however, never stated except in narrative evidence, and an average age at death is still an elusive piece of information. It is clear that archaeological work will further our knowledge in relation to this question. Nevertheless, it is true to say that grandparents figure very rarely in our documents, suggesting that lives extended only two generations, that is 35-40 years. Death did not, however, end an individual's participation in his or her family's life. Family churches were used both to worship and to bury. Ancestral names were given to children, particularly, although not exclusively, down the male line. And deceased relatives were commemorated every time a piece of inherited property formed part of a land transaction. It is possible that this continued presence rendered death a less frightening prospect in the early medieval period, a familiar and frequent event that signalled a change in the deceased individual's status, but which might affect the family group very little. I have suggested above that it was only when the coherence of the family's activities came under threat from the twin prongs of church reform—attacking *eigenkirchen*—and a new urgency in the preaching of personal salvation that death became more unnerving. Such preaching, I would argue, had much to do with the advance of medical knowledge from the late eleventh century onwards. In the next chapter I shall briefly explore this advance.

---

[59] *Translatio Sancti Severini*, chapter 3.
[60] da Costa-Louillet, "Saints de Sicile", p.117.

PART THREE

MEDICAL ACHIEVEMENT:
SOUTHERN ITALY IN CONTEXT

CHAPTER SEVEN

PATTERNS OF KNOWLEDGE:
TEXTS AND THE SCHOOL OF SALERNO

Although southern Italy is best known for its production of high-quality medical texts in the period under review, the previous chapters have indicated that medical activity, and indeed the issue of health, extend far beyond the scholarly tradition. Having surveyed the documentary and literary evidence for the knowledge and experience of disease and medicine in southern Italy, we can perhaps now put the production of medical manuscripts and the flowering of the medical school at Salerno in the late eleventh and twelfth centuries into context.

The desire on the part of historians to see a deliberate intellectual centre being set up at Salerno derives in part from the undeniable wealth of medical texts emanating from southern Italy from an early date (see Appendix 5). Ancient medical authors were preserved in the Byzantine world in their original forms and in compendia, and the Byzantine enclaves of Italy, both at Ravenna and then in the South, participated in this preservation. Examples of the type of material transmitted in this way include a ninth-century list of beneficial plants attributed to the abbot of Montecassino, Bertarius (d. 883)[1] and a tenth-century Cassinese manuscript of Dioscurides' (*fl.* AD 50-79) *Materia Medica*, which describes almost 1000 drugs of vegetable, animal and mineral origin, with extremely realistic depictions of the effects of some of the remedies (plates 5 and 6).[2] The tenth century also saw the translation in southern Italy of Paul of Aegina's *Epitome*,[3] and in addition many compilations, or *Summae*, were made.[4]

The *Institutiones* of the Roman senator Cassiodorus reveals that Dioscurides' work was already being translated in the sixth century. Its reference to that author's *Herbarium*, among the list of texts to be

---

[1] A. Russo, "Di un poco noto 'Glossario' botanico-farmaceutico del IX secolo (Cod. Cassinese 69)", *Atti dell'Accademia*, VII (1990), pp.213-7.

[2] L. Mackinney, *Medical Illustrations in Medieval Manuscripts*, (London, 1965), figures 35-37. The manuscript itself is in Munich, MS Latin 337.

[3] A. Beccaria, *I Codici di Medicina del Periodo Presalernitano (Secoli IX, X, e XI)* (Rome, 1956), p.27.

[4] Two of these, *Casin.Lat.* 92 and *Vat.Barb.Lat.* 160, were preserved at Montecassino and date to the tenth and eleventh centuries respectively: Beccaria, *Codici di Medicina*, p.32.

used at Cassiodorus' monastery of Vivarium in Calabria, is likely to mean the abbreviated version of the *Materia Medica* and containing just 71 descriptions of herbs.[5] This is one of the earliest examples of the part played by religious houses in conserving and translating ancient authors. A Greek text of Dioscurides, a seventh-century manuscript of uncertain origin, is now preserved at Naples.[6]

Beccaria lists three other surviving medical texts from Montecassino. The first, a compilation of the ninth or tenth century, includes a variety of extracts from Hippocratic work and authors such as Galen, Alexander of Tralles, Apuleius, Dioscurides and Sextus Placitus. The other two were produced during the abbacy of Desiderius in the eleventh century: translations of Paul of Aegina and Johannitius, the latter from the Arabic.[7]

Apart from Montecassino's own production, it also received gifts including medical books. We know of one such gift of books to the abbey in the tenth century. In the *Registrum* of Peter the Deacon, Leo the priest, of Larino in the Molise, is recorded as having donated in 945 'medicinales iii, Galenum, Aforismum et Genicia et Asclepium'.[8] Despite the source of this information (Peter was a notorious forger of land donations to the abbey), it is unlikely that a gift of books would have been invented.

A major question which does not seem to have been addressed in any great depth is where such manuscripts and books were being produced. Ieraci Bio comes to no clear opinion, suggesting that 'la materia medica, eminentemente "testo d'uso" ... poteva interessare entrambi gli ambienti'; that is, laymen or ecclesiastics may have acted as writers and patrons.[9] This is of course true, but this gets us no nearer to likely sources. We must begin therefore with the places active in transcribing texts, whether medical or not.

The obvious place to start, in that it preserves the earliest material, is Montecassino itself. Monastic interest in medical texts is much in evidence in southern Italy, particularly in examples from the

---

[5] H. E. Sigerist, "The Latin medical literature of the early middle ages", *Journal of the History of Medicine*, XIII (1958), p.131.

[6] G. Cavallo, 'La circolazione dei testi greci nell'Europa dell'alto medioevo', in *Rencontres de Cultures dans la Philosophie Médiévale: Traductions et Traducteurs de l'Antiquité Tardive au XIVe Siècle*, ed. J. Hamesse and M. Fattori (Louvain-la-Neuve/Cassino, 1990), p.56.

[7] Montecassino 351 and 225 respectively: Beccaria, *Codici di Medicina*, p.57.

[8] *Reg.Pet.Diac.* no.211, cited in Beccaria, *Codici di Medicina*, p.85.

[9] A. M. Ieraci Bio, "La trasmissione della letteratura medica greca nell'Italia meridionale fra X e XV secolo", in *Contributi alla Cultura Greca nell'Italia Meridionale*, ed. A. Garzya (Naples, 1989), pp.133-255, at pp.146-7.

Cassinese house. But we hear very little of transcription work or actual medical practice on the part of the monks. Nevertheless, Flint makes the valid point that early medieval Benedictine monks may have acquired skills or adapted previously pagan practices such as giving out prognoses on the basis of lunar cycles in order to win friends in their rural surroundings.[10] Her argument works equally well for more overtly medical practices: the ability to help sick people could be a potent means of establishing a monastery's authority with the local community. It could also be an effective way to convert pagans to Christians, if the hagiography of the South is to be believed. The life of St Elias of Enna (d. 903) includes him curing sick Saracens and persuading them to be baptised during a period of captivity with them.[11] However, this may represent wishful thinking on the part of a biographer with first-hand experience of the constant raids on Calabria and Sicily in the ninth and tenth centuries. Other saints' lives reveal them simply protecting local people from the intruders[12] or, perhaps more sensibly, fleeing to safety.

It has been argued that, elsewhere in Europe, the existence of medical texts in monasteries may not be evidence of medical practice, as such. The collection of texts on prognosis and signs of death arose as much from the liturgical duties of the monks in rituals surrounding the deceased as from any desire to care for the living patient.[13] This viewpoint must be treated with caution; it is highly unlikely that the collection and preservation of medical texts was carried out without some rudimentary medical knowledge being acquired. Monasteries, even the most remote, still attracted visitors and had lay servants to care for as well as the monks.

Indeed, to judge from hagiography and other sources from the South, it appears extremely likely that most text production took place within a monastic context. The *typikon* or foundation document of the Theotokos at Rossano in Lucania, for example, includes among the complement of the monastery a *kalligraphos*, evidence of a *scriptorium* in the monastery.[14] Santo Lucà illustrates that many of the

---

[10] Flint, *Rise of Magic*, p.145. Compare the early life of St Barbatus of Benevento, cited in an earlier chapter and also focusing on conversion.

[11] da Costa-Louillet, "Saints de Sicile", p.99.

[12] E.g. St Vitalis who, having avoided death through the intervention of a cloud which hid his attacker's sword and a bright halo surrounding his own body, persuaded the band raiding his monastery not to attack Christians: da Costa-Louillet, "Saints de Sicile", p.129.

[13] F. S. Paxton, "*Signa mortifera*: death and prognostication in early medieval monastic medicine", *BHM* LXVII (1993), pp.631-50.

[14] S. Lucà, "I Normanni e la 'rinascita' del secolo XII", *ASCL*, LX (1993), pp.1-91, at p.23.

Byzantine saints of the South, particularly in the tenth century, are also depicted as men of letters, including St Fantinus and St Elias Speleotis.[15] St Fantinus' occupation at his monastery in Calabria, for example, is described as *kalligraphein*, the transcribing of texts.[16] In addition, fragmentary pieces of evidence can suggest other centres of text production or preservation. In the margins of a compilation of Galenic and other recipes, made in the tenth century, a certain Urso attests to the text having been offered to the church of St Vincentius. Beccaria raises the interesting question whether this is the monastery of St Vincent on the Volturno river, but does not elaborate further as to a possible date for the marginal text nor his reasons for making the suggestion.[17] Nevertheless, recent excavations at this monastery have revealed an astonishing culture of the written word, with writing ostentatiously displayed throughout the monastery's public decorative scheme.[18] It would be strange, therefore, if this foundation did not have a library.

The potential for the dissemination of medical knowledge is underlined by Anna Maria Ieraci Bio, citing the pronounced presence of texts from the Alexandrian medical tradition of the sixth and seventh centuries, and the attested travel of St Nilus of Rossano within southern Italy from his home city through Capua and Gaeta and then to Grottaferrata.[19] St Elias, too, stayed in the Valle Metelliana in the territory of Salerno in the tenth century.[20]

Another tradition of medical text production existed among the Jews of southern Italy, of whom the most famous was Shabbetai Donnolo of Oria (913-after 982), discussed in an earlier chapter.[21] His 'Book of Mixtures', a herbal with over a hundred prescriptions, is the earliest extant medical text in Hebrew of European origin, and the earliest southern Italian medical text.[22] The book used both Byzantine and Jewish recipes, reflecting the environment in which he lived.

---

[15] "Normanni", p.67.

[16] *Vita di San Fantino*, chapter 21. This activity is not referred to when the saint arrives in Greece, however.

[17] The text is now in Vienna, ms 68: Beccaria, *Codici di Medicina*, p.67.

[18] J. Mitchell, "The display of script and the uses of painting in Longobard Italy", in *Settimane di Studio del Centro Italiano sull'Alto Medioevo*, XLI (1994), pp.887-951, esp. 904-925.

[19] "Trasmissione", pp.144, 143.

[20] *Le Pergamene di S. Nicola di Gallucanta (secc. IX-XII)*, ed. P. Cherubini (Altavilla Salentina, 1990), p.11.

[21] See above, chapter 4.

[22] A. Sharf, *The Universe of Shabbetai Donnolo*, (Warminster, 1976), p.vii. J. Shatzmiller, *Jews, Medicine and Medieval Society* (London, 1994), p.11, discusses this and another text, the 'Book of Remedies'.

We must not exclude from this survey of medical knowledge the likelihood that much was imported from other sources along with the constant travel between southern Italy and other parts of the Mediterranean. Jews may have been instrumental in this. The written evidence provides no explicit examples, but the links between Jewish communities in southern Italy and their counterparts elsewhere are well attested. For example, the correspondence of the Jewish treasurer of the caliph of Cordoba, Hisdai ibn Shaprut, on behalf of the Jews in Christian Europe includes contact with the communities of Apulia.[23]

Moreover, the interaction between Jew and Christian may have led to other transfers. A later letter of a Jewish physician from Asia Minor, whose daughter had married a Lombard merchant from one of the Apulian cities, provides circumstantial evidence of a possible route for the dissemination of medical knowledge.[24] The Cairo Genizah, in which this letter is preserved, reveals that the Jews in the Middle East had access to scientific works in Arabic. The medical works contained in one man's library are listed only in a twelfth-century document,[25] but it is legitimate to speculate that such collections existed much earlier.

By the time of the first references to Salerno as a medical centre in the tenth and early eleventh centuries, therefore, southern Italy already had a long history of medical text production and of the transfer of knowledge via saints and other travellers on its roads. As we have already seen, there are frequent references to local physicians in both the Salernitan and Neapolitan evidence prior to that date, and Kristeller acknowledges that this at least establishes a 'flourishing of medical practice in southern Italy.'[26] The later evidence for the school in the eleventh century seems to stress the practical nature of Salernitan medicine over the intellectual. Desiderius, the abbot of Montecasssino and later pope, went there in the late eleventh century. Orderic Vitalis reports that a monk, Rudolf the Badly-Tonsured was equalled in medical arts only by a 'certain matron' when he went to Salerno.

---

[23] J. Mann, *Texts and Studies in Jewish History and Literature*, I (Cincinnati, Ohio, 1931), pp.3-15.

[24] S. D. Goitein, "Sicily, and Southern Italy in the Cairo Geniza documents", *Archivio Storico per la Sicilia Orientale*, LXVII (1971), pp.9-34, at p.13.

[25] See S. D. Goitein, "The medical profession in the light of the Cairo Geniza documents", *Hebrew Union College Annual*, XXXIV (1963), pp.177-94, cited in Shatzmiller, *Jews, Medicine and Medieval Society*, p.13.

[26] P. O. Kristeller, "The school of Salerno: its development and its contribution to the history of learning", *BHM*, XVII (1945), p. 143, n.18.

[27] Kristeller, "School", p.145

Given that it did briefly find fame across Europe, with an anecdotal tale of the bishop of Verdun seeking a cure there in the 980s,[27] and the report that in 1085 princess Sikelgaita, the wife of Robert Guiscard, tried to kill her stepson with poison using the arts she had learnt in the city,[28] the lack of documentation of Salerno's institutional history has been the subject of comment by its historians. Nor is the actual site of the school securely established. In both contexts, historians may have been asking the wrong questions of their available documents. A 'school' does not have to be a formalised institution, so long as its members are recognised as carrying on a local tradition. That the lack of formalised documentation was felt to be a problem earlier than this century is suggested by a notorious forgery of the fifteenth century, in which the twelfth-century king Roger is supposed to have made an agreement with the city of Salerno about the licensing of medical practitioners and the running of the 'school'.[29]

What then are we to make of this? The previous chapters in this study have illustrated the presence of a substantial number of physicians in the communities of southern Italy, with something of a concentration in the more highly-urbanised Campania. It is this tradition which we should mine for information about the possibility of a Salernitan medical school. Any convergence of medics in the tenth and eleventh centuries is likely to have been seen by historians as deliberate, and the growth of schools and university training in the twelfth ensured that Salerno would be swept up into a categorisation that perhaps was not entirely appropriate. As the Jewish traveller Benjamin of Tudela reminds us:

> Inde unius die itinere Salernum devectus sum, urbam medicorum scholis illustrem; in qua Iudaei fere sexcenti erant...[30]

That is, when he visited the city in the mid-twelfth century, the city was famed for its *schools*, not just *a school*. This contemporary evidence conveys the sense of fluidity within the city at that time, and warns us against recognising a definite institution there. Piero Morpurgo is also dubious about the existence of a fully-developed medical school in the eleventh century, and suggests that the city may have been the location of an active book market by the twelfth, leading to its image as a

---

[28] D. Herlihy, *Opera Muliebra: Women and Work in Medieval Europe*, (London, 1990), p.105.
[29] Kristeller, "School", pp.162-4.
[30] Quoted from C. Colafemmina, "L'itinerario pugliese di Beniamino da Tudela", *Archivio Storico Pugliese*, XXVIII (1975), p. 97.

place of learning.[31] Scholars might certainly congregate there, but this does not necessarily mean that the debate they engaged in was at all institutionalised.

Nevertheless, Salerno's fame in the eleventh century was partly due to the undeniable presence in and around the city of men (and women, if we are to believe Orderic Vitalus) skilled and learned in medicine.

A central figure in the development of a Latin *corpus* of medical texts in central-southern Italy may have been bishop Alfanus of Salerno (*fl.* 1058-85), to whom Baader attributes a crucial role in creating a Latin technical terminology when translating Nemesius' *On the Nature of Man*. Such a terminology was an essential precondition to the reception of Arabic medicine in the later eleventh and twelfth centuries.[32] But where did Alfanus gain access to the Greek text in the first place? We know that he was a monk at Montecassino before taking on the archbishopric, and so this may be one possibility. However, historians appear to have ignored a far richer source of material literally on Alfanus' doorstep. For there is plenty of evidence from the tenth century onwards of a Greek presence in and around Salerno and its outlying coastal settlements. In particular, the recent publication of documents relating to the church of St Nicolas di Gallucanta, near Vietri, highlights the activities of Greek monks there. Although we know very little about the internal life of the monastery (for example, we are entirely ignorant of whether it had a *scriptorium*), nor when it gained a Greek community, it is clear that the family patronising it in the eleventh century, descendants of one Lambert the count, had strong associations with medical practitioners in the area. Such links may have arisen from the activities of the monastery itself, which had been founded as a private church dedicated to St Felix in the late tenth century.

Also in the tenth century, the church of St John by the sea in Vietri had been founded by St Sabas, who had lived there for a few years.[33] We have a record of the foundation dated 986, when 'Savas and Cosmas, Greek monks', purchased it (or perhaps paid an entry fee to govern it) from a certain Iaquintus son of Mascini and his

---

[31] P. Morpurgo, "L'ingresso dell'Aristotele Latino a Salerno", in *Rencontres de Cultures*, ed. J. Hamesse and M. Fattori (Louvain-la-Neuve/Cassino, 1990), pp.273-93, at p.273.

[32] G. Baader, "Early medieval Latin adaptations of Byzantine medicine in western Europe", in *Symposium on Byzantine Medicine*, p.259.

[33] *Pergamene di S. Nicola*, p.19.

nephews.[34] Again, this church may have had medical connections, if it is the same St John's mentioned in gifts to the abbey of the Trinity at Cava by Mascinus cleric son of Romaoald in 1064 and Romoald son of Peter, cleric and medic, in 1091.[35]

The evidence is circumstantial of course, but if we add the information that Alfanus in 1057 succeeded a Calabrian Greek, Basil, as abbot of St Benedict's in Salerno before achieving the archbishopric,[36] we see that he had plenty of opportunities to mine the knowledge available locally as well as at Cassino. As Cuozzo points out, Alfanus was already forty when he went to Montecassino, and he only stayed there fifteen months: his intellectual development was surely complete by this time.[37] Indeed, Alfanus extols the virtues of his city's medical tradition, and it is from him that we learn that abbot Desiderius visited the city in search of a cure.[38] The significance of this visit has also, I feel, been overlooked: if Montecassino was a centre of medical learning, surely someone in the community there might have picked up practical skills as well? It seems not: Desiderius had to come to Salerno to receive care, which supports the idea of the city's primacy by the late eleventh century.[39]

In the course of the twelfth century, the medicine of Salerno seems to have become more theoretical and more orientated toward formal, academic medical education.[40] Primacy in the translation work which made this possible must be given to Constantine the African (1010-1087). Constantine, who became a monk under Desiderius' abbacy, translated the *Pantegni* and much more besides from Arabic.[41] However, neither he nor Alfanus, archbishop of Salerno can be directly linked with a medical school as such.[42] Katherine Park is therefore overinterpreting the evidence when she suggests that the school of

---

[34] *CodCav*, II, doc. 382. Unfortunately, the list of books handed over to Iaquintus by the monks does not include any medical texts.

[35] *Pergamene di S. Nicola*, doc. 87 and note. The name Mascinus is not especially common in the Salernitan evidence, and given the frequent practice among southern Italian families of handing down 'lead names' through the generations, it is highly likely that the two transactions in the eleventh century are made by descendants of the original tenth-century author.

[36] *Pergamene di S. Nicola*, p.14.

[37] E. Cuozzo, "Un vescovo della longobardia minore: Alfano arcivescovo di Salerno (d. 1085)", *Campania Sacra*, VI (1975), pp.15-29, at p.17.

[38] Kristeller, "School", p.146.

[39] Of course, since our source for Desiderius' visit is Alfanus, the visit or its purpose may be fictitious and designed to *support* Alfanus' contention.

[40] Siraisi, *Medieval and Early Renaissance Medicine*, p.13.

[41] Siraisi, *Medieval and Early Renaissance Medicine*, p.14.

[42] Kristeller, "School", p.149.

Salerno developed 'in co-operation with the great Benedictine monastery of Montecassino'.[43] Nevertheless, the proximity of the Benedictine house to Salerno may explain why half of the prescriptions in the Salernitan *Antidotarium* are found also in Book X of the Practica of the *Pantegni* of Constantine, a somewhat abbreviated translation of the *Liber Regius* of Ali ibn el-Abbas. The linking of the study of philosophy with medicine at both Salerno and Naples[44] by the end of the twelfth century suggests perhaps that there was more of an intellectual tradition than a practical one. Most texts to come from the city are twelfth-century in date.[45] By the early thirteenth century, Salerno was already in decline. Formal university organisation was not introduced there until after the end of its period as a predominant centre of medical education.[46] Practical medicine, including surgery, seems to have been set apart from the intellectual tradition, and was practised by barbers and women.[47] This separating out of roles may also be reflected in the evidence of the necrology of the church of St Matthew in Salerno, where twelfth- and thirteenth-century names are given the title *doctor in phisica* rather than the earlier, and more general *medicus* found in the charter material.[48]

In a sense, the work done by scholars of medicine to try to establish the existence of a formalised school at Salerno from the tenth century onwards reflects the wealth of evidence for medical practice and texts surviving from before that date and Salerno's later, documented, history as a centre of text production in the twelfth century. And yet the evidence of southern Italian practice throughout the period suggests that it was individuals, not associations, who promoted and spread medical knowledge in the peninsula; and that it is in ecclesiastical circles that much of this dissemination took place. That clerics took the greatest part in such activities is significant, for it lessened the need for the development of a dedicated institution in which medical knowledge could be preserved and disseminated. Montecassino in the ninth and eleventh centuries was already, in some sense, a medical school. Naples in the tenth was a city of lay medical practitioners, and yet has never acquired a 'medical school' in the historiography. Salerno's fame, I think, is partly a result of the

---

[43] Park, "Medicine and society", p.67.

[44] Salerno: P. Kristeller, "Nuovi fonti per la medicina", *Rassegna Storica Salernitana*, (1957), pp.61-75; Naples: M. Fuiano, 'L'insegnamento della medicina a Napoli nei secoli XIII e XIV', *Studi Storici Meridionali*, V (1985), pp.275-85.

[45] Kristeller, "School", p.154.

[46] Siraisi, *Medieval and Early Renaissance Medicine*, p.57.

[47] Fuiano, "Insegnamento", p.276.

[48] See above, chapter 6.

high profile of some of its medical protagonists, especially archbishop Alfanus, whose links with Montecassino, Desiderius and Constantine in a 'golden age' for the abbey naturally lead to the assumption that a renaissance of medical knowledge was taking place. In some senses such a rebirth was happening, with the growth of Arabic influences in western knowledge. But in documenting this, historians have ignored the fact that Salerno as a medical centre has a history long before its textual tradition, and that other parts of the South were also places of medical practice. Instead of attempting to create an entity which may never have existed, it is far more rewarding to document the activities of those whose skills undoubtedly promoted the image of Salerno throughout Europe. In conclusion, we shall see how the different fragments of evidence can be put together, and how the importance of the problem of a 'medical school' at Salerno diminishes.

CONCLUSIONS:
INTEGRATING THE SOUTHERN ITALIAN EVIDENCE

The chapters in this book have attempted to address a variety of themes with bearing on the health of the early medieval population of the peninsula. They have drawn on different types of source material, each with its own problems of interpretation. Each has, in the past, been studied in isolation: the medical texts have attracted the attention of palaeographers and medical historians; the charters have been mined for the illumination they shed on social structures; the archaeology will gradually provide more information on those whose lives may never show up in the written evidence; and charter evidence and surviving structures and landscapes inform us about the conditions in which the population lived. In this study I have tried to investigate these very disparate strands of evidence to address a basic problem for the medieval population: ill health and how it was alleviated. In this final chapter, I shall attempt to demonstrate my belief that these strands can be read as parts of a whole. They can be linked to each other to provide a greater insight into how different classes of an early medieval society faced up to disease. I am not arguing for a coherent, managed healthcare system in southern Italy. Nothing in this area of the peninsula could have been achieved on such a scale, even if anyone had wanted to create such a system. (The regulation of later rulers such as Frederick II was, I would argue, prompted more by the desire to raise revenue from regulation than any care for the health of the population.) Simply, the pattern of southern Italian historiography has led to many, excellent local studies, following the scheme dictated by the fragmented political history of the area, but little attempt to stand back and look critically at the whole. As a result, the common links between many, disparate pieces of evidence may have been overlooked.

The key to understanding the patterns of medical knowledge and dissemination in southern Italy may lay in examining the political life of the peninsula. In an earlier chapter I stressed the probability that the medical practitioners we see documented, the *medici*, congregated in places where they were likely to receive patronage. Thus although we have documents from rural settings, most of the documented *medici* are seen in towns, whence political power was exercised and where the nobility lived. The political changes occurring between the ninth and eleventh centuries had implications for all aspects of medical practice. *Medici* might have to move to gain employment again; monasteries might find themselves subject to conflicting claims of sovereignty; the arrival of outsiders may have brought new and differing theoretical ideas and opened up the peninsula to the wider Mediterranean. All of this might affect the patterns of written knowledge that survive. A second, strong thread linking many of the themes addressed in this study has been the intervention of the Christian church, although, as we have seen, there were flourishing medical traditions outside the Christian milieu. How did the political and religious life of the peninsula from the ninth to the twelfth centuries influence the development of medical knowledge and practice?

In the ninth century, much of the peninsula suffered from Arab raids, but this also opened it up to other parts of the Mediterranean apart from the Byzantine world. Bari was briefly an emirate until 871, when it was taken over by the Byzantines with the help of the Frankish emperor Louis. The cities of the Campanian coast, at the same time, drifted away from Byzantine sovereignty and openly colluded with Saracen mercenaries. Michael McCormick has recently argued, convincingly it seems to me, for a transfer of travellers in the Mediterranean onto Arabic routes and shipping.[1] This may explain the prominance of Alexandrian texts appearing in early Italo-Greek collections. At the same time there is evidence of a flourishing text tradition in central-southern Italy. At Montecassino, abbot Bertarius produced a medical treatise. Strikingly, his close contemporary and the *praepositus* of the monastery, Ragemfrid, is also described as *medicus* in three documents preserved in the later *Register* of Peter the Deacon.[2] It may be coincidence that at this time (883-900), the Cassinese monks were esconced at Capua, their own monastery having been sacked by the Arabs in 883. Capua, as we know from the Chronicle of Ahimaaz, had a flourishing Jewish community in the ninth century. Nearby, the first *medicus*, Iosep, is recorded in the documents from the Cava archive. Iosep, however, appears not to have lived in Salerno but in the far South of the city's territory in the Magliano area of Lucania. The significance of this fact may have been overlooked for if, as Kreutz argues, he was Jewish, he might have had contacts with other communities. If a Christian, the fact that he ap-

---

[1] M. McCormick, "Mediterranean communications in the eighth and ninth centuries: the prosopographical evidence", in *L'Eredità di Arechi. Convegno Internazionale, Ravello 17-19 June 1995*, ed. J. Mitchell and P. Peduto (forthcoming).

[2] All three are documents of the princes of Salerno, dated 883, 897 and 900: H. Taviani-Carozzi, *La Principauté Lombarde de Salerne*, 2 vols, (Rome, 1991), I, p.456, n.28.

pears to have lived less than fifty kilometres (as the crow flies), from the monastery of St Anastasius at Carbone, a possible centre of text production, and certainly on a main route from Calabria into Campania, may be significant. It is unlikely that he, as a country practitioner, was on the mainstream of the transmission of written knowledge, but people from the southern tip of Salernitan territory nevertheless travelled to the city, about 30km away, to make their documents. So the movement of knowledge was entirely possible.

In the tenth century, the Arabic presence was still more pronounced, as Sicily remained out of Byzantine hands. Tenth-century saints' lives provide evidence of continued medical activity. The concerted reconquest under Basil I in the late ninth century laid the foundations of an expansion of the Greek population in the southernmost parts of Italy until the Norman conquest in the eleventh century. The expansion of the Greek community is embodied by the travels of the Calabrian saints northwards, and the foundation of new Greek monasteries in Campania and Lazio in these centuries. For example, St Nilus's travels brought him, and presumably knowledge, northwards to both of these regions. At the same time, St Peter *de Foresta* was founded near Pontecorvo in 999, run by Greek monks, and St John near Vietri also dates to this period. The usual explanation for this phenomenon is sought in the persecution of Greeks in Sicily by the Arabs from the ninth century onwards, leading to an exodus to the mainland and further North. However, a recent revision of this picture has been proposed by Vera von Falkenhausen, who argues that very few Greeks in fact left the island. She suggests that we should seek the origins of the immigrants in Rome or the Peloponnese, the latter invaded by the far less tolerant Slavs.[3] This theory gains weight if we remember that St Nilus himself may have had dealings with the Saracens. One of his remedies for a mentally-ill person sounds very Arab-influenced. Of course, if the Greek monks of Campania did come from further afield than has always been thought, this only widens the possibility of new medical influences reaching southern Italy in the tenth century.

There is evidence of the ability to translate from Greek to Latin in Naples in this century. The ease with which Greek was understood in the city at this date may be indicated by passages from hagiographic texts written at Naples. In the tenth-century *Vita* of Athanasius, bishop of Naples in the late ninth century, the author comments on the fact that he was able to read both Greek and Latin texts, and to

---

[3] *Le Pergamene di S. Nicola*, pp.15-16.

summarise the contents of a text in one language in the other.[4] The
continued singing of both Greek and Latin liturgies at Naples in the
tenth century is also attested to in John the Deacon's account of the
translation of St Sossus.[5]

Jewish communities continue to be attested, with documented
north African connections. The early tenth century also saw the rise
of autonomous small states further north, with opportunities for the
establishment of an intense court culture in Naples and Salerno. This
is reflected in lively exchanges between both cities and Constantinople. Naples had a particularly close relationship, which resulted in the
import of a number of eastern goods, including texts. The dukes
themselves were interested in the patronage of writing and translation
work, but the only attested medical book was owned by a church.
Nevertheless, the majority of medics here in the tenth century were
laymen. Clerics were the largest group of medics in Salerno, and they
included the future bishop, Peter. Medical practice in Amalfi may
also have been confined to the church. Beccaria cites a document of
1007 from Atrani, in which one John the priest leaves to the monastery of St Maria a *flores evangeliorum cum aliquanta antidota scripta*.[6] The
lack of a stable ducal dynasty may explain why medical practitioners
preferred to congregate in nearby Salerno. Gaeta did have a very
strong ruling dynasty, but this city had a very lively exchange with
Naples and perhaps the larger centre offered better opportunities.

The eleventh century was a time of upheaval even before the
Normans. The conquests of Guaimarius IV were I think *crucial* to our
understanding of the development of medical practice. His establishment of a super-principate created in Salerno a focal point for the
whole of southern Italy. In the mid-eleventh century he was the only
viable ruler, until he was assassinated, but he had in the meantime
conquered most of the South. At the same time, the ruling dynasty of
Naples was temporarily ousted by Pandolf Ironhead of Capua; the
dynasty at Gaeta also fell, and that at Amalfi suffered a number of
factional changes of power. So really Salerno and Capua (less well
documented and itself taken over by Guaimarius) formed the main
centres of patronage. Salernitan territory also reached right down
into Lucania and northern Calabria, and so picked up influences
from monastic institutions there.

---

[4] *Vita Athanasii Episcopi Neapolitani*, in *MGH SRL*, p.441.
[5] *Iohannis Translatio Sancti Sosii*, in *MGH SRL*, p.463.
[6] A. Beccaria, *I Codici di Medicina del Periodo Presalernitano (Secoli IX, X e XI)* (Rome, 1956), p.84.

Who would foster this network of knowledge? Strikingly, a document of 1041 shows Guaimarius conceding a number of Jews at Capua, including the son of a *medicus*, to his count of the palace, Grimoald.[7] Guaimarius is also credited by the chronicler of Montecassino, Leo of Ostia, with summoning Alfanus from the abbey to become archbishop in Salerno.[8] Alfanus had been a monk there for two years, and was a friend and close contemporary of abbot Desiderius. It is interesting to note the presence in Salerno in 1078 of an Alfanus *cleric and medic*; this is unlikely to be the bishop, but must surely be a relative?[9]

So did Salernitan medical fame arise from or cause the clustering of eminent men we see in the late eleventh century? Did the triumvirate of Alfanus, Constantine and Desiderius move behind the activity? Or was the sudden opening out of the Salernitan principate in the middle of the century the key factor? Did Alfanus gain inspiration from texts he might meet for the first time then? Or was he drawing on his experiences at Montecassino, which had at least in the ninth century evidence of text production? I have already suggested that he had other, more local, sources besides Montecassino to draw upon.

The importance of early medieval southern Italy to the history of medical practice cannot be overstressed. Although it provides relatively little new material to deepen our understanding of diagnostic methods or innovative remedies in this period, it does furnish us with major information on the environment, diet, and day-to-day lives of its population and their interaction with those who provided care when they fell ill. The evidence is also filled with the possibilities of living in a multiracial, multilingual society. Latins, Greeks, Christians, Jews, and Moslems all inhabited parts of the peninsula. The literate culture of all but the last group is available to be studied, thanks to its preservation by powerful Christian abbeys and cohesive Jewish communities which lasted until Frederick II's programme of expulsion in the thirteenth century. Alongside the works produced in these milieux, we have thousands of charters. Whilst the vast majority of these do not concern medical practice or illness, the handful which do outline for us the mentality of this population when faced with disease. Even taking into account the obvious problems of preservation by those in whose interests it was to promote themselves, that is, the churches, we still get an overwhelming impression that faith was as

---

[7] Taviani-Carozzi, *Principauté*, 448. The concession is at the abbey of Montevergine, Archive, *pergamena* 47.

[8] Taviani-Carozzi, *Principauté*, 1009.

[9] *CodCav* X, doc. 98.

important to a successful cure as practical medicine. Indeed, we never see the numerous documented *medici* in a practising situation. Is this attributable to the nature of the evidence? It would appear not: when Adelina, a royal nurse, provided a valued service, she was rewarded in two charters with parcels of land. So we might expect that a grateful patient's gift to a successful doctor would take the same form. The fact that no such charter survives is of course no indication that it never existed, but then perhaps the doctor's fee was considered ample reward by those who sought their services.

The most striking feature of southern Italy's history in this period is the sheer movement of people along its roads, rivers and coasts. I have dealt elsewhere with this phenomenon of movement between the territories of the Tyrrhenian coast, but longer distances were also covered. The peregrinations of St Nilus have already been highlighted: his journey from Calabria to Lazio suggests the possibilities for a really determined traveller.[10] Long-distance travel, however, seems to have been something of a hallmark of the southern Italian Greek saint. Although Nilus's journeys appear to have been entirely genuine, we must be wary of accepting at face value the pilgrimages to Rome, for example, that many of his contemporaries made. Such a journey may indeed have been part of an unofficial *cursus honorum* for the saintly, but can equally be ascribed to the literary borrowings of one hagiographer from another. In favour of much genuine travel, however, is the fact that much of the hagiography of Calabrian and Sicilian saints was produced within a generation of their deaths. Whilst the biographers may have been writing with didactic aims, it is difficult to see why they should invent such journeys.

Natives from the Campanian cities, particularly Amalfitans, travelled to and settled in the coastal ports of Apulia. We must not forget either that the Amalfitans founded their own monastery on Mt Athos at the end of the tenth century. Pilgrims from the Lombard principalities made the arduous journey to the shrine of St Michael Archangel on Monte Gargano: a valuable chapter from the *Vita* of St Fantinus records that he and his companion, 'with difficulty' (*molis*), achieved the journey to the mountain from Calabria in eighteen days.[11] And all the while traffic frequented the sea routes along the coasts and across the Mediterranean to Sicily, North Africa and Con-

---

[10] He was not the only Calabrian to settle further North: one John *Calabritano*, 'now of Mairanu', appears as a tenant of land in that district near Salerno in 1020: *CodCav*, V, doc. 726.

[11] *Vita di San Fantino*, chapter 26. One assumes that this journey, like all of Fantinus' recorded overland travel, was accomplished on foot.

stantinople. In the 1130s, letters from the Cairo Genizah inform us, a ship from Gaeta regularly plied the route between Spain and Egypt, and was used by the correspondents.[12]

This movement, coupled with the mingling of different cultures in the towns of the South, should alert the historian of medicine in the peninsula to the possibility of mutual exchange between different communities when it came to healthcare practices and ideas. It was this relative openness that allowed a Saracen, Constantine, to become a monk at Montecassino and provide his new community with translations of Arabic medical texts. We know of at least one convert from Judaism to Christianity, Lando son of Samuel, who made a gift of all his property to the bishopric of Caiazzo in 1060.[13] Unfortunately, the possessions he lists do not include any books.

The crossover happened in the other direction, too. We know very little about converts to Islam and Judaism. The texts that we have usually feature those distinguished figures of society whose apostasy gained them infamy with the Christian community.[14] But these converts were able to gain access to the written culture of their chosen religious communities: again, even if there are no overt references to medicine, we should not assume that information of this type was not exchanged along with religious teaching, nor that such conversions were a rarity in this period.[15]

It cannot be argued with any conviction that southern Italy contributed anything particularly new to the study of medicine in the centuries leading up to 1100. What was special about this area was the combination of so many infuences in a comparatively limited geographical area from the ninth century onwards. Christian sources speak with animosity about the Arabs in the later ninth century, but still the merchants of the Tyrrhenian cities did business with them. The Jewish community was strong and confident throughout this

---

[12] Goitein, "Sicily and southern Italy", pp.12-13.

[13] *Caiazzo*, doc. 5.

[14] For example, in 1001/2, the *protospatharius* Gregory Trachaniotes condemned the 'unbeliever and apostate' Loukas, a convert to Islam, who had rebelled and seized some lands near Tricarico in Apulia: A. Guillou and W. Holtzmann, "Zwei Katepansurkunden aus Tricarico", *QFIAB*, XLI (1961), p.12. Around 1078 Andreas, the archbishop of Bari, converted to Judaism, and we have the autobiography of John-Obadiah, a Norman convert to the same faith in 1102: S. D. Goitein, "Sicily and southern Italy", pp.17-18.

[15] Indeed, church councils as early as the ninth century had preached against those who 'judaised', that is, rested on Saturday and ate a kosher diet: J.-M. Martin, "L'ambiente longobardo, greco, islamico e normanno nel Mezzogiorno", in *Storia dell'Italia Religiosa I: L'Antichità e il Medioevo*, ed. A. Vauchez (Bari, 1993), pp.193-242 at 198.

period, and had frequent contact with other parts of the Mediterranean. The ease of travel and exchange within the peninsula, in marked contrast to other parts of Europe where 'foreigners' were viewed with suspicion, is the key to understanding why so many strands of medical practice could survive and flourish here, and why the epithet *medicus* brought only prestige to its user.

A brief period of political ambition on the part of the prince of Salerno may have been the catalyst which dictated developments later on, however. The Salernitan hegemony over much of the South, combined with the apogee of one great monastery, Montecassino and the foundation of another at Cava, plus the exchanges and travel just outlined, meant that southern Italy in the early eleventh century provided a fertile garden in which the seeds of medical knowledge and practice could grow. Whilst Naples, so cosmopolitan in the tenth century, turned in upon itself and featured less and less in the political developments of this period, Salerno looked aggressively outwards, and may have become something of a magnet for those seeking patronage of any kind. The city was growing apace, as contracts providing for the erection of new houses on empty land reveal. This was *opulenta Salernum*, a city of opportunity.[16] Hence medics, just as other professionals and tradesmen, would be attracted here. But it is possibly time to jettison the notion of any kind of organised medical school in the city in this period. To outsiders, such gatherings of medics, apparently handing on their skills, may have seemed like a school or, as Benjamin of Tudela recorded, schools. But the reality is likely to have been much less institutionalised. Perhaps the gatherings happened around particular churches or streets in the city: we just do not know. Salerno's close links with both Montecassino and Cava perhaps make it inevitable that the actions of literate men (and women) should be recorded and preserved for posterity in a much more systematic way than for other parts of the South. It is striking that the other centre of medical excellence, which comes to light in the twelfth century, was the Reggio di Calabria/Messina area. But the pattern here was the same: would we have so much evidence of medical practice if Sicily and Calabria had not formed a focus of Norman power and monastic patronage?

Ultimately, a medieval charter can only provide a crystallised view of a particular moment in time, and the fact that *medici* show up in these

---

[16] The best short overview of the city in this period is P. Delogu, *Mito di una Città Meridionale* (Naples, 1977), chapter 4.

individual snapshots is of no value whatsoever unless we can set them into a wider world. The lay tradition of medical practice centred around the precociously urbanised Tyrrhenian region, and later around here and the straits of Messina. The ecclesiastical tradition, to which we can link much of the treatise material, was less focused, with a major centre at Montecassino, before and after its sacking, and further activity in the Cilento and Calabria among saints and their monastic communities. Every so often, these traditions intersected with each other and with the Jewish practitioners who seem to have been present in the South throughout our period, despite not being heavily-documented in what is a Christian archive. And all three strands of medical practice on the peninsula were touched by the Arab presence in Sicily and North Africa. Southern Italy was linked to much of the wider Mediterranean through trade, political ties and hostile acts. The latter did not have any significant impact on the other two. Rather, the continued movement between the peninsula and the wider world, and the ease of exchange within it, led to a medical culture that attracted visitors from the rest of western Europe.

APPENDICES

A MIRACLE OF ST TROPHIMENA PROVIDES
A CURE FOR THEODONANDA

35 Piissimi quoque temporibus Pulcharis prefecturii, puella quaedam, nomine Theodonanda, tradita est viro cuidam, nomine Mauro in matrimonio. Haec itaque viro suo copulata, quia necdum nubilis erat, plurimis moribunda iacens temporibus, quotidie sui cruciatus miserrimum praestolabatur interitum. Eodem itaque tempore archiater Salerni non mediocri medicinae salubritate pollebat Hieronymus, qui dum sibi adducta esset a parentibus, ut aliquo ei proficuo medicinae subveniret remedio, respuens eam, proiecit dicens: Incurabilis est passio eius, nequibo eam curare. Deprecantibus autem illis, ut sui misereretur, tandem aliquando precibus victus, interrogavit: Quot temporibus hoc laboraret exitio? Responderunt dicentes: Mensibus quatuor. Quapropter adducti desperationis tristes miseria venimus, ut, praeveniente clementia Dei, per te sospitatem recipiat.

36 His itaque precibus archiater, Dei famulus, victus, coepit suae artis quaerere librorum immensa volumina, si forte titulum infirmitatis huius per lectionis curam posset agnoscere: cumque has, et illas legeret valitudines passionem, et nusquam reperire potuisset, quali laboraret incommodo, ait: Regredimini fratres hinc, quia nullum medicinae solatium ei praebere queo; hoc autem scitote, quia aut misericordia Dei salvanda est, aut iusto iudicio punienda. His auditis, amarao luctu flere coeperunt, et valedicentes venerunt Rheginnas, ut depositam, secundum archiatri dictionem, ibi lugerent. Inter haec igitur ista et illa loquentes, mutuis exhortationibus surrexerunt, ut eam deferrent ad basilicam S. Trophimenis (erat autem in praediolo suo haud procul ab eiusdem ecclesiae septis). Adducta igitur puella ad sanctae tumulum Trophimenis apprehendens eam quaedam sanctimonialis, nomine Agatha, iactavit eam feminecem ante altare orans, et cum parentibus triduo exitum expectabat ipsius. Valetudo autem corporis talis erat; agitabat enim brachia sua sursum, rursum... deponens inferius, velut milvus, cum longo volatu aeram verberat.

Translation

35   In the time of the most pious prefect Pulchari, a certain girl named Theodonanda was given in marriage to a man named Mauro. Having consummated the marriage, because she was not yet nubile, she lay close to death for a long time, each day she expected the wretched end to her torture. At that time there was a powerful doctor, Hieronymus, [providing] good health with the best medicines at Salerno. When her parents brought her to him, in order that he might find some medicinal remedy for her, he rejected her, saying, 'Her illness is incurable, I will not be able to help her.' They pleaded with him to show her some pity and after several prayers, overcome, he asked, 'How long has this discharge troubled her?' They replied, 'Four months. Because of this, brought to desperation by her harsh misery, we came so that, with the mercy of God, she might receive good health through you.'

36   At these pleas the doctor, a servant of God, was overcome and began to consult immense volumes of books on his art, to see if by chance he could through reading recognise a cure for this illness: when he had read through all his diseases, and could find nowhere which illness she was suffering from, he said, 'Go away from here brothers, because I cannot offer her any medical help; know this, however; either she will be cured through the mercy of God, or she will be punished through just judgement.' Hearing these words, they began to shed bitter tears, and bidding farewell they came to Reginna so that, just as the doctor had said, they might mourn their dead. And discussing their plight and coming to agreement they got up to take her to the basilica of St Trophimena (it was not at all far from the same church's enclosure). The girl was brought to the tomb of St Trophimena, a nun named Agatha took her and laid her ?womanishly [in a ladylike way?] in front of the altar, praying, and then waited with her parents for three days for her to come out. Such was the illness of her body that she waved her arms back and forth ... laying down underneath just like a bird of prey calls with a long flight in the air.

37 At cum his languoribus fatigaretur puella, reliquerunt eam parentes eius cum praedicta sanctimoniale, paululum accepit ante altare soporis, et ecce puella pedetentim exiens, flumen petebat sola; necdum enim fluminis alveus properaverat. Et ecce vidit pucherrimam puellarum puellam, dantem sibi tres in dorso ferulas, ac dicentem: Cur ausa es de templo exire, revertere, et nostrum semper habeto pavorem. Cumque puella trepidans iret, et sanctimoniali narraret, gavisa protinus est, ut sancta ei Trophimenes specialiter appareret. His igitur beneficiis delibata, videns iterum eadem sanctimonialis oleo pavimentum sudare nimis, odorisque plenum, intentissime Deum orans, sanctam invocans Trophimenem; iussit, ut exuviis corpus exueret ... Quae unxit corpusculum eius oleo sancto, et statim sana est facta ab infirmitate.

37 And when the girl was tired by these fatigues, her parents left her with the nun, and she slept a little in front of the altar, and behold the girl went out on tiptoe and headed for the river alone; for the hollow riverbed was not yet hastened. And behold she saw the most beautiful girl of all, giving her three blows on the back and saying, 'Why have you dared to leave the church, go back, and always fear me.' When the agitated girl went back and told the nun, she rejoiced ceaselessly, that St Trophimena had appeared to her specially. Having sampled these benefits, the nun saw the pavement sweating large quantities of oil, full of perfume, and prayed intently to God, invoking the saint; she ordered the girl to undress and anointed her tiny body with the holy oil, and immediately she was cured from her illness.

URSUS THE DOCTOR ON TANCRED'S
ILLEGITIMATE BIRTH

From: Peter of Eboli, 'De Rebus Siculis Carmen', chapter VIII

lines 212—233

Hoc ego dum dubia meditaretur mente profundum,
Que res nature dimidiasset opus,
Egregius doctor et vir pietatis amicus
Explicuit causas talibus Ursus michi:
'Ut puer incipiat, opus est ut uterque resudet,
Ex quo perfectus nascitur orbe puer.
Non in Tancredo sementat uterque parentum,
Et, si sementent, non bene conveniunt.
Dux alter de stirpe ducum, de stegmate regum,
Altera de media stirpe creata fuit.
Naturam natura fugit: fornacis aborret
Gemma luem nec humus nobilitate coit.
Evomit humorem tam vilis texta virilem:
Concipitur solo semine matris homo.
Quantum materies potuit pauperrima matris,
Contulit et modicum materiavit opus.
Hunc habuisse patrem credamus nomine, non re:
Rem trahit a matre dimidiatus homo.
Qui purgata solo bene culto semina mandant,
In iolium versos sepe queruntur agros.
Sepius infelix comceptum vacca iuvencum
Monstriferumque pecus mollis abortit ovis.

CHRONOLOGY OF MAJOR EARLY MEDIEVAL
DISASTERS IN ITALY (AFTER CORRADI)

Medieval chroniclers were acutely sensitive to natural and manmade disasters. They also associated periods of poor health or bad harvests with signs and portents such as earthquakes or comets. What follows summarises Corradi's list of such events.

Date	Event
512	eruption of Vesuvius and earthquake
531-99	Justinianic plague, including the arrival of the Goths in Italy in 537, carrying plague with them to Rome; the surrender of Naples in 543, still in the grip of plague. In 563 the continuing plague *inguinaria* was noted in Paul the Deacon's *Historia Langobardorum*, Lombards arrived in 568 and there was famine; 590 another *inguinaria* plague
599	sickness in Rome: Gregory the Great, letter 50, writing in bed because of gout, commented on the 'populo tanti febrium languores irruerunt'
615	earthquake and flood in Rome: people dying of swellings
667	plague in Rome
680	high mortality in Rome and other northern cities
684	Vesuvius erupted
721	'Eo anno primo aprilis fuit mortalitas magna in civitate Neapolis, et mortua est decima pars personarum hominum et mulierum'
722	'In Campania Italiae frumentum combustum et legumina ceciderunt de coelo tamquam pluvia'
746-8	plague began in Sicily and Calabria 'velut igni sensim depascens'
767	plague 'quae medicis inguinaria vocatur' in Naples
832	Saracens invade Sicily
856	Tiber flooded, and an epidemic of *angine* (Rosen, *History of Public Health*, 7, equates this with difficulty in swallowing and inflammatory disease of throat = diphtheria?)
863	Naples: great snows
868	mortality of men and beasts in Naples

873	Benevento and Salerno hit by *cavalette* and *bruchi*, bringing poverty to all of Italy
877	*dolor oculorum*, plague and coughs in Italy and Germanic areas
878	siege of Syracuse by Saracens left citizens paying inflated prices for wheat, eating flesh of corpses, spreading disease
940-1	famine in Sicily
949	great disease in Salerno and Benevento
977	Salerno and Calabria great snows
992	great rains, poverty in Naples
993	plague in Capua; Vesuvius erupts
995	drought May-Dec in Italy
999-1000	Vesuvius erupts
1004	disease and hunger in Rome
1005-7	9 months of drought; poverty and plague; Saracen invasion of Calabria and Puglia
1011	wet winter with snow 2 months, wind and cold. Plants dried up, animals died of hunger, everyone on diet of *herbas agrestas* (Naples)
1015	*cavalette* May/June Calabria and Benevento
1028/9	rains 3 years in a row
1048	hunger because of dryness and cold
1079	principality of Salerno so cold in January that rivers froze. *Poscia* and illness and poverty
1083	Cava: fever with *peticulis* and *parotibus* and death of 9 brothers, 2 oblates and 4 lay servants
1084	great hunger and death
1102	hunger and death around Benevento
1105	snow Jan/Feb
1108	vines failed
1120	intensely hot May (Naples)
1139	Vesuvius erupts - dust over Salerno, Benevento, Naples and Capua
1169	huge earthquake Sicily 4 Feb, Catania ruined, 15000 dead inc bishop

A SURVEY OF MINIMUM AGES AT GAETA

Sample taken from *Codex Diplomaticus Cajetanus*. Only those appearing twice or more were counted. A minimum age of twelve was assumed for legal competence.

Name	First appears	Last appears	Minimum age (12+)
John	787	855	80
Elizabeth	839	866	39
Constantine	839	866	39
Marinus	839	866	39
Mercurius	851	862	23
Bonus	855	867	24
Docibilis I	867	906	51
Kampulus	890	949	71
Anatolius	890	918	40
Benedict	890	903	25
John I	890	933	55
Anatolius	906	924	30
Leo	906	930	36
Maria	906	924	30
Christopher	909	919	22
Stephen	914	923	21
Docibilis II	914	954	52
Stephen	922	936	26
Rodeipert	924	954	42
John II	933	962	41
Bona	934	959	49*
Leo	934	959	37
Leo	935	962	39
Docibilis	937	963	38
Atenolf	939	978	51
Gregory	939	981	54
Constantine	941	994	65
Leo	941	963	34

* Bona's age can be increased by at least 12, as her son appears with her in 934.

Name	First appears	Last appears	Minimum age (12+)
Peter Mirus	941	962	33
Marinus	945	984	51
Mirus	950	959	21
Gaetanus	950	964	26
Kampulus	957	974	29
Marinus	959	1020	73
Kampulus	963	974	23
Constantine	963	984	33
Ramfus	972	1041	81
John	976	996	32
Kampulus	978	1042	76
Kampulus	978	1019	43
John III	978	999	33
Docibilis	980	991	23
Docibilis	980	1010	42
Landolf	981	1013	44
Kampulus	983	993	22
Leo	991	1026	47
Sergius	991	1071	92
Maria	992	1026	46
Leo	992	1010	30
John IV	993	1010	29
Mastalus	999	1042	55
Mauro	999	1008	21
John	999	1006	19
John	1000	1032	44
Emilia	1002	1029	39
Gregory	1002	1024	34
John V	1002	1032	42
Marinus	1006	1021	27
Constantine	1009	1042	45
Marinus	1010	1024	26
Sergia	1017	1031	26
Docibilis	1020	1053	45
John	1020	1036	29
Leo	1020	1067	59
Peter	1020	1048	40
Ugo	1023	1040	29
Kampulus	1025	1036	23
Leo	1025	1036	23
John	1025	1041	28

Name	First appears	Last appears	Minimum age (12+)
Ederado	1025	1053	40
Leo	1026	1040	26
Gemma	1028	1053	37
Leo	1028	1049	33
Marinus	1030	1062	44
Franco	1030	1039	21
Letitia	1031	1054	35
Constantine	1038	1068	42
John	1040	1079	51
Atenolf	1047	1058	23
John	1052	1064	24
Stephen	1052	1087	47
John	1056	1064	20
John	1057	1068	23
Bernard	1058	1071	25
Marinus	1058	1084	38
Docibilis	1058	1123	77
Kampulus	1063	1071	20
Leo	1064	1089	37
Peter	1064	1091	39
Marenda	1064	1089	37
John	1067	1084	29
Mirus	1071	1096	37
Leo	1071	1093	34
Constantine	1091	1124	45
Anatolius	1094	1120	38
Stephen	1105	1124	31
Andrea	1105	1117	24

EXTANT MEDICAL MANUSCRIPTS
FROM SOUTHERN ITALY

(This list is based on information in Beccaria, *Codici di Medicina*, Morpurgo, "L'ingresso", and Ieraci Bio, "Trasmissione" up to the twelfth century. I am not aware of any other extant mss.)

Date	Texts	Origin	Shelfmark
7c	Dioscurides *Materia Medica*, alphabetical	Rome/S Italy	Neap Gr 1
8c	Five Greek medical mss from 5th-6th C		Neap Lat 2.ii
	Paul of Aegina's *Epitomae Medicae*, bks IV-VI	Italo-Greek	Bruxell Gr IV 459
9c	Dioscurides *Materia Medica*, original version		Paris Gr 2179
	Galen, *Succedaneis*, abbot Bertarius's work	Beneventan script	Casin Lat V 69
	Apuleius, Sextus Placitus, Dioscurides	S Italy	Laur LXXIII 41 ii
	Fragments and treatise on cautery	S Italy	Laur LXXIII 41 i
	Palimpsest of recipes	S Italy	Rome Cap S Pietro H4
	Aristotelian scientific works, list of Hippocratic works	Salento?	Vindobon. phil. gr.100
945	Libri medicinales, Galenum, Aforismum et Genicia et Asclepium given to Montecassino	Larino, Molise	Reg Pet Diac no 211
10c	Dioscurides *Materia Medica* 6th C version	S Italy	Munich Lat 337
	Galen compilation 'given to St Vincent'	S Italy	Vienna 68

	Contents	Origin/Script	Shelfmark
	Aphorisms, Galen's *De Methodo Medendi ad Glauconem*, Latin version of Stephen of Athens' Commentary on Hippocrates	Beneventan script	Hunter Lat V.3.2
	Galen, *De Methodo Medendi ad Glauconem, De Pulsibus ad Tirones, Definitiones Medice*, Oribasius' *Eclogae Medicamentum*, Stephen of Athens' *De Febrium*, Paul of Aegina *Epitomae Medicae* bk VI, Leo *Synopsis Artis Medicae* (9C), eye cures from Galen?	Asia Minor/ S Italy Italo-Greek	Paris suppl Gr 446 Messan Gr 84
	Aetius of Amida, *Libri Medicinales*, bks I-III *Prognosticon*, Theofilus' *Commentary on the Aphorisms*, Galen *De Methodo Medendi ad Glauconem* Stephen of Athens' *Commentary on the Hippocratic Aphorisms*	Italo-Greek	Vat Gr 2254
	Signa mortifera iuxta Hippocratis, Galen *De Methodo Medendi ad Glauconem* bk I, Latin excerpts of Alexander of Tralles' *Therapeutica*, Stephen of Athens' *Commentary on the Hippocratic Aphorisms*	Beneventan script	Casin Lat V 97
	Stephen of Athens' *Commentary on Hipp Aphorisms*		Scor 90 Σ II 10
10-11c	Dioscurides *Materia Medica* bk V, excerpts of Alexander of Tralles' *Therapeutica*, Paul of Aegina's *Epitomae Medicae* bks II, III and VI, *Geoponica*, anonymous treatises on diet, pulse, eyes, hair, urine, ?Soranus weights and measures	Malvito, Calabria	Paris suppl Gr 1297F

Date	Texts	Origin	Shelfmark
10-11c	Latin version Paul of Aegina's *Epitomae Medicae*, Beccaria: made under abbot Desiderius at MC	S Italy	Casin Lat V 351
1007	*aliquanta antidota scripta* with a *flores evangeliorum* given to church of St Maria by John the priest of Fontanella	Atrani	Camera, *Memorie* I,221
11c	Translation of Iohannitius from Arabic and other recipes	Beneventan script	Casin Lat 255
	unidentified palimpsests	S Italy	Rome, Angelica 1496
	gynaecological compilation of Muscio and Cleopatra, Oribasius and recipes group of texts by Apuleius	S Italy	Copenhagen 1653
	fragmented version of Iohannitius	S Italy	Turin K IV 3
	Apuleius, commentary on *Aphorisms*, Oribasius, Theodore Priscian, Quintus Serenus, Galen *De Methodo Medendi ad Glauconem*, Latin version of Stephen of Athens' *Commentary on the Hippocratic Aphorisms*, recipes and minor works	S Italy	Paris N A 1628
	Dioscurides, excerpts of *Dynameron* attributed to Alexander of Tralles, a practical pharmacy, recipes, ps. Dioscurides *De Venenis*	Dalmatia/Apulia	Vat Barb Lat 160
		Calabria/Campania	Scor 37 (R.III.3)

	Contents	Origin/Script	Manuscript
	Galen *De Succedaneis* Manual of practical medicine *Prognosticon*, Metrodora *De Mulierum Morbis*, anonymous weights and measures, recipe for a miraculous salt, other recipes and amulets	Beneventan miniscule Calabria/Campania	?Haun Gks 1653.4 Laur XXXV 3
	Theofilus *De Pulsibus* and *De Urinis*	Calabria/Campania ?	Laur LXXV 3 ?
11-12c	Theofilus *De Urinis* and *Commentary on the Hippocratic Aphorisms*	Italo-Greek	Laur LXXIV 11
	ps. Hippocratic text, miscellaneous others, astronomical texts, physiologus, *voces animalium*	Otranto	Ambr Gr 1 (A45 sup)
12c	*Aphorisms, Prognosticon*, ps.Hippocratic letters, Theofilus *Commentary on Hippocratic Aphorisms*	Reggio style script	Urb Gr 64
	John of Alexandria (attrib.) *Commentary on Hippocrates' De Popularibus Morbis*, Theofilus *De Urinis*, Abu Jaffar *Ephodia* Hippocratic corpus	Straits of Messina Sicily	Vat Gr 300 Vat Gr 276

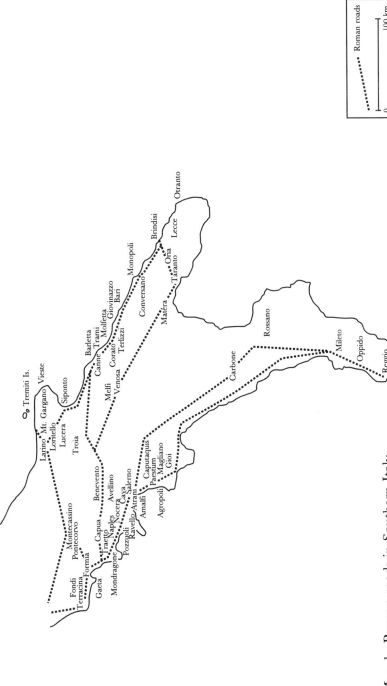

Map 1. Roman roads in Southern Italy

PLATES

Plate 1. Salerno, aqueduct

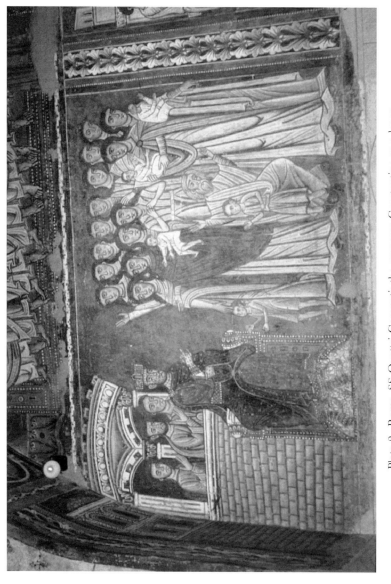

Plate 2. Rome, SS Quattri Coronati: the emperor Constantine as a leper

Plate 3. Trota of Salerno as depicted in a
14th-century manuscript (photograph courtesy
of the Wellcome Institute Library, London)

Plate 4. Salerno, tomb of Sergius Capograssa

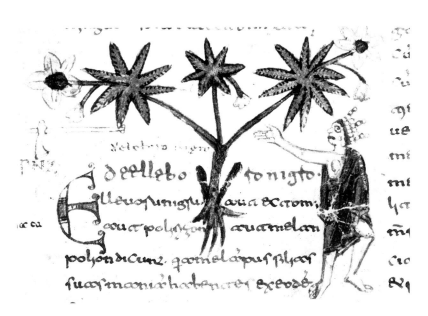

Plates 5 and 6. Dioscurides, *Materia Medica* (Munich,
ms 337, 10th century): cures for snakebite and insanity
(photographs courtesy of the Wellcome Institute Library,
London, and Bayerische Staatsbibliothek)

BIBLIOGRAPHY

Unpublished Primary Sources

Cava, Abbey of La Trinità, Archivio, *Arcae XIII-XXIV*.
Naples, Archivio di Stato, Sezione Politico-Diplomatica, *Monasteri Soppressi* 3437.

Primary Sources in Print

[Les] Actes Latins de S. Maria di Messina, ed. L.-R. Ménager (Palermo, 1963).
Anna Comnena, *Alexiad*, trans. E. R. A. Sewter (London, 1969).
[Le] Brébion de la Métropole de Règion (vers 1050), ed. A. Guillou (Vatican City, 1974).
R. Briscese, "Le pergamene della cattedrale di Venosa", *ASCL*, X (1940).
F. Caraballese, *L'Apulia ed il suo Comune nell'Alto Medioevo* (Bari, 1905).
[Le] Carte che si conservano nello Archivio del Capitolo metropolitano della Città di Trani, ed. A. Prologo, (Barletta, 1877).
[Il] Chartularium del Monastero di S. Benedetto in Conversano, ed. D. Morea (Montecassino, 1892).
Chronicon Episcoporum S. Neapolitanae Ecclesiae, in *Monumenta ad Neapolitani Ducatus Historiam Pertinentia*, ed. B. Capasso, I (Naples, 1881).
Codex Diplomaticus Cajetanus, I-II, (Montecassino, 1887-1891).
Codex Diplomaticus Cavensis, I-VIII, ed. M. Morcaldi *et al.*, (Milan, Naples, Pisa, 1873-93), IX and X, ed. S. Leone and G. Vitolo (Badia di Cava, 1984, 1990).
Codice Diplomatico Amalfitano, ed. R. Filangieri di Candida, I, (Naples, 1917), II, (Trani, 1951).
Codice Diplomatico Barese, I-II, ed. G. B. Nitto & F. Nitti, (Bari, 1897-99).
—, III, *Le pergamene della cattedrale di Terlizzi*, ed. F. Caraballese, (Bari, 1899).
—, IV, *Le pergamene di S. Nicola di Bari : periodo greco*, ed. F. Nitti, (Bari, 1900).
—, V, *Le pergamene di S. Nicola di Bari: periodo normanno*, ed. F. Nitti, (Bari, 1902).
—, VII, *Le carte di Molfetta*, ed. F. Caraballese, (Bari, 1912).
—, VIII, *Le pergamene di Barletta*, ed. F. Nitti, (Bari, 1914).
—, IX, *I documenti storici di Corato*, ed. G. Beltrani, (Bari, 1923).
—, X, *Le pergamene di Barletta del R. Archivio di Napoli*, ed. R. Filangieri di Candida (Bari, 1927).
This series is continued by the *Codice Diplomatico Pugliese*:-
—, XX, *Le Pergamene di Conversano*, ed. G. Coniglio, (Bari, 1975).
—, XXI, *Les Chartes de Troia*, ed. J.- M. Martin, (Bari, 1976).
Codice Diplomatico del Monastero Benedettino di S. Maria di Tremiti (1005-1237), ed. A. Petrucci (3 vols, Rome, 1960).
[Il] Codice Perris: Cartulario Amalfitano, I, ed. J. Mazzoleni & R. Orefice, (Amalfi, 1985).
[I] Diplomi Greci ed Arabi di Sicilia, ed. S. Cusa, Ii-II (Palermo, 1868-1882, repr. as one vol. Cologne, 1982).
[I] Documenti Inediti dell'Epoca Normanna in Sicilia, ed. C. A. Garufi (Palermo, 1899).
V. de Donato, "Aggiunte al *Codice Diplomatico Barese*," *Archivio Storico Pugliese*, XXVII (1974).
Ecclesiastical History of Orderic Vitalis, ed. M. Chibnall, I (Oxford, 1980), II (Oxford, 1968).

"Elenco delle pergamene già appartenenti alla famiglia Fusco ed ora acquistate dalla Società Napoletana di Storia Patria", *ASPN* (1883).

Gregory of Tours, *History of the Franks*, trans. L. Thorpe (London, 1974).

A. Guillou and W. Holtzmann, "Zwei Katepansurkunden aus Tricarico", *QFIAB*, XLI (1961).

Historia Inventionis ac Translationis et Miracula S. Trophimene, in *Acta Sanctorum, v Julii*.

W. Holtzmann, "Papst-, Kaiser- und Normannen-urkunden aus Unteritalien I: San Filippo - S Maria Latina in Agira", *QFIAB*, XXXV (1955).

W. Holtzmann, "Papst-, Kaiser- und Normannen-urkunden aus Unteritalien II: San Giovanni di Fiore, Erztbistum Rossano, Bistum Bova, Sant'Elia Carbone", *QFIAB*, XXXVI (1956).

Honorantie Civitatis Papie, ed. C.-R. Brühl and C. Violante (Köln-Wien, 1983).

H. Houben, *Il "Libro del Capitolo" del Monastero della SS Trinità di Venosa (Cod. Casin. 334)* (Bari, 1984).

Liutprand of Cremona, *The Embassy to Constantinople and other Works*, trans. F. A. Wright (London, 1930).

F. Magistrale, "Aggiunte al *Codice Diplomatico Barese*: documenti di Terlizzi", *Archivio Storico Pugliese*, XXVI (1973).

L.-R. Ménager, "L'abbaye bénédictine de la Trinité de Mileto, en Calabre, à l'époque normande", *Bullettino dell'Archivio Paleografico Italiano*, n.s. IV-V (1958-9).

A. Mercati, "Le pergamene di Melfi all'Archivio Secreto Vaticano", *Miscellanea Giovanni Mercati*, V (Vatican City, 1946).

Monachesimo e Mondo dei Laici nel Mezzogiorno Medievale: Il Necrologio di Montevergine, ed. M. Villani (Altavilla Salentina, 1990)

Monasteri Femminili e Nobiltà a Napoli tra Medioevo ed Età Moderna: Il Necrologio di S. Patrizia (secc.XII-XVI), ed. A. Facchiano (Altavilla Salentina, 1992)

Necrologio del Liber Confratrum di S. Matteo di Salerno, ed. C. A. Garufi (FSI 56, Rome, 1922).

Paul the Deacon, *History of the Langobards*, trans. W. Dudley Foulke (Philadelphia, 1907).

[Le] Pergamene degli Archivi Vescovili di Amalfi e Ravello, I, ed. J. Mazzoleni (Naples, 1972); II, ed. C. Salvati (Naples, 1974); III, ed. B. Mazzoleni (Naples, 1975).

Pergamene del Monastero Benedettino di S. Giorgio, 1038-1698, ed. L. Cassese (Salerno, 1950).

[Le] Pergamene del Monastero di S. Gregorio Armeno di Napoli, ed. J. Mazzoleni, I (Naples, 1973).

[Le] Pergamene dell'Archivio Vescovile di Caiazzo (1007-1265), I, ed. C. Salvati (Caserta, 1983).

[Le] Pergamene della Curia e del Capitolo di Nardò, ed. M. Pastore (Lecce, 1964).

[Le] Pergamene di S. Nicola di Gallucanta (secc. IX-XII), ed. P. Cherubini (Altavilla Salentina, 1990).

[Le] Più Antiche Carte dell'Archivio Capitolare di Agrigento (1092-1282), ed. P. Collura (Palermo, 1961).

Recueil des Actes des Ducs Normands d'Italie (1046-1127), I: Les Premiers Ducs, 1046-87, ed. L.-R. Ménager (Bari, 1980).

Regesta Neapolitana, in *Monumenta ad Neapolitani Ducatus Historiam Pertinentia*, ed. B. Capasso, IIi, (Naples, 1885).

Regesto di S. Leonardo di Siponto, ed. F. Camobreco (Rome, 1913).

Regii Neapolitani Archivii Monumenta, Ii, III, IV, eds. M. Baffi et al. (Naples, 1845-54).

G. Robinson, "The history and cartulary of the Greek monastery of S. Elias and S. Anastasius of Carbone", *Orientalia Christiana*, LIII (1929).

S. Jean-Théristes (1054-1264), ed. A. Guillou (Vatican City, 1980).

S. Nicolas de Donnoso, ed. A. Guillou (Vatican City, 1967).

[La] Theotokos de Hagia-Agathe (Oppido), ed. A. Guillou (Vatican City, 1972).

F. Trinchera, *Syllabus Graecarum Membranarum*, (Naples, 1865).
[Die] Urkunden der normannisch-sizilienischen Könige, ed. K. A. Kehr (Innsbruck, 1902).
Vita di San Fantino il Giovane, ed. E. Follieri (Brussels, 1993).
Vita di San Nilo, trans. G. Giovanelli, (Grottaferrata, 1966).
Vita Sancti Barbati Episcopi, in *MGH, Scriptores Rerum Langobardorum et Italicarum*, ed. G. Waitz (Hanover, 1878).

Secondary Works

J. Agrimi and C. Crisciani, *Medicina del Corpo e Medicina dell'Anima: note sul sapere del medico fino all'inizio del secolo XIII*, (Milan, 1978).
A. R. Amarotta, *Salerno Romana e Medievale: Dinamica di un Insediamento* (Salerno, 1989).
D. Amundsen, "Medicine and faith in early Christianity", *BHM*, LVI (1982).
P. Ariès, *Centuries of Childhood* (New York, 1962).
P. Arthur, "Archeologia urbana a Napoli: riflessioni sugli ultimi tre anni", *Archeologia Medievale*, XIII (1986).
P. Baker & G. Clark, "Archaeozoological evidence for medieval Italy", *Archeologia Medievale*, XX (1993).
A. Beccaria, *I Codici di Medicina del Periodo Presalernitano (Secoli IX, X, e XI)* (Rome, 1956).
M. Becker, "The human bones", in *Excavations at Otranto I: the Excavation*, ed. D. Michaelides and D. Wilkinson, (Lecce, 1992).
J.-N. Biraben and J. Le Goff, "La peste dans le haut moyen age", *Annales ESC*, XXIV (1969).
M. Bloch, *The Historian's Craft*, trans. P. Putnam, with preface by P. Burke, (Manchester, 1992)
F. Bonelli, "La malaria nella storia demografica ed economica d'Italia: primi lineamenti di una ricerca", *Studi Storici*, VII (1966).
J. Boswell, "*Expositio* and *oblatio*: the abandonment of children and the ancient and medieval family", *American Historical Review*, LXXXIX (1984).
J. Boswell, *The Kindness of Strangers: the Abandonment of Children in Western Europe from Late Antiquity to the Renaissance* (New York, 1988).
S. N. Brody, *Disease of the Soul: Leprosy in Medieval Literature*, (Ithaca, NY, 1974).
J. A. Brundage, *Law, Sex and Christian Society in Medieval Europe* (Chicago, 1987).
G. Buckler, "Women in Byzantine law about 1100AD", *Byzantion*, XI (1936).
H. Bush, "Concepts of health and stress", in *Health in Past Societies*
H. Bush and M. Zvelebil, "Pathology and health in past societies: an introduction", in *Health in Past Societies*
M. L. Cameron, "Anglo-Saxon medicine and magic", *Anglo-Saxon England*, XVII (1988).
G. Cassandro. "Il ducato bizantino", in *Storia di Napoli*, II, i (Naples, 1969/73).
U. Cassuto, "Nuove inscrizioni ebraiche di Venosa", *ASCL*, IV (1934).
U. Cassuto, "Ancora nuove inscrizioni ebraiche di Venosa", *ASCL*, V (1935).
U. Cassuto, "Iscrizioni ebraiche a Bari", *Rivista degli Studi Orientali*, XV (1935).
A. Chamberlain, *Human Remains*, (London, 1994).
N. Christie, *The Lombards* (Oxford, 1995).
The Church and Childhood, ed. D. Wood (Oxford, 1994).
The Church and Healing, ed. W. J. Sheils (Oxford, 1982).
N. Cilento, "Il significativo della 'translatio' dei corpi dei vescovi napoletani dal cimitero di S. Gennaro 'extra moenia' nella basilica della Stefania", *Campania Sacra*, I (1970).
G. Clark, "Town and countryside in medieval Italy", *Anthropozoologica*, XVI (1992).

G. Clark, "Animals and animal products in medieval Italy: a discussion of archaeological and historical methodology", *PBSR*, LVII (1989).

C. Colafemmina, "L'itinerario pugliese di Beniamino da Tudela", *Archivio Storico Pugliese*, XXVIII (1975).

R. Collins, *Early Medieval Spain*, (London, 1983).

Il Complesso Archeologico di Carminiello ai Mannesi (Scavi 1983-1984), ed. P. Arthur (Rome/Lecce, 1994).

M.-H. Congourdeau, "La société byzantine face aux grandes pandémies", in *Maladie et Société*.

L. Conrad, M. Neve, V. Nutton, R. Porter and A. Wear, *The Western Medical Tradition, 800B.C. to A.D.1800* (Cambridge, 1995).

A. Corradi, *Annali delle Epidemie Occorse in Italia dalle Prime Memorie fino al 1850*, 2 vols (Bologna, 1863, repr. 1972).

S. Crawford, *Age Differentiation and Related Social Status: a Study of Anglo-Saxon Childhood* (Oxford, D.Phil thesis, 1991).

E. Cuozzo, "Un vescovo della longobardia minore: Alfano arcivescovo di Salerno (d. 1085)", *Campania Sacra*, VI (1975).

G. da Costa-Louillet, "Saints de Sicile et de l'Italie méridionale aux VIII, IX, et X siècles", *Byzantion*, XXIX-XXX (1959-60).

Death in Towns: Urban Responses to the Dying and the Dead, 100-1600, ed. S. R. Bassett (Leicester, 1992).

P. Delogu, *Mito di una Città Meridionale* (Naples, 1977).

P. Delogu, G. Maetzke, P. Natella, P. Peduto, E. Tabaczynska and S. Tabaczynski, *Caputaquis Medievale*, I (Salerno, 1973).

Diet and Crafts in Towns: the Evidence of Animal Remains from the Roman to the Post-Medieval Periods, ed. D. Serjeantson & T. Waldron, (BAR British Series 199, Oxford, 1989).

H. Dillard, *Daughters of the Reconquest: Women in Castilian Town Society, 1100-1300* (Cambridge, 1984).

S. Epstein, *Wills and Wealth in Medieval Genoa, 1150-1250*, (London, 1984).

L. Faccini, "Storia sociale e storia della medicina", *Studi Storici*, XVII (1976).

N. Ferorelli, *Gli Ebrei nell'Italia Meridionale dall'Età Romana al Secolo XVIII* (Bologna, 1966).

V. J. Flint, "The early medieval *medicus*, the saint -- and the enchanter", *Social History of Medicine*, II (1989).

V. J. Flint, *The Rise of Magic in Early Medieval Europe* (OXford, 1991).

A. Forey, *The Military Orders from the Twelfth to the Early Fourteenth Centuries* (London, 1992).

M. Fuiano, "L'insegnamento della medicina a Napoli nei secoli XIII e XIV", *Studi Storici Meridionali*, V (1985).

V. Fumagalli, *Landscapes of Fear: Perceptions of Nature and the City in the Middle Ages* (Cambridge, 1994).

V. Fumagalli, "Il paesaggio dei morti: luoghi d'incontro tra i morti e i vivi sulla terra nel medioevo", *Quaderni Storici*, XVII, ii (1982).

P. Geary, *Living with the Dead in the Middle Ages* (Cornell, 1994).

B. Geremek, *The Margins of Society in Late Medieval Paris* (Cambridge, 1987).

M. Ginatempo, "Corpi e uomini tra scienza e storia: studi di osteo-archeologia umana per l'Italia medievale", *Archeologia Medievale*, XV (1988).

J.-L. Goglin, *Les Misérables dans l'Occident Médiéval* (Paris, 1976).

S. D. Goitein, *Letters of Medieval Jewish Traders*, (Princeton, 1973).

S. D. Goitein, *A Mediterranean Society, I: Economic Foundations*, (Berkeley, 1967).

S. D. Goitein, *A Mediterranean Society II: the Community*, (Berkeley, 1971).

S. D. Goitein, *A Mediterranean Society III: the Family*, (Berkeley, 1978).

S. D. Goitein, "Sicily and southern Italy in the Cairo Geniza documents", *Archivio Storico per la Sicilia Orientale*, LVII (1971).

A. Goodman, "Health adaptation and maladaptation in past societies", in *Health in Past Societies*.

A. Grauer, "Patterns of life and death: the palaeodemography of medieval York", in *Health in Past Societies*.

M. Green, "Constantinus Africanus and the conflct between religion and science", in *The Human Embryo: Aristotle and the Arabic and European Traditions*, ed. G. R. Dunstan (Exeter, 1990).

M. Green, "Recent work on women's medicine in medieval Europe", *Society for Ancient Medicine Review*, XXI (1993).

M. Green, "Documenting medieval women's medical practice", in *Practical Medicine from Salerno to the Black Death*, ed. L. Garcia-Ballester *et al.*, (Cambridge, 1994).

M. Green, "Estraendo Trota dal *Trotula*: ricerche su testi medievali di medicina Salernitana", *Rassegna Storica Salernitana*, n.s. XII (1995).

M. D. Grmek, "Préliminaires d'une étude historique des maladies", *Annales ESC* XXIV (1969).

A. Guillerme, *The Age of Water: the Urban Environment in the North of France, 300-1800* (College Station, Texas, 1988).

A. Gurevich, "Approaches of the 'Annales School' from the history of mentalities to historical synthesis", *Scandia*, LVIII (1992).

A. Gurevich, *Historical Anthropology of the Middle Ages*, ed. J. Howlett (Oxford, 1992).

Health, Disease and Healing in Medieval Culture, ed. S. Campbell, B. Hall and D. Klausner (London, 1992).

Health in Past Societies, ed. H. Bush and M. Zvelebil, (BAR Int. series 567, Oxford, 1991).

B. Henisch, *Fast and Feast: Food in Medieval Society*, (London, 1976).

D. Herlihy, *Opera Muliebra: Women and Work in Medieval Europe*, (London, 1990).

V. A. Higgins, *Health Patterns in Rural Agricultural Communities of the Late Roman and Early Medieval Periods, Including a Study of Two Skeletal Groups from San Vincenzo al Volturno* (Sheffield, Ph.D. thesis, 1990).

P. Horden, "Possession without exorcism: the response to demons and insanity in the earlier Byzantine middle East", in *Maladie et Société*.

P. Horden, "Responses to possession and insanity in the earlier Byzantine world", *Social History of Medicine*, VI (1993).

Hunger and History, ed. R. I. Rotberg and T. K. Rabb (Cambridge, 1983).

Hunger in History, ed. L. Newman *et al.* (Oxford, 1990).

A. M. Ieraci Bio, "La trasmissione della letteratura medica greca nell'Italia meridionale fra X e XV secolo", in *Contributi alla Cultura Greca nell'Italia Meridionale*, ed. A. Garzya (Naples, 1989).

J. Johns, *The Muslims of Norman Sicily, c.1060-1194*, (Oxford D.Phil. thesis, 1983).

W. R. Jones, "The clinic in three medieval societies", *Diogenes*, CXXII (1983).

A. Kazhdan, "The image of the medical doctor in Byzantine literature of the tenth to twelfth centuries", in *Symposium on Byzantine Medicine*.

B. Kreutz, *Before the Normans*, (Philadelphia, 1991).

P. O. Kristeller, "Nuovi fonti per la medicina", *Rassegna Storica Salernitana*, (1957).

P. O. Kristeller, "The school of Salerno: its development and its contribution to the history of learning", *BHM*, XVII (1945).

J. Kroll and B. Bachrach, "Sin and the etiology of disease in pre-crusade Europe", *Journal of the History of Medicine and Allied Sciences*, XLI (1986).

I. M. Lewis, *Ecstatic Religion: an Anthropological Study of Spirit Possession and Shamanism*, (Harmondsworth, 1971).

M. Livi-Bacci, *Population and Nutrition*, (Cambridge, 1991).

The Lombard Laws, ed. K. Fischer Drew, (Pennsylvania, 1973).

R. Lopez and I. Raymond, *Medieval Trade in the Mediterranean World* (Oxford, 1955).

S. Lucà, "I Normanni e la 'rinascita' del secolo XII", *ASCL*, LX (1993).

J. H. Lynch, *The Medieval Church: a Brief History* (London, 1992).

M. McCormick, "Mediterranean communications in the eighth and ninth centuries: the prosopographical evidence", in *L'Eredità di Arechi. Convegno Internazionale, Ravello 17-19 June 1995*, ed. J. Mitchell and P. Peduto (forthcoming).

L. Mackinney, *Medical Illustrations in Medieval Manuscripts*, (London, 1965).

Maladie et Société à Byzance, ed. E. Patlagean, (Spoleto, 1993).

J.-M. Martin, "L'ambiente longobardo, greco, islamico e normanno nel Mezzogiorno", in *Storia dell'Italia Religiosa I: L'Antichità e il Medioevo*, ed. A. Vauchez (Bari, 1993).

M. S. Mazzi, *Salute e Società nel Medioevo*, (Firenze, 1978).

Medicine in Society, ed. A. Wear, (Cambridge, 1992).

T. S. Miller, "The Knights of St John and the hospitals of the Latin West", *Speculum*, LIII (1978).

G. Minois, *History of Old Age from Antiquity to the Renaissance* (Cambridge, 1989).

J. Mitchell, "The display of script and the uses of painting in Longobard Italy", in *Settimane di Studio del Centro Italiano sull'Alto Medioevo*, XLI (1994).

R. I. Moore, *The Formation of a Persecuting Society: Power and Deviance in Western Europe, 950-1250* (Oxford, 1987).

J. Moreland, M. Pluciennik *et al.*, "Excavations at Casale San Donato, Castelnuovo di Farfa (RI), Lazio, 1992", *Archeologia Medievale*, XX (1993).

P. Morpurgo, "L'ingresso dell'Aristotele Latino a Salerno", in *Rencontres de Cultures*, pp.273-93.

R. Morris, "The powerful and the poor in tenth-century Byzantium", *Past and Present*, LXXIII (1975).

Mortality and Immortality: the Anthropology and Archaeology of Death, ed. S. C. Humphreys and H. King (London, 1981).

V. Nutton, "Velia and the School of Salerno", *Medical History*, XVII (1971).

E. M. O'Connor, "Peter of Eboli, *De Balneis Puteolanis*: manuscripts from the Aragonese scriptorium in Naples", *Traditio*, XLV (1989/90).

K. Park, "Medicine and society in medieval Europe, 500-1500", in *Medicine in Society*.

E. Patlagean, "Sur la limitation de la fécondité dans la haute époque byzantine", *Annales ESC* XXIV (1969).

F. S. Paxton, "*Signa mortifera*: death and prognostication in early medieval monastic medicine", *BHM*, LXVII (1993).

P. Peduto, M. Romito, M. Galante, D. Mauro and I. Pastore, "Un accesso alla storia di Salerno: stratigrafe e materiali dell'area palaziale longobarda", *Rassegna Storica Salernitana* (1988)

A. Petrucci, *Il Chronicon Salernitanum*, (Salerno 1988).

A. Petrucci and C. Romeo, *"Scriptores in Urbibus": Alfabetismo e Cultura Scritta nell'Italia Altomedievale* (Bologna, 1992)

Poverty in the Middle Ages, ed. D. Flood, (Werl, Westf., 1975).

Rencontres de Cultures dans la Philosophie Médiévale: Traductions et Traducteurs de l'Antiquité Tardive au XIVe Siècle, ed. J. Hamesse and M. Fattori (Louvain-la-Neuve/Cassino, 1990).

J. M. Riddle, "Ancient and medieval chemotherapy for cancer", *Isis*, 76 (1985).

J. M. Riddle, *Contraception and Abortion from the Ancient World to the Renaissance* (Harvard, 1992).

G. Rosen, *A History of Public Health* (2nd ed, Baltimore, 1993).

A. Russo, "Di un poco noto 'Glossario' botanico-farmaceutico del IX secolo (Cod. Cassinese 69)", *Atti dell'Accademia*, VII (1990).

San Vincenzo al Volturno 1 & 2, ed. R. Hodges (London, 1994, 1995)

Self and Society in Medieval France: the Memoirs of Abbot Guibert of Nogent (1064?-c.1125), ed. J. F. Benton (New York, 1970).

S. Shahar, *Childhood in the Middle Ages* (London, 1990).

S. Shahar, "Who were old in the middle ages?", *Social History of Medicine*, VI (1993).

A. Sharf, *The Universe of Shabbetai Donnolo*, (Warminster, 1976).

J. Shatzmiller, *Jews, Medicine and Medieval Society* (London, 1994).

H. E. Sigerist, "The Latin medical literature of the early middle ages", *Journal of the History of Medicine*, XIII (1958).

N. Siraisi, *Medieval and Early Renaissance Medicine: an Introduction to Knowledge and Practice*, (London, 1990).

P. Skinner, *Family Power in Southern Italy: the Duchy of Gaeta and its Neighbours, 850-1139* (Cambridge, 1995).

P. Skinner, "Women, wills and wealth in medieval southern Italy", *Early Medieval Europe*, 2 (1993).

P. Skinner, "Women, literacy and invisibility in medieval southern Italy", in *Women, the Book and the Worldly*, ed. J. Taylor and L. Smith (Woodbridge, 1995).

P. Skinner, "Gender and poverty in the medieval community", in *Medieval Women in their Communities*, ed. D. Watt (forthcoming).

P. Skinner, "Urban houses and households in medieval southern Italy", in *Houses and Households in Towns*, ed. R. Holt (forthcoming).

P. Stuart-Macadam, "Anaemia in Roman Britain: Poundbury Camp", in *Health in Past Societies*.

Symposium on Byzantine Medicine, ed. J. Scarborough, (*Dumbarton Oaks Papers*, XXXVIII, 1984).

H. Taviani-Carozzi, *La Principauté Lombarde de Salerne*, 2 vols, (Rome, 1991).

P. Vovelle, "L'histoire des hommes au miroir de la mort", in *Death in the Middle Ages*, ed. H. Braet and W. Verbeke (Leuven, 1983).

S. Vryonis *The Medical Unity of the Mediterranean World in Antiquity and the Middle Ages*, (Crete, 1991).

T. Waldron, "The effects of urbanisation on human health: the evidence from skeletal remains", in *Diet and Crafts in Towns*.

C. J. Wickham, *Early Medieval Italy*, (London, 1981).

C. J. Wickham, *Land and Power: Studies in Italian and European Social History*, (London, 1994).

D. Wilson, *Signs and Portents: Monstrous Births from the Middle Ages to the Enlightenment*, (London, 1993).

INDEX

THE

MEDIEVAL MEDITERRANEAN

PEOPLES, ECONOMIES AND CULTURES, 400-1453

Editors: Michael Whitby (Warwick), Paul Magdalino, Hugh Kennedy (St. Andrews), David Abulafia (Cambridge), Benjamin Arbel (Tel Aviv), Mark Meyerson (Notre Dame).

This series provides a forum for the publication of scholarly work relating to the interactions of peoples and cultures in the Mediterranean basin and the Black Sea area and is intended for readers with interest in late antiquity, the Middle Ages (Italy, Spain, the Latin East), Byzantium, Islam, the Balkans and the Black Sea. Manuscripts (in English, German and French) should be 60,000 to 120,000 words in length and may include illustrations. The editors would be particularly interested to. receive proposals for monograph studies; studies with texts; editions with parallel translations of texts or collections of documents; or translations provided with full annotation.

1. Shatzmiller, M. (ed.), *Crusaders and Muslims in Twelfth-Century Syria.* 1993. ISBN 90 04 09777 5
2. Tsougarakis, D., *The Life of Leontios, Patriarch of Jerusalem.* Text, Translation, Commentary. 1993. ISBN 90 04 09827 5
3. Takayama, H., *The Administration of the Norman Kingdom of Sicily.* 1993. ISBN 90 04 09865 8
4. Simon, L.J. (ed.), *Iberia and the Mediterranean World of the Middle Ages.* Studies in Honor of Robert I. Burns S.J. Vol. 1. Proceedings from Kalamazoo. 1995. ISBN 90 04 10168 3
5. Stöckly, D. *Le système de l'Incanto des galées du marché à Venise (fin XIIIᵉ-milieu XVᵉ siècle.* 1995. 90 04 10002 4.
6. Estow, C., *Pedro the Cruel of Castile, 1350-1369.* 1995. ISBN 90 04 10094 6
7. Stalls, W.C., *Possessing the Land.* Aragon's Expansion into Islam's Ebro Frontier under Alfonso the Battler, 1104-1134. 1995. ISBN 90 04 10367 8
8. Chevedden, P.E., D.J. Kagay & P.G. Padilla (eds.), *Iberia and the Mediterranean World of the Middle Ages.* Essays in Honor of Robert I. Burns S.J. Vol. 2. Proceedings from 'Spain and the Western Mediterranean', a Colloquium Sponsored by *The Center for Medieval and Renaissance Studies,* University of California, Los Angeles, October 26-27, 1992. 1996. ISBN 90 04 10573 5
9. Lev, Y. (ed.), *War and Society in the Eastern Mediterranean, 7th-15th Centuries.* 1997. ISBN 90 04 10032 6
10. Ciggaar, K.N., *Western Travellers to Constantinople.* The West and Byzantium, 962-1204: Cultural and Political Relations. 1996. ISBN 90 04 10637 5
11. Skinner, P. *Health and Medicine in Early Medieval Southern Italy.* 1997. ISBN 90 04 10394 5

12. Parry, K., *Depicting the Word*. Byzantine Iconophile Thought of the Eighth and Ninth Centuries. 1996. ISBN 90 04 10502 6
13. Crisafulli, V.S. & J.W. Nesbitt, *The Miracles of St. Artemios*. A Collection of Miracle Stories by an Anonymous Author of Seventh-Century Byzantium. 1997. ISBN 90 04 10574 3